Delta Democracy

BRIDGING THE GAP

Series Editors
James Goldgeier
Bruce Jentleson
Steven Weber

*The Logic of American Nuclear Strategy:
Why Strategic Superiority Matters*
Matthew Kroenig

*Planning to Fail:
The US Wars in Vietnam, Iraq, and Afghanistan*
James H. Lebovic

*Delta Democracy:
Pathways to Incremental Civic Revolution in Egypt and Beyond*
Catherine E. Herrold

Delta Democracy

*Pathways to Incremental Civic Revolution in
Egypt and Beyond*

CATHERINE E. HERROLD

OXFORD

UNIVERSITY PRESS

Oxford University Press is a department of the University of Oxford. It furthers
the University's objective of excellence in research, scholarship, and education
by publishing worldwide. Oxford is a registered trade mark of Oxford University
Press in the UK and certain other countries.

Published in the United States of America by Oxford University Press
198 Madison Avenue, New York, NY 10016, United States of America.

Library of Congress Cataloging-in-Publication Data
Names: Herrold, Catherine E., author.
Title: Delta democracy : pathways to incremental civic revolution in Egypt
and beyond / by Catherine E. Herrold.
Description: New York, NY : Oxford University Press, [2020] |
Series: Bridging the gap | Includes bibliographical references and index.
Identifiers: LCCN 2019041565 (print) | LCCN 2019041566 (ebook) |
ISBN 9780190093235 (hardback) | ISBN 9780190093310 (paperback) |
ISBN 9780190093259 (epub) | ISBN 9780190093266 (online)
Subjects: LCSH: Democratization—Egypt. | Non-governmental organizations—Egypt. |
Civil society—Egypt—21st century. | Egypt—Politics and government—2011–
Classification: LCC JQ3881.H47 2020 (print) |
LCC JQ3881 (ebook) | DDC 320.962—dc23
LC record available at https://lccn.loc.gov/2019041565
LC ebook record available at https://lccn.loc.gov/2019041566

1 3 5 7 9 8 6 4 2

Paperback printed by LSC Communications, United States of America
Hardback printed by Bridgeport National Bindery, Inc., United States of America

For Khaldoun and Mona

Contents

Acknowledgments   ix

Introduction: Civil Society and Egypt's Arab Spring   1

1. The Co-Optation of Egypt's NGO Sector   27

2. The Widening and Narrowing of Egypt's Civic Space   50

3. The West's Democracy Promotion Playbook   79

4. All You Need Is Tea: An Alternative Democracy Promotion Playbook   90

5. Promoting Democracy in the Face of Autocracy   123

Conclusion   138

Notes   159
Bibliography   187
Index   203

Acknowledgments

In mid-2011, I arrived at the Cairo office of an Egyptian human rights NGO for a conversation with one of its staff members. My phone began buzzing around the time of our scheduled appointment. My interviewee would be late, his text messages informed me. He was busy supporting protesters in Tahrir Square, which was still home to demonstrations months after the country's January 25 uprisings. But the staff member asked me to wait and promised that he would come back to the office as soon as possible. He arrived about thirty minutes later, breathless and exhilarated. He told me that he would return to the square after our conversation, but that he could talk for as long as I wished.

I conducted the bulk of the fieldwork for this book in the years directly following Egypt's January 25, 2011, uprisings—a period of major political turmoil in Egypt. At first, it was a moment of opportunity, and local nongovernmental organizations (NGOs) worked overtime as they took advantage of Mubarak's ouster and mobilized citizens in an effort to transition Egypt to democracy. Later, trepidation settled in as successive transitional governments cracked down on civil society organizations and arrested outspoken activists. NGO staff members became more cautious about who they talked to, especially as the government tried to smear their organizations as being agents of Western intruders. Throughout this period—both when NGO leaders were busy fighting for a revolution and when they were guarding their safety—the interviewees whose words are featured in this book took the time and the risk to answer my questions. Like the human rights activist just mentioned, they interrupted their own very important work to tell me their stories and share their perspectives on all that was happening. I am profoundly grateful for my interviewees' time, insights, and trust. I hope I have done them justice in the following pages.

By the time the 2011 uprisings broke out, I had already made significant inroads into research on Egypt's grantmaking foundation sector thanks to support from Barbara Ibrahim—founding director of the American University in Cairo's (AUC) John D. Gerhart Center for Philanthropy and Civic Engagement. Barbara not only introduced me to key interlocutors who would help me get my project off the ground but she and her husband, Saad Eddin Ibrahim, also, and more importantly, became close friends and confidants. The hospitality that Barbara and Saad showed me during my many visits to Egypt made me feel at home from my earliest days in the country. Our long discussions about Arab civil society fed my curiosity and honed my thinking. That I managed to complete this project and write this book is thanks in no small part to Barbara and Saad Ibrahim.

Many more experts on Arab civil society also patiently and generously devoted many hours to describing local and regional NGO sector dynamics to me. The observations shared by Heba Abou Shnief, Judy Barselou, Marwa el-Daly, Naila Farouky, Hilary Gilbert, Ayman Ismail, Mudar Kassis, Atallah Kuttab, Noha el-Mikawy, Sherine el-Taraboulsi-McCarthy, and Sarah Sabry helped to contextualize and triangulate interview data and correct for Western biases. Conversations with Michal Almog-Bar, Flannery Becker, Souheil Gabriel Chad, Amy Johnson, Michelle Lanzoni, Andrew Reynolds, and Steven Rosenbaum—who all have many years of experience working in the Middle East—expanded my thinking and helped me clarify my arguments for wider audiences.

On one of my first bus rides out to AUC's New Cairo campus, I met AUC faculty members Kim Fox and Rashmika "Gogo" Pandya, who invited me to a dinner party hosted by their friend and colleague, Anne Justus, that evening. At the party, Jason Beckett, Nathan Fischer, Kim, Anne, Gogo, Bonnie Settlage, and Shereef Zein welcomed me into their circle of friends. I subsequently spent countless late nights with this group on Anne's balcony, where we reflected on the revolutionary events we were witnessing and shared stories of our everyday lives in Cairo. As Anne's delicious dinner spreads fueled our (often exhausted) bodies, the conversations I shared with these friends fed my mind and nourished my soul.

During my time in Egypt, I swam competitively with the Gezira Sporting Club Master's Swim Team. In the pool, I took advantage of one of the few quiet places in Cairo to reflect on my daily discoveries. After Friday trainings, debates with teammates over *ful* and *ta'amiya* helped me to sort through lingering confusions and questions. Captain Mohsen, Nadia el-Araby, Khaled el-Ayat, Hoda el-Ridi, Osama Momtaz, and Aisha Rashad are my lifelong teammates no matter where I happen to be swimming.

As I penned this book, I thought often about my teachers. My love of research was born on the sixth floor of Mount Holyoke College's Williston Library, where I wrote my undergraduate senior thesis under the tutelage of Michael Robinson and James Monks. This book began as a PhD dissertation project at Duke University's Sanford School of Public Policy, where my dissertation committee chair, Kristin Goss, along with advisors Nicholas Carnes, Charles Clotfelter, Joel Fleishman, Timur Kuran, Charles Kurzman, Mbaye Lo, Frederick Mayer, Guillermo Trejo, and Jacob Vigdor provided exceptionally smart and patient guidance. To all of my teachers, thank you.

The book took form at my current intellectual home, Indiana University, where my colleagues stopped by my office with encouragement and high fives. In the classroom, my students inspire and prod my thinking with their insightful comments and questions. Special thanks to fellow faculty member Tyrone Freeman and former students Kinga Horvath, Manal Issa, and Afsoon Mohseni for their persistent interest in the book's progress.

I benefited from colleagues' keen questions, comments, and criticisms when I presented parts of this work at the Bush School of Government and Public Service at Texas A&M University, the Center for Effective Philanthropy, the Gerhart Center for Philanthropy and Civic Engagement at AUC, the Paul H. O'Neill School of Public and Environmental Affairs at Indiana University, and conferences of the Association for Research on Nonprofit Organizations and Voluntary Action, the International Society for Third Sector Research, the International Studies Association, and Takaful: Annual Conference on Arab Philanthropy and Civic Engagement.

Cristina Balboa, Kevin Bolduc, Thomas Hiatt, Lesley Lenkowsky, and Mickey Levitan read and commented on various parts of this book's proposal and manuscript. Their feedback helped me conceptualize the book's main takeaways and think through the feasibility of its policy recommendations. Another group of colleagues demystified the academic book publishing process. The useful tips offered by Jennifer Brass, Jennifer Brinkerhoff, Philip Cook, David Craig, Erica De Bruin, Brent Durbin, Kristin Goss, Turan Kayaoglu, Nancy Robertson, Mark Sidel, Josh Stacher, and Haley Swedlund helped me find the right home for this book and prepare my manuscript for submission.

Heartfelt thanks to Ali Aslam, Edward Curtis, Joy Lisi Rankin, Marianne Wokeck, and Gizem Zencirci for picking up the telephone whether I was calling to celebrate or to cry. These friends and mentors not only helped me navigate the logistics of book publishing; more importantly, they remained steadfastly by my side during the emotional ups and downs of writing, revising, and getting this book to press.

The feedback offered by two anonymous reviewers was invaluable. The reviewers' concrete, detailed suggestions helped me strengthen the book's argument and clarify the book's policy recommendations. Thank you, Reviewer 1 and Reviewer 2, for your intellectual generosity. The book also benefited from the sharp eyes and red pens of editors Amy Sherman, Katie Van Heest (Tweed Editing), and Audra Wolfe (The Outside Reader), all of whom helped me tighten my argument and streamline my prose. Claire Boyd, Dana Doan, and Krisztina Tury, my research assistants, masterfully dug up data and recommended literature that I had overlooked.

The extensive time I spent in Egypt researching this book was financially supported by the Duke University Graduate School, the Mount Holyoke College Alumnae Association, and the Sanford School of Public Policy at Duke University. I am indebted to these institutions for their commitment to this project.

I am immensely proud to be part of a book series that does the important work of connecting academic scholarship and foreign policymaking. James Goldgeier, Bruce Jentleson, and Steven Weber, the three coeditors of the Bridging the Gap Series, saw potential in this book from the very start and advocated for it throughout the publication process. Jim carefully read the manuscript's first full draft, coached me through the reviews, and connected me to foreign policy experts whom this book seeks to engage in conversation. The publicity created by Bridging the Gap's Leila Adler and Kristina Biyad will undoubtedly help this book reach the widest possible audiences. At Oxford University Press, I was fortunate to work with David McBride, who, along with his talented assistant Holly Mitchell, worked tirelessly to shepherd this book through its various stages of review and production.

I am enormously grateful to my friends who cheered me through authoring this book, even when my focus on writing detracted from my sociability. Lehn Benjamin, Angela Bies, Loïc Binard, Cathie Carrigan, Kevin Connolly, Holly Graham, Blade Hauth, Kate and Les Lenkowsky, Don Lundberg, Chris Maroldo, Jim Obermeier, Sally Perkins, Martina Schuldt, Mike Spilbeler, Robert Uhlenhake, Marlene Walk, and Megan Young, I look forward to being a better friend now that this book has gone to press.

I crafted countless paragraphs of this book while swimming my daily laps in the Indiana University (IU) Natatorium. Without the self-discipline cultivated under the stopwatch of my late YMCA swimming coach, Bill Schmidt, I never could have persevered in writing, rewriting, and revising this book.

Deep thanks as well to my IU Natatorium lane mate, whose encouragement and support kept me going during the long hours I spent back at my desk.

My parents, Jan and John Herrold, drove me to the airport in early February 2011 as I set off to embark on what would turn out to be nearly two years in Egypt. Squabbles over "too many" reminders to pack my passport and debates about whether to weigh my suitcase one last time revealed my parents' love and betrayed the tension we all felt as I prepared to fly into an ongoing revolution. Mom and Dad taught me from an early age to venture down side streets whenever and wherever I traveled, and that habit served me well as I probed deep into post-uprising Egypt. Visiting Andrew, Danielle, and Jed in Texas gave me welcome respites from my research. Their hospitality and love also fueled me with warm energy and renewed self-confidence when I returned to my pen and paper. Thank you, Mom, Dad, Andrew, Danielle, and Jed, for everything.

Jérôme Dumortier read and commented on the entire first draft of this book and, despite that version's many flaws, always believed in the book and its author. Jérôme, in addition to your devotion to my manuscript, I thank you for your savvy career mentorship, your irreverent humor, and our lengthy dinner conversations that always end too soon. Most of all, thank you for your care. Our friendship enriches my life exponentially.

Khaldoun AbouAssi and Mona Atia entered my life as I first embarked on fieldwork in Egypt. Khaldoun and Mona, just like the country that I came to call home, you quickly lodged yourselves into a special corner of my heart. Thank you for the lessons you teach me, the fun times we share, and your fierce loyalty. Thank you for your ululations. Thank you for your friendship and love. I dedicate this book to you.

Introduction:
Civil Society and Egypt's Arab Spring

On May 6, 2011, leaders of Egypt's largest grantmaking foundations gathered in Beirut, Lebanon, with their counterparts from across the Arab region to discuss how their organizations should respond to the wave of uprisings that had recently swept through much of the Arab world—the so-called Arab Spring. These foundation leaders had convened for the annual meeting of the Arab Foundations Forum, a platform for networking, coordination, and information sharing among a burgeoning group of Arab philanthropies. The session entitled "The Role of Philanthropy in Supporting Reform Agendas" was the most anticipated of the conference, and the room was packed with participants eager to explore their organizations' roles in what seemed to be a new Middle East.

Most of the foundations represented at the conference had been established within the previous decade and had little experience in the realm of political reform. While charitable giving is deeply rooted in Arab cultures, modern-day grantmaking foundations proliferated primarily in the 1990s and early 2000s—when Arab rulers maintained tight control over civil society. Many of the foundations headquartered in the monarchies were governed by royals; those in other Arab states were mostly run by businesspeople who maintained close connections to their countries' ruling regimes. The donors to these foundations had no interest in disrupting the status quo that prevailed at the time, nor in getting thrown in jail for breaking the rules. Throughout their early years, then, the Arab region's foundations had carefully avoided any activities that could be deemed political or contentious.

But times had changed, and the foundation leaders who gathered in Beirut just months after the removal of Tunisia's former president Zine el-Abidine Ben Ali and Egypt's former president Hosni Mubarak saw the writing on the wall. They anticipated the downfall of other Arab dictators and knew that to remain relevant they would need to disentangle themselves from corrupt relationships with authoritarian rulers and realign with social change actors in civil society. During that session on reform agendas, foundation leaders vowed to learn lessons from the protesters' messages, connect with social movements and informal social change initiatives, better support under-served populations, and identify political reform as a key priority. To do so, they would need to "overcome an ingrained avoidance of all things political, controversial, or difficult."[1]

Leaders of Egypt's major grantmaking foundations were at that meeting, and a number of them spoke publicly about their commitment to change. They highlighted the need for a new map both for themselves and for Egypt's civil society organizations—many of which had, like the foundations, been caught up in too-cozy relationships with the Mubarak regime. They partici-pated in group breakout conversations to brainstorm how Arab foundations could be torchbearers of change. And they emphasized that the ideas con-ceived at the conference had to be translated "from flowery speeches . . . into reality."[2] At the end of the session, music boomed from a stereo as the participants held hands and danced around the room. The spirit of optimism and change that had infused Cairo's Tahrir Square during Egypt's January 25, 2011, uprisings flowed through that meeting of grant makers in Beirut.

When the conference attendees got back home to Egypt, though, their foundations did not seem to change course. Nor did the foundations' grantees or, for that matter, the vast majority of Egypt's forty thousand non-governmental organizations (NGOs). Instead of transforming into advocates of democratic political reform and creating new democracy promotion projects, most of Egypt's grantmaking foundations and NGOs remained doggedly focused on socioeconomic development. As a result, they appeared to squander what outside observers and Egyptian civil society leaders alike viewed as a major political opportunity—to bring democracy to Egypt. When the reticence of local foundations and NGOs to act was contrasted with the rapid response of Western donors and Egyptian human rights organizations—bringing increased budgets for democracy promotion to Egypt and working overtime on projects related to electoral, legislative, and judicial reform—it appeared that much of Egypt's NGO sector was being left behind.

There is a straightforward explanation for why the foundation leaders' flowery speeches about embracing political reform failed to translate into reality. For decades, Egypt's NGO sector had operated within a culture of fear wrought by strict government control, coercion, and persecution. Organizations that dared to challenge Mubarak's authoritarian rule faced harassment at best, closure at worst. In order to survive, they worked on projects that were government sanctioned and that advanced the Mubarak regime's development priorities. Some—including and especially Egyptian foundations—formed collaborative and mutually beneficial relationships with Mubarak and his government. Philanthropy and economic development work served as a mechanism through which organization leaders could curry favor with the government—be they monopoly rights for organization leaders' corporations, government grants, or simply the ability to go about their work without harassment from government officials. Disentangling themselves from webs of loyalty to the Mubarak regime would take time.

Moreover, despite the sense of euphoria that electrified Egypt after the uprisings, the political and economic climate was tumultuous, which made strategic decision making difficult. The Supreme Council of the Armed Forces (SCAF) that came to power after Mubarak's deposal governed arbitrarily and increasingly harshly, ultimately cracking down on Egyptian civil society in draconian ways. At the same time, Egypt's economy spiraled downward as foreign investment slowed and tourism dried up. Organization leaders feared being targeted by the SCAF if they took on political activities, and it was unclear how future elected governments would regulate Egypt's NGO sector. Furthermore, as Egypt's economic situation became more precarious, foundations' existing grantees and NGOs' existing beneficiaries needed financial support more than ever. To siphon money away from existing socioeconomic development projects and into political reform activities seemed both dangerous and unfair.

A closer look, however, reveals that a number of Egyptian grantmaking foundations and development NGOs—a subset of Egypt's NGO sector—*did* take advantage of the political opening created by the 2011 uprisings.[3] Publicly, their response was to double down on their socioeconomic development activities. But behind this public façade of staying the course, a number of Egyptian foundations and NGOs structured their work to advance the democratic aspirations of the uprisings. The democracy building work of these organizations was not explicit; it was subtle, veiled, and never publicly presented as "democracy promotion." Yet in quiet conversations, development NGO and foundation leaders proudly explained that democratic political reform was a priority that their organizations embraced and covertly nudged forward.[4] Their efforts were remarkably consistent across organizations and exhibited two key characteristics: 1) they integrated democracy building work into existing, public-facing socioeconomic development programs; and 2) they adopted a participatory approach aimed toward cultivating democratic citizens at grassroots levels.

Most aid programs administered by Western organizations such as the United States Agency for International Development (USAID) and the European Union (EU) clearly distinguish between funding for socioeconomic development projects and funding for democracy and good governance projects. Programming in education, healthcare, job training, arts and culture, and community infrastructure, for example, fall under socioeconomic development. Initiatives related to human rights, elections, legislative and judicial reforms, and other political topics are considered democracy and good governance programs. By contrast, Egypt's development NGO and foundation leaders conceptualized economic and political issues as tightly linked, and they integrated lessons about democratic rights and responsibilities into their socioeconomic development projects. In health clinics, for example, patients not only received medical services but also learned about their right to demand high-quality healthcare for themselves and their families. Groups of handicraft makers discussed the meaning of the Arab uprisings while learning new skills. Some organizations built voter education and registration drives into community meetings that were ostensibly convened to identify local development priorities. These organizations' activities were diverse, but their strategies for couching democratic political reform efforts within socioeconomic development programs were notably similar— even though no development NGO or foundation leaders publicly described their work as constituting "democracy promotion."

Development NGO and foundation leaders recognized that for democracy to take hold in Egypt, national political institutions would need to be reformed. But they also believed that an equally important component of building democracy was the cultivation of democratic citizens, and these NGO and foundation leaders focused their efforts here. Their approach centered on three sets of participatory democratic practices: 1) discussion, debate, and collective problem solving; 2) free expression; and 3) rights claiming. In the first realm, organization leaders convened groups of beneficiaries to discuss local challenges, debate priorities, and develop and implement solutions through collaborative initiatives. Whether around coffee and tea, in libraries, or through summer camp programs, NGO leaders facilitated deliberation and collective action in ways that raised consciousness and habits of collective agency and citizen sovereignty. Organization leaders turned to arts and culture initiatives to promote free expression, a democratic right that was suppressed during decades of authoritarianism. And in the course of their organizations' daily activities, they educated beneficiaries about their rights as citizens and encouraged small-scale mobilization to claim those rights from local government officials. Across all of these activities, organization leaders worked to construct citizens who were mindful of their rights and primed to work collectively to demand those rights from their government.

The understated nature of the democracy building work of Egyptian development NGOs and foundations, coupled with the fact that their leaders never publicly used the words "democracy promotion" to describe what they were up to, allowed these organizations to continue even in the face of government repression. In late 2011, the SCAF launched a campaign against Egypt's NGO sector that smeared organizations for promoting Western political agendas. The SCAF raided and shut down seventeen NGOs and placed forty-three NGO employees on trial for operating their organizations illegally. While this early crackdown focused primarily on international and human rights NGOs, it injected fear into the entire NGO sector and portended future governments' more widespread restrictions on, and repression of, NGOs and foundations. Ultimately, as a result of the government's hostile stance toward organizations working on political reform projects, many Western donors decreased their democracy promotion budgets while international NGOs either scaled back their political reform work or exited Egypt entirely.[5] Meanwhile, employees of Egypt's human rights organizations packed "prison bags" for the day they would be arrested.[6]

By contrast, the Egyptian development NGOs and foundations featured in this book continued to nurture democratic political reform while operating under the radar. As they showcased their government-approved socioeconomic development programs, Egyptian development NGOs and their local funders redoubled efforts to help marginalized groups—including the poor, uneducated, unemployed, and disenfranchised—raise their voices, claim their rights, and fight for greater freedoms. Within their development projects they sought to cultivate collective agency among beneficiaries to claim sovereignty as well as political, economic, and social justice. Their efforts continued even as subsequent ruling regimes dissolved, or forced out, an increasing number of democracy promotion organizations and even after the government ratified a new law that further constrained the types of activities NGOs could pursue.

While Egypt remains under autocratic rule at the time of this writing, the ongoing democracy building work of local development NGOs and foundations deserves our attention for several reasons. First, it suggests that civil society organizations operating in autocratic and semi-autocratic states may have a greater capacity to mobilize citizens for change and promote democratic political reform than much of the scholarly literature concludes. Scholars studying the associational revolution in the Global South since the 1980s have shown that liberal theories of civil society—which portray NGOs as harbingers of democracy—fall short when applied to nondemocratic contexts. Studying the NGO sector in Egypt, China, Russia, Ethiopia, Kenya, and other countries throughout Africa, Asia, and Latin America, scholars have found that a proliferation of NGOs does not necessarily spur democratization and in some cases can actually reinforce authoritarianism.[7] In states that witnessed rapid NGO sector growth, organizations helped autocratic rulers consolidate power by serving as partners in providing social services in eras of welfare state retrenchment. At the same time, the proliferation of professional NGOs divided and weakened once-vibrant civil society spheres by causing social change activists to sequester themselves in bureaucratic institutions and busy themselves with the technical demands of organizational sustainability rather than mobilizing collectively for substantive change.[8] NGOs also created institutional channels through which savvy dictators could monitor and suppress political dissent while simultaneously ensuring that they could meet their socioeconomic development goals.

Most studies of NGOs operating in autocratic and developing countries conclude that NGOs in such contexts have limited capacity to build democracy. While NGOs may enhance human welfare by providing vital social services, they are unlikely agents of political change so long as governmental institutions remain under autocratic control.[9] In other words, civil society organizations must operate in reasonably democratic contexts to be able to carry out the democratic functions typically prescribed to them by liberal theories. The case of Egypt shows that when faced with a political opening, shrewd organizations can, carefully, step into that space. After the 2011 uprisings, the development NGOs and grantmaking foundations featured in this book managed to adopt and maintain democracy building initiatives even as successive governments cracked down on civil society and did their best to extinguish all forms of dissent, which suggests that formerly co-opted organizations may be more resourceful than past research would have it. Their work may not be the magic bullet of democratization that liberal theories of civil society claim,[10] but their agility and persistence indicates that they can contribute to incremental progress toward democratic political reform.

Second, the work of Egypt's development NGOs and foundations has important foreign policy implications for US aid agencies. Democracy aid has come under fire for failing to bring about meaningful democratic political reforms in many parts of Africa, the Middle East, and Central Asia.[11] Funds earmarked for democracy and good governance rarely flow to the types of civil society organizations that are mobilizing rural and grassroots communities. Instead, democracy aid targets a small cluster of organizations that are in the business of generating information.[12] Recipients of democracy promotion grants are primarily professional organizations—some with international headquarters and others that are local—that employ highly trained staff who write reports, host workshops and conferences, offer legal aid, and train would-be democratic political leaders. Democracy aid's technical approach and its concentration among intellectual elites and human rights activists means that it often fails to reach or resonate with large swaths of local populations. As a result, it has a poor track record in catalyzing popular support for democracy or including broad and diverse groups.[13] Moreover, its overt focus on democracy per se makes such aid an easy target for dictators who easily feel threatened.

The efforts of the Egyptian development NGOs and philanthropic foundations chronicled in the following pages offer an alternative way forward. Though not normally considered players in the political reform arena, these organizations' efforts to create spaces for public deliberation and free expression and to facilitate collective problem solving and rights claiming—all decidedly democratic acts—make them effectively partners in democracy promotion. Not only do development NGOs far outnumber human rights organizations in most nondemocratic states; they also tend to have broader constituencies and a less confrontational approach to rallying citizens for democratic change. Their participatory approach to cultivating substantive democracy at local levels can be instructive for the reform of US democracy aid.

The democracy building work by development NGOs and foundations featured in this book was not intended to bring about a rapid transition from authoritarianism to democracy. Instead, it was designed to coax the country toward democratization in a more incremental way. *Delta Democracy* refers to this mode of changemaking, with the uppercase Greek letter *delta* representing, in mathematics, a modicum of difference. The title of this book is of course also a nod to Egypt, whose population pools in the Nile River Delta and whose famous pyramids of Giza resemble the character itself: Δ.

Researching Civil Society in Egypt

I first arrived in Egypt in January 2010, a year prior to the uprisings, with a mind to understand how philanthropic foundations operated in liberalized autocracies—were they, like NGOs, resigned to serving as tools of the state, or were they somehow working surreptitiously to build a more autonomous civil society? A 2002 revision to Egypt's NGO law allowed for the creation of local philanthropic foundations, or *mu'assasat*. In the ensuing years, around one thousand foundations were established. Most were small, operating programs rather than making grants. In fact, their work more closely resembled that of NGOs than what one might associate with foundations. But some wealthy Egyptian businesspeople also created larger grantmaking foundations that were similar to well-known US institutions such as the Ford and Carnegie Foundations. My early research focused on these. The answer to my original question seemed clear: prior to 2010, Egypt's grantmaking foundations not only were controlled by the state; they were co-opted to such an extent that one foundation program officer described the foundation sector as "part of the [Mubarak] regime."[14]

Nevertheless, when the 2011 uprisings broke out, I was curious about how these organizations would respond. Would they refashion themselves as underwriters of civil society's political reform efforts, as most existing theories of philanthropic foundations would predict?[15] Or would they shrink back, as the regime to which they were so closely connected was discredited and partially dismantled? Philanthropic foundations in liberalized autocracies had not yet been widely studied, and extant research on the roles of foundations in supporting social movements was predominantly post hoc.[16] In January 2011, I realized that I had an opportunity to uncover the role of foundations in non-democracies and contribute to understanding how foundations navigate, in real time, a major social movement.

To get a handle on whether or not Egyptian foundations began to promote democracy after Mubarak's fall, I originally thought I should compare their responses to the uprisings with those of Western aid organizations, international democracy-promotion NGOs, and Egyptian human rights organizations—the three groups of organizations typically considered to constitute the democracy promotion establishment. During the first year after the uprisings, I primarily interviewed leaders of Egyptian foundations, Western aid agencies, international NGOs, and human rights organizations. Through conversations with directors and senior program staff members of these groups, it became clear that Egyptian foundations were not adopting the democracy promotion techniques of international organizations or human rights NGOs—for example, advocating publicly for democracy and human rights or building projects around electoral, judicial, and legislative reform. Foundation leaders did narrate the uprisings as a major opportunity for change and vowed to join forces with civil society activists fighting for freedom and democracy. But these foundations did not initiate new grantmaking programs expressly aimed at building democracy. As a result, leaders of the international and human rights NGOs with whom I spoke criticized the local foundations for being uninterested in democracy. They also speculated that foundation leaders profited from the status quo under Mubarak and were either leery of or downright opposed to a more democratic future.

But the sample of organizations whose leaders I interviewed in 2011 constituted just a fragment of Egypt's NGO sector. There are approximately forty thousand registered NGOs (or *gam'iyyat*, which transliterates to "associations") in Egypt, including charitable, development, and human rights organizations. Human rights NGOs number less than one hundred; meanwhile, charitable and development NGOs form the vast majority of registered organizations, providing social welfare and economic development services throughout Egypt. Because I was familiar with theories of NGOs in liberalized autocracies, I assumed these latter organizations were not likely to be engaged in democracy promotion after the uprisings. If they did engage, I assumed their efforts would be fledgling and not a standard by which to evaluate the efforts of local foundations.

I was wrong. Early in 2012, a conversation with the founder of a development NGO changed the trajectory of my research. He articulated a more substantive form of democracy predicated on a new social contract between the government and citizens—one in which the Egyptian people held the power to determine the conditions under which they lived, express and debate their views in the public sphere, and demand responsiveness and accountability from the government. At that moment I realized that by focusing only on international and human rights NGOs as prototypical democracy promotion organizations, I was potentially overlooking other groups that might be working to advance democratic political reform in ways not typically funded by Western democracy aid. I therefore expanded my sample of organizations to include a wide variety of development NGOs, from small, volunteer-based, grassroots groups to more professional NGOs working in villages throughout the country.

When I asked the leaders of these organizations how they understood the goals of the uprisings and what steps, if any, they were taking to help achieve those goals, they shared remarkably similar insights. First, they believed the uprisings reflected deeply held and widely shared economic and political grievances and that these injustices were tightly linked. Concentrated political power within the Mubarak regime, they believed, allowed high-ranking government officials to structure the economy in such a way that political and economic elites prospered while many working-class Egyptians received substandard education and healthcare and had trouble finding jobs. Therefore, democratic political reform would need to encompass the assurance of basic human rights and access to a decent standard of living for all citizens. Development NGO leaders also believed that cultivating democratic values and skills among everyday citizens was just as important as reforming national political institutions. They focused their organizations' political reform efforts on discussion and deliberation, free expression, and rights claiming, and integrated their initiatives into the existing socioeconomic development programs on which their beneficiaries relied. This strategy not only respected the intertwining of the economic and the political, it also masked organizations' democratic proclivities and kept them relatively free from government repression.

As I continued my fieldwork and circled back to Egypt's grantmaking foundations, I realized that they *did* seize the opportunity to realign with civil society after the uprisings. Like development NGOs, they took a citizen-oriented, participatory approach. Their story was more complex than that of the NGOs, though, because many of the foundations' board members had been closely connected to Mubarak. Some were even considered his cronies. Therefore, it wasn't enough for foundation staff members to view the 2011 uprisings as a major opening for civil society. Foundation staff also had to convince their governing boards that 2011 marked a moment when the foundations could choose on which side of history they would be remembered. Remarkably, most chose the side of change. But due to old ties to the Mubarak regime, the foundations had to be particularly careful in their efforts to support democratic political reform. Creating new democracy grant programs or bearing the torch of human rights proved out of the question; such actions were too risky for foundation board members who were skittish about provoking Egypt's new political leaders. So, instead of sending grants to human rights NGOs or bankrolling projects to reform national political institutions, Egypt's grantmaking foundations partnered with existing development NGO grantees to cultivate a culture of participatory, democratic citizenship at grassroots levels.

The bulk of my fieldwork took place between February 2011 and July 2012. I was also on the ground in Egypt from January through March 2010, from May through August 2014, and for two weeks in October 2017. During those periods, I was based in Cairo and traveled throughout the country to visit organizations, meet their leaders, and observe their activities. I conducted over one hundred interviews with leaders of Egyptian philanthropic foundations, development NGOs, and human rights NGOs; leaders of international donor agencies and NGOs; and activists, academics, and close observers of Egyptian civil society.[17] I spoke, less formally, with countless other Egyptians familiar with the local civil society landscape. Because I did not have access to official government lists of registered NGOs, I identified organizations and contacts through snowball sampling—in which the researcher relies on existing contacts to introduce new ones—and through lists that I cobbled together from a variety of sources, including the Gerhart Center for Philanthropy and Civic Engagement at the American University in Cairo (AUC), the Arab Foundations Forum, the United Nations Development Programme's Development Partners Group, Western donor agencies, and local grantmaking foundations.

There is a risk of selection bias inherent in nonrandom sampling,[18] and in fact most of the organizations in my sample were similar in that, first, they were in some way connected to national, regional, and global networks of NGOs and foundations; and second, they were professional enough to receive grants (even if very small ones from local funders) and be listed in databases and registries. These groups constitute only one segment of Egypt's vast NGO landscape, and a relatively small one at that. Most NGOs in Egypt are small, charitable groups that lack the basic managerial structures and global reach of the organizations I studied. Nevertheless, certain characteristics of nonrandom sampling enabled me to gain access to organizations I would have missed through purely random sampling. In particular, snowball sampling opened countless doors to organizations that most likely would have remained closed if I had relied strictly on cold calling. Moreover, the select groups of organizations included in this study are the most eligible contenders for foreign democracy aid; their unique efforts to nurture democratic political reform should therefore command the interest of policymakers.

The ethnographic nature of my research allowed me to complement and corroborate interviews with direct observation. I watched and sometimes participated in organizations' activities and also sat in on their workshops, seminars, and press conferences. I often attended the protests that continued to spring up throughout 2011 and 2012, albeit always as an observer at the back of the crowd. I also sat in on national and regional conferences of Arab NGO and foundation leaders including the annual conference of the Arab Foundations Forum, the annual meeting of the World Congress of Muslim Philanthropists, and Takaful: Annual Conference on Arab Philanthropy and Civic Engagement.

Formal interviews generally lasted one hour but sometimes stretched for multiple hours. Many extended into daylong site visits. Most interviews were prearranged and semi-structured, but some were less structured and occurred spontaneously. While I am conversant in Arabic, I conducted interviews in English or with the assistance of an Arabic translator. Questions were open-ended so as to encourage interviewees to expound on their perspectives on the uprisings and their organizations' responses. I asked my interlocutors about their views on the meaning of the uprisings; whether or not they believed their organizations played a role in the uprisings; the opportunities and challenges the uprisings and their aftermath posed for the organizations and their beneficiaries; what they believed were the most important roles for civil society organizations in the wake of the uprisings; whether their organizations changed the nature of their work after the uprisings and, if so, why; and their views on the wider response of civil society groups to the uprisings.

Because organizational leaders may conscientiously and selectively present themselves in particular ways to researchers—especially foreign researchers—I took steps to ensure the validity of my interview data. I embedded myself in networks of local NGOs, social change actors, and everyday Egyptians to build trust and hear a variety of perspectives in casual conversations. I also triangulated my findings with ethnographic participant observation and conversations with in-country experts. Finally, I returned to Egypt on four trips between 2010 and 2017 in order to meet with organization leaders multiple times and confirm that their accounts were consistent over time.

In light of the sensitive political context, the culture of fear and intimidation that had permeated the NGO sector for decades, and the ubiquitous presence of Egypt's state security apparatus, I guaranteed interviewees anonymity and took notes by hand instead of using a recording device.[19] Many contacts were so fearful of talking to a foreign researcher that they insisted on providing oral, rather than written, consent. Some also suspected that their electronic devices were being monitored, so our messages to coordinate meetings were brief and veiled. In order to protect organizations, I occasionally met interlocutors at cafés rather than at their premises or at an activity site.

Due to all of these precautions, along with the fact that many organizations whose leaders I spoke with and whose activities I observed have since been shut down or forced out of Egypt, I cannot provide the list of organizations included in my sample.[20] I can, however, shed light on these organizations' characteristics. The Egyptian philanthropic foundations self-identified as private, corporate, and community foundations and gave grants primarily to development NGOs. Some also operated their own development programs. All were established after 2002 and, regardless of the religious backgrounds of their donors, they all described themselves as secular organizations interested in economic development. Foundation board and staff members were predominantly fluent in both Arabic and English. They were familiar with the development industry and connected to other foundation leaders in the region through the Arab Foundations Forum, the Gerhart Center for Philanthropy and Civic Engagement at the AUC, and the Global Fund for Community Foundations. Although still in its infancy, Egypt's foundation sector was growing and institutionalizing rapidly and the organizations I connected with were at the forefront of the sector's expansion. Most foundations were based in and around Cairo while their grantees were located throughout Egypt. Foundation program staff traveled throughout the country to meet with grantees and observe their activities.

The international organizations in my sample included bilateral and multilateral aid agencies, private philanthropic foundations, and international democracy and development NGOs. Most were headquartered in the United States and Europe and maintained offices in Cairo. All were large, professional organizations whose names are well known in democracy and development sectors throughout the world. Staff members were fluent in English and many spoke Arabic as well. Many of the donors were members of the Development Partners Group, a group of Western donors convened by the

United Nations Development Programme (UNDP) to coordinate international aid efforts in Egypt. The international NGOs in my sample received funding from these Western donors, among others. These organizations were all based in Cairo and had varying levels of outreach to other parts of Egypt, with democracy aid heavily targeting Cairo and development work spread further afield.

The Egyptian NGOs in this study included self-identified human rights NGOs and development NGOs. The human rights NGOs were based in Cairo and received funding almost exclusively from Western donors. Offices were professional and outfitted in current technologies, but they were not fancy by Western standards. Staff members were fluent in both Arabic and English and were well versed in universal vocabularies of human rights, democracy, and development. Their activities centered on human rights advocacy and included trainings, workshops, reports, and legal aid.

The development NGOs in my study ranged in size and level of professionalization. Some had ten or more paid staff members and offices that resembled those of the human rights NGOs. Others were smaller, relied heavily on volunteers, and operated in multifunctional spaces. Most received funding from both local and international donors. They worked across a wide spectrum of program areas, including education, job training, health and human services, arts and culture, environmental protection, women and youth empowerment, and community development. Their office locations and activities spanned the country. Staff members were fluent in Arabic and many spoke English as well.

It is important to note the types of organizations that I did *not* include in this study, and they are many, given the vast size and scope of Egypt's NGO sector. I excluded three main groups of organizations: Islamic charitable and development organizations, small charitable groups, and small operating foundations. I excluded Islamic organizations because other scholars have extensively these groups,[21] and I excluded small charitable organizations and small operating foundations because they were not the typical recipients of local foundation grants or democracy aid. Since Islamic organizations, small charities, and operating foundations constitute the vast majority of organizations in Egypt, the reader should not assume that my findings pertain to the entire Egyptian NGO sector.

The organizations I did include in this study are, by and large, the types of organizations most eligible for Western democracy aid. Most, no matter how small, are professional enough to apply for grants and manage the logistical hurdles involved in receiving funds from abroad. Those that do not seek funding from abroad are eligible for grants from local foundations (who, in turn, could accept and regrant funds from Western donors). Therefore, these organizations' ability to take advantage of the political opening created by the uprisings and to incorporate democracy building efforts into their programs should be of interest to Western democracy brokers—and, as I argue in this book's concluding chapter, instructive for the reform of US democracy aid.

Organizations and Powers That Be at Cross Purposes

The agility of Egypt's development NGOs and foundations after the uprisings offers lessons for theoretical understandings of civil society organizations. The story of authoritarian regimes' ability to manipulate and coerce NGOs and foundations into doing the government's bidding usually ends bleakly, with civil society organizations acknowledged as important social service providers but thought of as unable to work in any sort of adversarial capacity. The maneuverability of the organizations featured in this book suggests that co-optation is not a death knell. Just as savvy autocrats can adapt to political openings and reassert power, so too can civil society organizations take advantage of political openings to realign with the people and engage in forms of concealed contestation.

Liberal theories of civil society, which continue to guide much scholarship and foreign aid, frame NGOs and philanthropic foundations as hallmarks of a vibrant civil society and liberalized, democratic state.[22] Scholars describe NGOs as key sites of collective empowerment where citizens come together to express a plurality of interests and mobilize to promote change.[23] In addition to cultivating tolerance, respect, and civic participation among members, NGOs are thought to act as watchdogs over the state and vehicles through which citizens advance their interests in policy arenas. Through their efforts to safeguard the interests of marginalized groups, pluralize the public sphere, and check state power, NGOs are considered part and parcel of a healthy civil society and, by extension, of strong democracy.[24] In addition, NGOs are theorized to be sites of mobilization to build collective demand for a more democratic future.[25] Philanthropic foundations are also considered well situated to support citizen empowerment and mobilization. Endowed with financial assets in perpetuity and accountable only to the mandates of the founding donor, foundations are presumed to be uniquely positioned to support movements for transformative change and to fight for policy reforms that advance social goals.[26]

These theories, which were constructed primarily through studies of civil society in established or transitioning democracies, fail to hold up when applied to non-democracies—including liberalized autocracies such as Egypt. Liberalized autocracies—also referred to as semi-autocratic states or hybrid regimes—are states that have partially opened their political, economic, and civic sectors but remain ruled by autocrats. They are characterized by elections that are neither free nor fair, opposition parties that are divided and weak, privatized economies marked by crony capitalism, and NGO sectors that are tightly regulated by the government.[27] Partial liberalization presents the guise of liberalization and democratization to both international observers and local citizens, but maintains a structure that prevents potential opposition groups—be they political parties, corporations, or NGOs—from gaining strength and collaborating to unseat the ruling regime. Instead, the autocratic ruler pits these groups against one another in a strategy that political scientist Daniel Brumberg refers to as "divide and rule."[28] But it is not only in liberalized autocracies that NGOs have mushroomed in recent years—NGO sectors have also emerged and rapidly expanded in single-party states and absolute monarchies such as China and Saudi Arabia. Yet democracy has not taken hold. On the contrary, rulers maintain absolute power despite the many NGOs operating within their respective borders.

The idea that autocrats can simultaneously promote NGO sector growth and retain dictatorial power suggests that in autocratic and semi-autocratic states, the proliferation of NGOs need not signal an inevitable march toward democracy. Rather, NGO sector expansion may be part of the ruling regime's strategy to retain power.[29] Autocrats have developed a range of techniques to co-opt and control NGOs. As governments privatize their economies and their systems of providing welfare, they use NGOs to pick up the slack left by shrinking government agencies. Regimes bolster their reputations by promoting, supporting, and even collaborating with NGOs that provide social services. One might wonder whether the transfer of service provision from governments to NGOs would erode the state's legitimacy among populations that traditionally relied on the government to provide for their basic welfare. But studies indicate that most people don't care who provides services, so long as they are delivered.[30] And since NGOs are often more flexible than bulky government agencies, they can sometimes provide higher-quality services more effectively and efficiently than government service providers can.

Recognizing this, in many states that are semi- or non-democratic—including, for example, Kenya, China, Jordan, and Palestine—governments have built collaborative, consultative, and co-optative relationships with local NGO sectors.[31] These arrangements often lead to enhanced service provision and government learning, as NGOs provide government officials information about target population priorities and advocate on their constituents' behalves for improved service delivery. But at the same time, organizations that develop such close relationships with the state tend to become reliant upon and supportive of it. In such cases, NGOs are unlikely to criticize their government patrons.[32] Ultimately, government legitimacy is enhanced as citizens receive relatively high-quality services and NGOs endorse—rather than question—the government.

Autocrats deliberately control and fragment NGO sectors and, in doing so, divide society and prevent citizens from mobilizing against regime dominance. Autocratic rulers develop regulatory schemes that allow them to monitor and control organizations' operations. Laws governing NGOs clearly delimit the types of activities that organizations may pursue—generally prohibiting activities related to politics or policy—and also include strict rules regarding organizations' registration, governance, and fundraising. These laws, which are often vaguely worded so as to allow government officials to interpret them however they see fit, are designed to channel NGO activity into spheres of socioeconomic development approved by the regime and prevent governing boards or external funders from steering the organizations along more oppositional paths. In addition, unwritten rules govern the size and collaborative activity of NGOs, preventing organizations from growing too large or working together, thus minimizing their collective strength.[33]

Government bureaucrats enforce NGO laws through formal and informal monitoring. They review reports about organizations' activities, board meetings, and finances, and have been known to eavesdrop on the correspondence of NGO leaders and show up unannounced to observe board meetings and activities.[34] The monitoring stokes fear and distrust within NGO sectors and also gives government officials a window into civil society, allowing them to identify and quell potential citizen mobilization before it has the opportunity to erupt into mass uprisings.[35]

Autocrats' strategies for co-opting NGOs operate like a pressure-release valve. Within semi-autocratic states, NGOs provide some of the few spaces in which citizens can gather to try to create change. They provide a rare outlet for participation, however circumscribed, and allow members to "blow off steam."[36] NGOs thus funnel citizens' desires for meaningful participation into organizations that are nominally autonomous but in fact are tightly regulated by the state. These groups serve to mollify citizens, allowing them a space to gather and feel empowered while simultaneously lowering the risk of collective opposition to, and action against, the regime.

While monitoring independently formed NGOs, autocratic rulers also set up government-organized NGOs, or GONGOs, to manage debates on politically sensitive topics such as human rights and women's empowerment.[37] By stacking the boards of GONGOs with government officials and regime sympathizers, rulers can control national conversations surrounding issues of democracy and good governance while projecting the image of a regime dedicated to citizen rights and freedoms. Thus, the large NGO sectors that exist alongside many hybrid and autocratic regimes give an impression of genuine liberalization, but they do not portend democracy. Instead, NGOs can enhance regime legitimacy by ensuring that citizens' human welfare needs are met while simultaneously serving as channels through which astute autocrats cripple the opposition. NGOs understand that in order to survive, they cannot be autonomous from the state or adopt adversarial relationships with the government.[38] Instead, they must position themselves as cooperators and collaborators in realms of service provision, submit to intrusive monitoring and control by government officials, and relinquish any hope for independence.

In the years leading up to 2011, Egypt was a quintessential liberalized autocracy. It was home to elections that were neither free nor fair, an economic system that rewarded party loyalists with government contracts and monopoly rights, and a tightly controlled NGO sector. The Mubarak regime was demonstrably skilled in techniques of control and co-optation. Through formal legislation and informal harassment, the regime prevented NGOs from conducting political or policy-related activities that might challenge the government's power. In addition, the regime provided incentives—for example, funding opportunities and preferential treatment—for organizations to align their work with the government's development priorities. Projects in areas such as job training, education, healthcare, social services, and economic development were encouraged, while activities related to human rights, rule of law, and political reform were almost entirely prohibited. As a result, most Egyptian NGOs and foundations adopted complementary and cooperative, rather than adversarial, relations with the Mubarak regime. They helped to legitimate the regime's neoliberal economic development strategy by filling gaps in welfare service provision rather than working to build opposition to the government's policies or its authoritarian form of rule.

When the 2011 uprisings broke out, the bulk of Egypt's NGOs and foundations were experienced in socioeconomic development work but had no background in promoting democracy. Some organizations not only were resigned to working within the government's development priorities and policies, they actively partnered—or even colluded—with the government to make the authoritarian status quo palatable for those who otherwise might have created a formidable opposition. As a result, Egyptian NGOs and foundations were not primed to serve as democracy builders.

But despite being ill positioned to promote democracy, many Egyptian NGOs and foundations *did* actively work to cultivate democracy in Egypt in the years following Mubarak's deposal. However, they did so in ways that went unrecognized by most observers—including, importantly, subsequent government rulers. The democracy building work of these organizations did not resemble the techniques commonly used by the democracy promotion establishment and was deliberately subtle, masking political reform efforts behind socioeconomic development projects. Citizen-led and participatory, the programs nurtured values of democratic citizenship through projects as innocuous as education, literacy, job training, arts and culture, and healthcare.

Promoting Democracy under Qualified Autocracy

Western democracy aid constitutes a specific strand of foreign aid that is separate from humanitarian and development aid. It is expressly political in its aims and is designed to bring about democratic reforms of national-level institutions, particularly in the electoral, legislative, judicial, and civic realms. Democracy aid is an important foreign policy tool within the aid frameworks of a variety of Western states, particularly the United States, European Union, and distinct European countries. Democracy promotion grants are administered primarily by bilateral and multilateral aid agencies, quasi-governmental foundations whose mission is to promote democracy globally, and large private foundations. Grants are distributed primarily to a group of international NGOs explicitly focused on democracy building and to local advocacy and human rights organizations in the target country.

While the specific policies and practices of democracy aid vary by both donor and target country, Western democracy aid exhibits relatively consistent characteristics across funders and regions. First, such programs attempt to spread procedural democracy through a top-down approach that targets national political institutions. Goals include free and fair elections, broadly representative legislatures, independent judiciaries, and autonomous civil society organizations that can serve as watchdogs over the state and bring a variety of citizens' voices into the political sphere.

Second, democracy aid funds technical projects that are carried out by trained professionals. Organizations are staffed with highly educated, well-paid employees conversant in the language of democracy promotion and skilled in drafting grant proposals and measuring progress toward clearly stated goals. Typical projects produce reports, trainings, and workshops and involve consultations with national political figures. Quantifiable outputs are included in regular reports to the donor.

Third, democracy aid focuses expressly on political institutions. It typically does not include funding for socioeconomic development reforms. It targets elections, legislatures, judiciaries, political parties, and the media. Projects in fields such as education, healthcare, arts and culture, and infrastructure fall under aid budgets allocated for socioeconomic development.

Scholars of democracy aid have argued that these programs fail to challenge dictators or instigate radical forms of collective action.[39] Instead of mobilizing citizens to engage in the protests, sit-ins, and demonstrations that characterize most social movements, democracy aid funds the production of outputs that satisfy technical grant requirements but fail to appeal to everyday citizens. Lacking widespread recognition and respect, professional NGOs that receive the bulk of democracy aid tend to be more upwardly accountable to their donors than downwardly accountable to local populations. As political scientist and democracy aid expert Sheila Carapico has argued, and as evidence in this book confirms, Western democracy aid neither undergirded the 2011 uprisings nor spurred grassroots mobilization in their aftermath.[40] And, because the aid was so overtly political, it was quickly roadblocked by government repression.

The democracy building techniques used by the Egyptian development NGOs and supported by the local foundations featured in the following pages present an alternative approach. Rejecting the notion that democracy is best formulated by highly trained professionals and must be bankrolled through grants for knowledge production and trainings, Egyptian development NGOs and foundations operated by the philosophy that "All you need is tea." With social rituals such as drinking tea, these organizations could bring together community members to discuss their problems, debate priorities, and work collectively to both create their own solutions and claim their rights from government officials. The NGOs and foundations featured in this book cultivated an ethos of citizenship and the development of a democratic culture instead of trying to impose it. This form of democracy was more relevant to the lives of long-time subjects of a dictator than voting in elections or serving in parliament. It was the real stuff of democracy that had been denied to Egyptians for decades. And by weaving this form of democracy promotion into socioeconomic development programs, organizations both respected the intertwined nature of politics and economics in Egypt and avoided government suspicion. This citizen-oriented, participatory approach—which through its subtlety allowed organizations to persist even in the face of government crackdowns—offers a model for reforming US democracy aid in ways that make it more accountable to local citizens and sustainable through political tumult.

While most Western *democracy* aid programs neglect a widespread appeal to local citizens, the idea that citizen participation is critical to fundamental and sustainable change is relatively orthodox in international *development* realms.[41] American foreign policymakers, donors, and international development practitioners have asserted since at least the 1950s that sustainable development happens most effectively when members of the target community contribute to the design and implementation of development projects.[42] As a result, small-scale community development programs that rely on local participation feature prominently, alongside large-scale modernization projects, in US-sponsored development programs throughout the Global South.[43]

Development experts' contemporary enthusiasm for participation can be traced in part to Robert Chambers's work in the mid-1990s on the Participatory Rural Appraisal (PRA). PRAs comprise a group of development methods that claim to "enable rural people to share, enhance, and analyze their knowledge of life and conditions, to plan and to act."[44] While lofty in its goals, the methods of PRA are quite technical and include mapping development sites; producing diagrams, calendars, and charts to analyze environmental conditions; conducting transects (systematic walks and observations); and assessing, through scores and ranks, various development interventions. Such activities are carried out jointly between development professionals and local residents. Participatory development programs built on the same logic as the PRA have been implemented throughout the Global South in a wide range of fields, including healthcare, environmental conservation, agriculture, and poverty alleviation.[45]

In notable instances, the international community's enthusiasm for participation has extended to democracy building. Participatory democracy schemes, which have been deployed in a number of emerging democracies, including Kenya, Brazil, and Chile,[46] consist of formal institutions designed to provide opportunities for citizens to interact directly with governing authorities and influence political priorities and public policies.[47] Participatory democracy programs aim to broaden the range of voices heard in policymaking processes and to amplify the interests and concerns of citizens directly affected by the decisions made. In turn, governments are supposed to become more responsive and accountable to the people served and, ultimately, deliver better outcomes. Structures and opportunities for participation are diverse and range from neighborhood councils and associations to participatory budgeting initiatives, participatory urban planning exercises, and public policy management councils.[48] In these forums, citizens are brought face to face with government bureaucrats in discussions, debates, and consultations that, if successful, influence public policies.

Participatory development and democracy programs take an important step in acknowledging the value of local voices in both development design and policy deliberations. Yet they have a poor record of fundamentally shifting power relations in society, and a chorus of scholars have criticized participatory programs for depoliticizing development and public policy processes.[49] If citizen participation is conceptualized on a continuum from weak to strong—with weak participation suggesting that local citizens are consulted and informed about development projects and public policies and strong participation suggesting that citizens contest and negotiate power with development and government officials while realizing their rights, exercising their voices, and attaining a degree of control over goals and processes— then participatory development and democracy programs tend to fall on the weak end of the scale.[50] Development experts and politicians may consider citizens' perspectives when devising projects and policies, but participatory encounters rarely challenge the prevailing social order or encourage a radical rethinking of the social, economic, and political structures that shape societal relations.[51] As a result, communities that take part in participatory initiatives may wind up with better infrastructure and services, but the development and government officers who orchestrate the programs remain in dominant positions.

Some of the development NGOs featured in this book took part in participatory development programs administered by Western aid organizations. (Notably, these programs were part of socioeconomic development aid programs, not democracy promotion programs.) Doing so brought in valuable funds to organizations operating on shoestring budgets. But the directors of these Egyptian NGOs criticized the programs for failing to address or dismantle existing structures of power and control. One NGO leader, particularly frustrated by his organization's involvement in a PRA, said that participatory programs gave Egyptians the ability to "play and have fun" but didn't provide the resources or power necessary for local people to truly solve problems. Development NGO leaders widely believed that participation matters, but that most programs funded by Western aid organizations imposed bureaucracy, stifled local innovation, and resulted in projects that were more aligned with Western donor priorities than with local community needs.

Meanwhile, typical participatory democracy schemes were out of the question since Egypt's transitional governments seemed to have no interest in building channels for truly open communication and consultation with citizens. Instead of inviting perspectives, critiques, and advice from local Egyptians, the rulers who came to power after the uprisings harassed and suppressed individuals and organizations that questioned or challenged their decisions. Human rights organizations and prominent activists in particular were targeted, with organizations shut down and individuals slapped with jail time, asset freezes, and travel bans. Even when the government did claim to welcome citizen input, few Egyptians believed they could express their genuine points of view if those diverged from the government's agenda.

Yet Egyptian development NGO and foundation leaders did believe in the power of participation and actively created spaces for it. The subtle yet striking difference between the initiatives that these organizations facilitated and the ones typically administered by international development groups was the former's focus on politics and power. The 2011 uprisings gave local NGO and foundation leaders the opportunity to tie engagement and participation directly to political outcomes. Throughout their programs, organization leaders sought to shift participants' political subjectivities from subjects to citizens. They consistently framed their work around issues of freedom and justice, reminding participants of their rights as democratic citizens and encouraging them to mobilize and claim their rights through contentious acts. They emboldened participants to directly confront government officials about their grievances and to reclaim public spaces as their own. Organizations' efforts were subversive; they were not sanctioned by the state. But, by integrating what amounted to democracy building work into socioeconomic development projects, organizations managed to evade government repression.

In the years following Mubarak's ouster, the space for civil society in Egypt contracted. Successive governments—led by the SCAF, Mohammed Morsi, and Abdel Fattah al-Sisi—escalated an assault on NGOs and donors operating throughout the country. Organizations explicitly promoting democracy—including Western aid agencies, international NGOs, and local human rights organizations—bore the brunt of government crackdowns. Some international NGOs and Egyptian human rights organizations were forced out of Egypt, while certain Western aid agencies scaled back their democracy promotion budgets.

Throughout this turmoil, the foundations and development NGOs featured in this book persevered in their attempts to incubate democracy in Egypt. Their approach offers a timely model for the reform of US democracy aid relevant to both regional and global trends. NGO and foundation sectors are proliferating throughout the Arab region and Global South as leaders privatize their economies and look to foundations and NGOs to fill the gaps. At the same time, governing regimes have learned strategies of co-optation and repression that strangle local opposition groups and restrict foreign funds for democracy.[52] NGOs and their donors are finding novel ways of contesting government rule and advocating for freedom while evading government suppression. This book tells their story.

***

The book begins with an account of Egypt's NGO sector as it existed under Mubarak. Tracing the growth of Egypt's NGO sector through the latter half of the twentieth century, chapter 1 introduces the reader to the types of organizations established and shows how the Mubarak regime used them to simultaneously divide Egyptian civil society and advance the government's neoliberal economic agenda. Through official laws, unofficial harassment, and clientelist relations, the Mubarak regime molded an NGO sector that addressed social welfare needs and presented a guise of liberalization while failing to unite in a cohesive oppositional bloc.

In the wake of Mubarak's overthrow, Egyptian citizens expressed a new-found desire to participate in bringing freedom and democracy to the country. Egyptian NGOs and foundations played an important role in harnessing that energy and involving activists in organized activities related to democratic political reform. Yet by late 2011, Egypt's transitional government began to crack down on the NGO sector even more harshly than the Mubarak regime had. In addition, Egypt's economy declined precipitously. Chapter 2 lays out the opportunities and challenges that the 2011 uprisings created for Egyptian civil society organizations and briefly describes how two sets of donors—Western aid organizations and Egyptian philanthropic foundations—responded in the months following Mubarak's removal.

Chapter 3 outlines the West's democracy promotion playbook and presents its promise and perils. Democracy aid has been criticized by both scholars and Egyptian NGO leaders for failing to effectively confront dictators or to resonate with local populations. Yet democracy aid provides crucial funding for organizations that otherwise have limited sources of cash. This chapter introduces a range of perspectives on the strengths and weaknesses of the West's democracy promotion strategies.

Chapter 4 presents the democracy building strategies of Egypt's philan-thropic foundations and development NGOs. These organizations harnessed citizens' desires to take part in Egypt's trajectory and positioned themselves as facilitators of citizen-led initiatives. Instead of creating and imposing their own reform initiatives, Egyptian foundations and development NGOs worked closely with grassroots communities to cultivate democracy on their terms. This approach both respected grassroots priorities and cultures and allowed the organizations to evade government crackdowns.

When Abdel Fattah al-Sisi was installed as president in 2014, he quickly moved to consolidate power and repress Egypt's NGO sector. In 2017 the Egyptian government ratified an even more oppressive NGO law that fur-ther restricted foreign funding, eliminated loopholes for human rights or-ganizations, curtailed permissible activities, and instituted more severe punishments for violating the law. Rather than a transition to democracy, Egypt seemed to have settled into even deeper autocracy, as President Sisi curtailed civil society even more repressively than Mubarak. Still, development NGO and foundation leaders persevered, finding new and creative ways to continue to fight for reform. Drawing upon data collected in October 2017, chapter 5 presents their efforts.

The concluding chapter ties together lessons learned and offers a set of policy recommendations aimed at making US democracy aid more relevant, sustainable, and effective.[53]

1

The Co-Optation of Egypt's NGO Sector

I rose early on the morning of the 2011 Eid al-Adha, eager to witness the festivities in my Cairo neighborhood. I was warned that rivers of blood would flow through the streets, but instead I found streams of people carrying small bags of meat while laughing and talking cheerfully. This was clearly a special day. Venturing back a side street from which people were emerging, I spotted an open garage. As Figure 1.1 shows, the skin of an animal was stretched on the floor of the garage, and behind the skin a group of men were carving the carcass on a large table. The family responsible for the animal's sacrifice invited me in to watch and told me with satisfaction that the meat would be given to all needy people who came by. Throughout the day, Egyptian friends told me about their own animal sacrifices and their gifts to the needy. The happiness that their giving brought them was palpable.

Each year, Muslims throughout the world celebrate Eid al-Adha, one of two *eid* holidays. Also known as the feast of the sacrifice, the festival honors the prophet Ibrahim's willingness to sacrifice his son in submission to God. God intervened through an angel that placed a sheep in the son's place, saving the boy. During the holiday, Muslims sacrifice animals as a symbol of Ibrahim's devotion to God. Those who can afford to do so slaughter their best animals and distribute the meat to those in need, including family members, friends, neighbors, and the poor.

The distribution of meat during Eid al-Adha reflects a much broader tradition of charitable giving in Egypt. Beginning in Ottoman times, wealthy people of the lands that we now call the Middle East established private endowments to fund a wide variety of public services and local infrastructure. Today, private charitable giving takes place not only during religious holidays, when it is especially pronounced, but throughout the year in the forms of religious tithes (*zakat* in Islam, *ushur* in the Coptic faith), secular gifts (*sadaqa*), and volunteering to provide services for others. Conducted largely between individuals, or between individuals and religious institutions, these forms of charity are deeply rooted in Egyptian society and reflect a strong spirit of *takaful*, or social solidarity.

Figure 1.1. Eid al-Adha.
Source: Author's photo.

The NGOs and philanthropic foundations that proliferated in Egypt from the 1950s to the present and are the focus of this book intersect with traditional forms of individual charity but constitute a distinct sector of development organizations encouraged, facilitated, and managed by the state. Whereas idealized notions of NGOs assume that they arise from and operate according to the mandates of grassroots populations, Egypt's modern NGO sector was both propelled and tightly orchestrated by successive ruling regimes that used NGOs to advance their respective visions for Egypt's political economy. This state-led growth created a field of organizations that served to legitimize each regime's development priorities while simultaneously undermining the NGOs' capacity to band together as an oppositional force for change. By the time of the 2011 uprisings, Egypt's NGO sector was in a weak position vis-à-vis the government and unskilled in standard techniques of democracy promotion. To show how Egypt's NGOs found themselves in this debilitated situation, this chapter begins by tracing Egypt's evolving political economy of charity from the time of Mohammed Ali's rule to the presidency of Anwar Sadat.

The Political Economy of Charity in Egypt

Although the influence of Egypt's charitable organizations and private philanthropic institutions has ebbed and flowed based on the political economy of the state, these organizations have been important providers and funders of social welfare and public services throughout the country's history. Consecutive ruling regimes carefully managed Egypt's NGO sector expansion and used organizations within the sector to push their social welfare agendas. During the Middle Ages, public services and infrastructure were funded and administered mostly through private charity. Wealthy philanthropists formed *awqaf* (sing. *waqf*), or Islamic endowments, as religious acts and in doing so laid the bedrock for the social welfare system.[1] A *waqf* could be formed by an individual, family, or group of unrelated individuals and could consist of a variety of types of capital including land, buildings, machinery, and cash. Revenues earned from the assets were designated in perpetuity to finance the provision of public services or the construction and maintenance of public infrastructure. Throughout the Middle Ages, *awqaf* supported soup kitchens, mosques, schools, hospitals, roads, parks, wells, and cemeteries, creating a system that relied on private benevolence to provide for the public good.

As early as 1812, Mohammed Ali—regarded as the founder of modern Egypt—began to confiscate *awqaf* and bring them under the state's jurisdiction. Ali began buying up *waqf*-owned land and in 1835 he established the Ministry of Endowments to oversee Egypt's *waqf* system.[2] At the same time, Ali created a centralized state bureaucracy that began to assume responsibility for welfare services such as poor relief, health, and education.[3] Such state intervention in the welfare arena did not wipe out private charity: philanthropists continued to establish and administer *awqaf*, and Egypt's first NGOs—including the Gamey al-Maaref publishing organization, the Geographical Society, the Islamic Benefit Society, and the Coptic Benevolent Society—were created between 1868 and 1891.[4] But Ali's insertion of the state into the public service arena set into motion a practice of state management of social welfare that would be strengthened by subsequent ruling regimes.

Egypt's private charitable sector expanded during Britain's colonial rule of 1882–1952, but so too did state oversight. In 1939 the Ministry of Social Affairs (MOSA) was created to institutionalize the state's role in overseeing poor relief, and in 1945 Law 49 subsumed all charities under the ministry's purview. The 1952 revolution that won Egypt's independence brought Gamal Abdel Nasser to power and ushered in a new wave of state centralization. Nasser launched a state-led development strategy designed to broaden and deepen the role of the government in welfare provision and simultaneously nationalize vast swaths of private enterprise.[5] Under Nasser's rule, state-owned enterprises came to dominate banking, manufacturing, transportation, and foreign trade sectors. In addition, the national welfare state expanded as the state instituted programs to provide free education and healthcare for all Egyptians, offered subsidies for basic foodstuffs, fixed low prices for manufactured products, and guaranteed employment for all high school and university graduates.

As in Ali's time, Nasser's expansion of the state bureaucracy did not sideline NGOs. Rather, the Nasser regime encouraged the formation of NGOs within an increasingly corporatist state system.[6] While simultaneously championing the expansion of Egypt's NGO sector, Nasser built a set of regulations and monitoring technologies designed to give the government control over organizations' leaders, activities, and networks. In 1956 the government passed Law 348 to legally sanction state regulation of the NGO sector. Law 348 was soon superseded by Law 32 of 1964, which further enshrined the state's authority over NGOs, requiring all organizations operating at the time to re-register under the current licensing rules, and called for any organizations that failed to re-register within six months to be dissolved. It also gave MOSA jurisdiction over NGOs' activities and fundraising and allowed the ministry to dissolve any organizations deemed to violate the law or threaten national security. In 1969 the Nasser regime created the General Federation of NGOs and Foundations to supervise the state's Regional Federations of NGOs.[7] Chaired by presidential appointees and charged with overseeing all governorate-level federations, which in turn represented local NGOs, the General Federation added another level of state supervision to Egypt's NGO sector. In effect, the Nasser regime "succeeded in transforming NGOs into appendages of its bureaucracy" and deployed the sector to fulfill its welfare priorities.[8]

Nasser's welfare state expansion was short-lived. Soon after Anwar Sadat came to power in 1970, he rolled back the state's responsibility for welfare provision and privatized Egypt's economy. Sadat decreased the state's responsibility for managing the economy, opened the country to foreign investment, and looked to the private sector to step in and support an overburdened public service system. Through the policy of *infitah* (open door), enacted in 1974, Sadat opened Egypt to foreign investment. The law encouraged joint ventures between foreign investors and Egyptian capital, eased currency restrictions, and established free trade zones.[9] *Infitah* marked the beginning of an alliance with the West, and the United States Agency for International Development (USAID) began funneling aid to Egypt in 1975.[10] While collecting these external rents, Sadat simultaneously cultivated a new class of local capitalists charged with doing business internationally and investing locally. These new business leaders would ultimately serve as important patrons of Egypt's NGO sector, which continued to expand under Sadat's rule. Businessmen's associations grew particularly rapidly, and the government also encouraged Islamic groups to create more NGOs.[11] By urging ideologically diverse groups to register as formal organizations, Sadat both brought various factions into the government's monitoring apparatus and fostered a sector rife with divisions and rivalries—a strategy that would later be reinforced by Mubarak.

Under Hosni Mubarak, Egypt's economic privatization intensified, a system of crony capitalism took hold, and the NGO sector grew to the point of being bloated. Mubarak was installed as president in 1981, and in the mid-1980s Egypt's economy began to decline due to falling oil prices. As the economy spiraled downward, with ballooning external debt, increasing budget deficits, and high inflation, Mubarak turned to the World Bank and International Monetary Fund (IMF) for support.[12] In 1987 Egypt signed a reform agreement with the IMF, committing to reducing public spending, liquidating public sector companies, liberalizing the private sector, and devaluing the Egyptian pound against the US dollar. In exchange, Egypt's foreign debt was rescheduled. The country did not stop spending, however, and by 1990 the economy was in crisis. In 1991 the Mubarak government entered a structural adjustment program with the World Bank designed to further privatize Egypt's economy. Together, the IMF agreement, which extended into the 1990s, and the World Bank agreement constituted a comprehensive reform package titled the Economic Reform and Structural Adjustment Program (ERSAP).[13] Reflecting the increasingly global spread of the Washington consensus, which stressed neoliberal economic reform,[14] the ERSAP required Egypt to reduce government spending, lift price controls, freeze wage rates, impose new taxes, privatize public sector enterprises, and further liberalize foreign trade.

Mubarak formed agreements with the IMF and World Bank with some reluctance. On one hand, he had to shore up an economy that was in shambles.[15] On the other hand, Mubarak had witnessed the country's 1977 Bread Riots, which broke out when Sadat lifted subsidies on essential foodstuffs in compliance with IMF reform agreement regulations. The sight of mass protests and riots in the wake of subsidy withdrawal was an important lesson about how Egyptians would respond to economic austerity, and as a result Mubarak adopted economic privatization and liberalization reforms slowly, episodically, and cautiously.[16]

Over the next two decades, privatization and deregulation hurt members of Egypt's poor and working class as jobs in the public sector were slashed and services and subsidies were scaled back.[17] At the same time, a new class of corporate elites thrived within a system marked by crony capitalism.[18] As Mubarak encouraged private businesses to grow and produced an economic climate in which they could flourish, he developed close ties with the leaders of Egypt's largest corporations and brought them into clientelist relations with his administration.[19] In exchange for political loyalty, Mubarak gave corporate magnates the right to purchase state-owned enterprises, exemptions from duties and fees, priority access to contracts, monopoly rights, and immunity from prosecution.[20]

In addition, Mubarak brought some business leaders directly into the government itself. Businessmen increasingly represented Mubarak's National Democratic Party (NDP) in Parliament, and by 2005 they also dominated his cabinet. In 2003 the NDP's Policy Unit, headed by Hosni Mubarak's son Gamal, laid out a set of policy prescriptions designed to advance ERSAP reforms and enhance opportunities and incentives for private enterprise. A new cabinet led by Ahmed Nazif was formed in 2004 and charged with accelerating ERSAP. After Mubarak's re-election in 2005, Nazif formed a second cabinet that appointed businesspeople to six ministries, including trade and industry, housing, transportation, health, agriculture, and social welfare.[21]

Unable to maintain Egypt's welfare state in an era of public expenditure austerity, Mubarak increasingly looked to NGOs to pick up the slack. Along with Western donors, who were engaged in a global effort to expand NGO sectors in developing states under the rubrics of civil society building and sustainable development, the Mubarak regime actively encouraged Egypt's NGO sector to balloon.[22] The sector grew rapidly, more than doubling in size from approximately fourteen thousand registered NGOs in 1993[23] to around thirty thousand in 2011.[24]

Egypt's modern philanthropic foundation sector also emerged under Mubarak's reign. Nasser's appropriation of *waqf* properties in the 1950s and 1960s led Egyptians to abandon the institution as a vehicle for private philanthropy.[25] The leader of one NGO described the current state of *waqf* as "defunct," no longer a legitimate or desirable mechanism of private philanthropy due to the perception that the Ministry of Endowments was overbearing, corrupt, secretive, and intent on transforming all *waqf* properties into arms of the government.[26] Private institutionalized philanthropy was revived in 2002, however, when the new Law 84 allowed for the establishment of *mu'assasat*, or philanthropic foundations. Unlike NGOs, which required a minimum of ten founders in order to register, foundations were constituted by a financial endowment and could be created by a single founder. Thousands of these organizations were created between 2002 and 2011.[27]

While liberal theories of NGOs and foundations might read the proliferation of these organizations in Egypt as a sign of civil society strengthening, empowerment of poor and marginalized populations, and a movement toward democratization, in fact the expansion of Egypt's NGO sector was part and parcel of a tightly orchestrated, state-led strategy to partly liberalize Egypt's political economy. As the remainder of this chapter will explain, the Mubarak regime used a series of control and co-optation mechanisms to mold a sector that would help to fulfill the regime's development priorities and be unable to coalesce into a formidable opposition group. Rather than operate as a force for economic justice and democratic political reform, Egypt's NGO sector served as a tool for maintaining the regime's power.

Egypt's Current NGO Landscape

The law governing Egypt's NGO sector at the time of the 2011 uprisings, Law 84 of 2002, recognized three official forms of organizations: associations (*gam'iyyat*), foundations (*mu'assasat*), and federations (*ittihad*). Associations—which I hereafter refer to as NGOs—constitute the largest segment of the organizational landscape. These groups vary across a wide range of factors including size, ideological underpinning, relationship to the government, and nature of work. Most Egyptian NGOs are thought to be very small, charitable organizations that provide basic welfare services to local constituents. Others are larger, with headquarter offices in major cities and staff who lead development projects in various towns and villages. Islamic associations maintain a formidable presence in Egypt, and Coptic NGOs also play important roles in the country's charitable landscape. Other groups stress their secular orientations.

Under Mubarak, most NGOs negotiated tenuous relationships with the regime, balancing their organizational goals with careful adherence to government rules and regulations. Human rights groups took a more adversarial stance, regularly testing the limits of government regulation by engaging in advocacy, while community development associations (or CDAs, a classification held over from Law 32 of 1964) hosted government sympathizers on their boards and faithfully implemented the administration's development priorities.

Despite this variety of organizations, Law 84 offered no official NGO classification scheme.[28] However, my interlocutors—including local NGO and foundation leaders as well as international aid staffers and local academics—clearly articulated the types of NGOs they believed to constitute the sector. Rather than focusing on the organizations' religious identity or the field of service in which these organizations work (e.g., education, healthcare, food and shelter, arts and culture, human rights, etc.), they distinguished organizations by their overarching approach to social welfare and social change: charity, development, or advocacy.[29] More than simply the result of a natural human inclination to classify, these distinctions reflected deep divisions and rivalries within the sector that were produced less through formal legal codes than through insidious government efforts to weaken the sector. I use these three classifications to distinguish NGOs throughout the remainder of the book.

Charity NGOs form the bulk of the sector and are often religiously affiliated and connected to a mosque or church. These organizations, according to my interlocutors, offer the proverbial bandage for social problems. That is, they seek to alleviate suffering and provide temporary relief from social challenges but do not try to solve underlying structural causes of the problem. Charitable organizations focus primarily on social welfare services, providing housing for orphans and the poor, basic healthcare, food, and other forms of social care. Such organizations are particularly active during religious holidays and situate their work within Egypt's deep traditions of social solidarity. Charities rely heavily on individual donations and religious tithes for their funding and enjoy a great deal of trust and support among both their donors and the beneficiaries of their services.

Development NGOs distinguish themselves by a well-known proverb: rather than giving a man a fish—as they claim charitable organizations do—development NGOs aim to teach the man how to fish. That is, instead of providing handouts to needy groups, development NGOs seek to address the underlying causes of poverty and other social problems and ultimately eliminate them. Often my interlocutors deployed the term "sustainable development" to signify that they intended their interventions to help communities solve their own problems and increase their long-term living standards. Development NGOs work primarily in education, job training, micro-enterprise, healthcare, environmental protection, arts and culture, and civic engagement, and their contributions to these fields made them the darlings of the Mubarak regime. The government viewed development NGOs as key partners in implementing its neoliberal economic agenda, and it was these organizations that grew in number most rapidly under Mubarak's rule. They are also the organizations favored by local philanthropic foundations. In addition to receiving grants from these foundations, development NGOs look to the government, international private foundations, and international aid agencies to round out their financial support.

The only NGOs that overtly acknowledged engaging in public policy advocacy were Egypt's advocacy NGOs. Often referred to as human rights organizations, they number less than one hundred by most estimates. These organizations are funded almost entirely by Western donors, are based in Cairo, and situate themselves squarely in the political realm by working on national-level issues such as human rights, democracy, and rule of law. They issue policy briefs, provide legal aid to human rights activists, host conferences, and talk to the press about topics of public policy such as environmental conservation, consumer rights, citizen advocacy, and so forth. Technically, Law 84 prohibited NGOs from doing "political" work. Some human rights organizations wiggled around this restriction by registering as law firms or civil corporations. Others relied on Mubarak turning a blind eye toward the political nature of their work in order to curry praise and favors from Western donors, who were important allies of the regime. Human rights NGOs were also careful not to cross certain red lines, such as criticizing the president or his family, and were generally able to go about their work without excessive harassment from the government. The regime tolerated these human rights organizations because they allowed Egypt to project the guise of liberalization to international observers.[30]

Since 2002, thousands of small *mu'assasat* have been established. Most of these operate their own programs and are nearly indistinguishable from NGOs. But a class of wealthy businesspeople also created larger grantmaking foundations modeled after well-known US foundations such as the Ford Foundation, the Rockefeller Foundation, and the Carnegie Endowment. Of the approximately twenty large grantmaking foundations I was able to identify, most resemble what in the United States would be classified as private and corporate foundations.[31] The main difference between Egypt's private and corporate foundations is their registration: private foundations register as *mu'assasat* while corporate foundations are simply arms of the parent corporation. Nevertheless, the lines between the two are fuzzy. All relied on a corporation's profits to fund their annual grantmaking budgets and all were subject to government surveillance, whether they registered under Law 84 or not. Moreover, the corporate foundations included in this study were actively seeking to build endowments, which would render them more similar to private than corporate foundations.

Whether private or corporate, all of these foundations were in some way connected to a corporation via their donors, board members, and funding schemes. For example, the Sawiris Foundation for Sustainable Development is a private family foundation but was created and is governed by members of the Sawiris family, who own Orascom Construction Industry, Orascom Telecom, and Orascom Hotels and Development. The EFG Hermes Foundation is also an independent private foundation but receives its funding from the EFG Hermes Holding Company and is governed by the company's top executives. Other foundations, such as the Mansour Foundation for Development, are directly tied to their corporate parents—in this case the Mansour Group—as grantmaking arms of the company. These foundations' funding schemes further strengthened their links to their founding donors' corporations. In 2011, both types of foundations were in the very early phases of building endowments and thus continued to rely on annual contributions from the founding donor, the donor's corporation, and foundation board members (who were often board members of the corporation) for their annual grantmaking budgets.

Unlike private and corporate foundations, self-identified community foundations were not affiliated with big businesses. Instead, they were created by community development experts and raised their funds from members of the local communities they served. And unlike the private and corporate foundations that based themselves on Western models, community foundations sought to merge local and international influences by tying the concept of *waqf* to the modern form of community foundation. In doing so, they aimed to revitalize the idea of a private endowment dedicated to serving local public purposes.

In 2011, while still in the early stages of development, Egypt's philanthropic sector was "experiencing a boom" as both corporations and wealthy individuals embraced new vehicles through which to institutionalize their philanthropy.[32] Both corporate social responsibility (CSR) and foundation-based giving had become increasingly recognized and popular, as foundations and CSR departments held public fundraisers and encouraged employees to participate in offsite volunteer days. Promotion by prominent regime members raised private philanthropy's profile even further. Suzanne and Gamal Mubarak (Hosni Mubarak's wife and son, respectively) were both involved in philanthropic pursuits and encouraged members of the business community to support the development of a hospital, library, and other capital projects that the state could not afford to build on its own. While foundation leaders were reticent to share information about the size of their endowments or grantmaking budgets, the information I gathered suggests that their grantmaking ranged from around $5 to $10 million annually. These funds provided important sources of income for local NGOs on limited budgets. Moreover, the foundations' prominence—both within the NGO sector and among regime officials—positioned them as a potentially significant force in the trajectory of Egypt's NGO sector.

Coinciding with the resurgence of philanthropy in Egypt was the proliferation of foundations throughout the Arab region. While locally born and bred (and, in the monarchies, often directly sponsored by members of the ruling family), the Arab region's new foundation sector is also heavily influenced by Western standards of philanthropy. At conferences and in one-on-one interviews, leaders of these foundations stressed that they were inspired by Western notions of "effective" and "strategic" philanthropy and were thinking about how those concepts relate to the Arab regional context. Supporting these conversations are two groups led by Arabs but sponsored in part by Western donors—the Arab Foundations Forum and the Gerhart

Center for Philanthropy and Civic Engagement at the American University in Cairo. The World Congress of Muslim Philanthropists also convenes foundation leaders and individual philanthropists with high net worth to discuss how to deploy their funds strategically in support of sustainable development and "social change."[33]

The federation, or *ittihad*, was the third form of organization recognized by Law 84 of 2002.[34] Federations are ostensibly designed to serve as networking bodies, helping NGOs to better coordinate their work and liaise with the government. In practice, however, federations served as a mechanism through which the Mubarak regime monitored and regulated NGOs and foundations. After the General Federation of NGOs was established in 1969, additional regional foundations were established at the governorate level. Law 84 brought all of these regional federations under the jurisdiction of the General Federation, which itself was governed in significant part by Mubarak-appointed board members.

In addition to a rapidly growing number of local NGOs and a surge in private institutionalized philanthropy, Egypt is also home to international NGOs and attracts significant funding from abroad. Major humanitarian, development, and advocacy NGOs have—or in some cases had, as a number of democracy promotion NGOs were forced to shut down after the uprisings—offices in Egypt, including CARE International, Mercy Corps, Oxfam, Caritas Internationalis, the National Endowment for Democracy, the National Democratic Institute, the International Republican Institute, and many more. The international community also helps to bankroll Egypt's local NGO sector through its support for civil society development.[35]

International donors coordinate their development aid to Egypt through the Development Partners Group (DPG). Launched in the late 1990s by the United Nations Development Programme (UNDP), in 2013 the DPG consisted of twenty-three bilateral aid agencies, seventeen multilateral aid agencies, and two philanthropic foundations. The DPG at first consisted primarily of aid agencies of Western nations including Canada, Switzerland, the United States, Australia, and the United Kingdom, as well as the European Union. In 2009, the group expanded to include representatives from Latin America, Asia, and Africa, and in 2010 it expanded further by welcoming international private donors such as the Ford Foundation and the Population Council. Members of the DPG meet regularly, both among themselves and with Egyptian government officials, to harmonize aid strategies and discuss opportunities and challenges confronted in their grantmaking.

Mubarak's Strategies of Control and Co-Optation

Hosni Mubarak used classic maneuvers deployed by savvy dictators to mold an NGO sector that would advance the government's priorities and fail to challenge its far-reaching rule. Mubarak's tactics can be grouped into two broad categories—control (the proverbial stick) and co-optation (the carrot). Through control tactics of official laws and informal harassment, the regime closely monitored and constrained all aspects of organizations' operations. Through tactics of co-optation, the regime brought organizations into its fold and incentivized good behavior. The primary tool that the Mubarak regime used to control Egyptian NGOs was Egypt's NGO law, Law 84 of 2002, which gave the government sweeping powers over all registered organizations operating in Egypt.[36] Egypt's Ministry of Social Solidarity (MOSS), the government agency charged with overseeing Egypt's NGO sector, had the jurisdiction to regulate each organization's registration, governance structure, activities, fundraising, and dissolution and worked in collaboration with Egypt's Ministry of Foreign Affairs to monitor international NGOs with registered branches in Egypt.

Law 84 created hurdles for NGOs as early as the registration stage. To operate, organizations acting in the capacity of NGOs or foundations were obliged to register or face dissolution. Leaders of organizations that failed to register could be imprisoned for up to six months and/or fined up to two thousand Egyptian pounds (Article 76). In order to register, organizations had to specify their founders, capital, board members, the activities they would pursue, and the premises they would occupy. The law's vague language gave MOSS officials significant discretion to approve or reject organizations' registration applications. While MOSS was officially obligated to make its decision within sixty days, it regularly left organizations in limbo for months or even years. As the director of one foundation said, "Dealing with the Egyptian bureaucracy is a nightmare, including setting up a foundation. It took eighteen months to register."[37] Although by law organizations were to be considered registered if the sixty days passed without notification from MOSS (Article 6), in practice, NGO leaders knew that proceeding with operations prior to MOSS approval could send them to jail and lead to the dissolution of their organizations.

The law also gave the government discretion over the activities organizations could pursue. Article 48 of Law 84's Executive Statute indicated that approved activities included those "aimed at realizing continuing human development, whether the educational, health, cultural, or social; economic or environmental services; consumer protection; enlightenment as to the constitutional or legal rights, social defense, or human rights." Meanwhile, Article 11 of Law 84 expressly prohibited organizations from engaging in activities that could be deemed political, threatened national unity, or violated public order or morals. Again, the law's vague language allowed government officials to interpret these strictures arbitrarily. NGO leaders clearly understood that they needed to secure government approval before moving ahead with any projects or activities. "We could end up in jail if we go ahead without approval," explained a program officer of a private foundation. "It is not effective to go ahead without the government on board. The point is to help people. It is not useful to fight the government."[38] When asked if NGOs were allowed to participate in policy debates, a program officer at another private foundation quickly emphasized, "No we don't go into that. The government won't let organizations have a say." But the program officer went on to explain that the government looked to foundations and NGOs to support their local communities and that, as a result, it was a "common practice for civil society organizations to work with the government."[39]

Law 84 further constrained NGOs' activities by regulating their fundraising. Grants from donors in Egypt largely escaped scrutiny; recipients simply needed to declare them to the government. Article 17 of the law, however, required NGOs seeking funds from abroad to gain approval from MOSS. The ministry regularly failed to approve grants intended for projects that it considered hostile, although interviewees indicated that they often did not understand what elements of their proposed projects were objectionable. Technically, the beneficiary organization could go to court to argue for the release of funds not approved by MOSS, but, according to an Egyptian lawyer, this option was considered "a nightmare" and organizations would opt instead to wait, often up to a year or more, for MOSS's decision and thus put the funded activities on hold.[40]

Organizations' governance also fell within the confines of the law. NGOs needed MOSS approval to form their boards of directors, set the dates and times of their board meetings, and determine the quorums needed to convene meetings and elect board members. In addition, organizations were required to keep detailed notes of all of their activities, financials, and meeting minutes and make these freely available to MOSS officials, who often arrived at NGOs' premises unannounced to inspect their records. During one of my visits to a foundation, the program officer showed me a room filled with notebooks. "We must tell the Ministry of Social Solidarity about everything we do," this program officer explained. "We keep notebooks of all of our activities and finances. Every NGO must do this. We have a notebook for board meeting minutes, for the budget (every revenue and expense), for donations, for capital and assets. It is illegal to do anything without the Ministry knowing. It takes a lot of time and stops our work."[41] Interviewees grumbled regularly about MOSS's excessive monitoring. The leader of a development NGO said, "Whenever you need permission from the government it takes a very long time. In the last few weeks we have had an auditor from the Ministry of Social Solidarity here to review all of our files since 2001. They have been working for five weeks to review all of these files."[42] But NGO leaders understood that they needed to put up with this surveillance in order to proceed with their work. " 'Control' is the word," observed the director of an umbrella organization of NGOs and foundations. "You have to get permission to do anything."[43]

While the law technically did not restrict the size of these organizations, NGO leaders believed the government felt threatened by large organizations and collaborative efforts and therefore discouraged both. Organization leaders stressed that they felt pressure to remain small and to work in isolation, citing an unwritten rule that if they became too large they would be harassed.[44] They also reported that they were prohibited from sharing office space. "Ninety percent of MOSS branches don't allow NGOs to share offices," complained one, pointing out that while the law did not technically prohibit shared space, local MOSS officials had the jurisdiction to forbid it.[45]

Formal oversight by MOSS was only part of the government surveillance NGOs faced. Members of the state security (SSI) were also known to keep a close watch over the NGO sector. SSI representatives showed up unannounced at meetings, phoned NGO employees to let them know that "Big Brother is watching," and were assumed to screen employees' phone calls and emails.[46] This led many NGOs to "keep their heads down, not wanting to be exposed" and prevented organizations from taking on activities that could draw attention.[47] "The truth of the matter is that behind the Ministry of Social Solidarity are security agencies that monitor the NGO sector," stated the Egypt office director of an international foundation. "They clamp down on human rights. If you want to set up a meeting in a hotel, they demand that you get permission. The government makes it difficult to challenge the government. If you challenge the government, you must do it in a sophisticated and clever way."[48]

While Law 84 and SSI harassment served as mechanisms of control and repression, the Mubarak regime exploited systems of clientelism and co-optation to incentivize NGOs to adopt its development priorities and refrain from politically contentious or threatening activities. Clientelist relations between the regime and NGO sector were particularly conspicuous among Egypt's philanthropic foundations. The business men and women who created these foundations built their corporate empires under Mubarak's system of crony capitalism, in which business success was contingent upon loyalty to the regime.[49] Philanthropy served as an important act of devotion through which business leaders helped to advance the state's economic privatization strategy. Foundation support for NGOs providing development services helped to fill in gaps left by welfare state retrenchment and was tacitly traded for tax exemptions, contracts, and other business favors, legal or otherwise.[50]

There was a widespread belief among my interlocutors that the majority of Egypt's foundation leaders were in bed with the government and that their foundations' philanthropy was deployed in ways that would advance the regime's priorities. "They are in cahoots," said one foundation program officer when asked about foundations' relations with the government. "The heads of foundations in Egypt have vested interests in maintaining the status quo. At the NDP conference the government highlights areas where it needs support from business. This will impact the agendas of foundations." This program officer clearly tied the foundations' strategies to their founders' business interests, going on to say, "Big foundations are founded by big business men and women. To successfully run a business in Egypt you must conform to a system set by the government. In many cases funding will go to semi-governmental institutions. For example, the National Council for Childhood and Motherhood, established by Suzanne Mubarak. There is an exchange of favors."[51]

In fact, Egypt's most prominent philanthropists and foundations cultivated relationships with the Mubarak regime's highest officials and leaders. Mohammed Mansour, CEO of the Mansour Group holding company and founder and chair of the Mansour Foundation for Development, served as Mubarak's Minister of Transport from 2006 to 2009. Gamal Mubarak—a strong proponent of neoliberal economic policies—held an 18 percent share in EFG-Hermes's Private Equity Group, a corporate parent to Egypt's EFG-Hermes Foundation. Members of the Sawiris family, who govern the Sawiris Foundation for Social Development, maintained complex relationships with the Mubarak regime. There is little doubt that the Sawiris family benefited from the monopoly rights that Mubarak granted Orascom. Yousriya Loza Sawiris, chairwoman of the board, was a Mubarak appointee to the People's Assembly in 1995 and a member of the National Council for Childhood and Motherhood.[52] Nassef Sawiris, a foundation board member, was a member of the Business Secretariat of Mubarak's NDP party.[53] Yet Naguib Sawiris, vice chairman of the foundation's board, supported relatively independent media outlets—he was a shareholder in the daily newspaper al-Masry al-Youm and owner of the television channel ONtv[54]—and bankrolled the political opposition party Democratic Front Party.[55]

The National Council for Childhood and Motherhood is an example of a GONGO (a government-organized NGO), another form of government co-optation of the NGO sector. GONGOs are NGOs founded and governed by government officials and sympathizers to steer policy agendas and manage debates on contentious topics such as human rights and women's empowerment. Egypt's most prominent GONGOs were set up as councils, and their boards were stacked with regime and regime-friendly officials as well as by some independent activists. Other examples included the National Council for Human Rights, and the National Council for Women, the latter of which was also championed by Suzanne Mubarak. While these GONGOs lacked official policymaking power, they created a façade of government interest in liberalization, democratization, and human rights.[56]

GONGOs served regime interests: they steered discussions away from radical ideas or initiatives that threatened or called into question the manner by which the government ruled. At the same time, GONGOs allowed the regime to feign progress toward liberalization while simultaneously sidelining the work of independent NGOs working on human rights and democratization issues. The leader of an Egyptian foundation pointed out that in the later years of Mubarak's rule, "there was a trend of advocacy, changing policies, and campaigns" but that this "wasn't successfully done by NGOs. It was done by the government; for example, campaigns for family planning, female genital mutilation, and girls' education" were all initiatives that the government led and NGOs tangentially supported.[57] GONGOs also created divisions within Egypt's independent NGO—and particularly human rights NGO—community. Activists who chose to serve on GONGO boards in order to try to have some input into policy debates generally lost legitimacy among colleagues who perceived them as selling out. This introduced a culture of suspicion into the sector and resulted in the formation of various cliques.

The deleterious effects of state-led NGO sector growth cannot be overstated. The Mubarak regime's strategy to flood Egypt's NGO field with many small organizations, burden them with bureaucracy and surveillance, and bring certain organizations into its fold created a fragmented sector that was uncoordinated, competitive, and fearful of government repression.[58] In addition, while charitable NGOs were well known, the development NGOs, foundations, and human rights organizations that proliferated under Mubarak were not well understood or trusted by the general public, leading to a crisis of confidence in the sector.

The Mubarak regime encouraged development NGOs to proliferate as part of its economic privatization and liberalization strategy. The aim was twofold. First, these NGOs provided new channels through which to attract Western aid. Under the Washington Consensus, NGOs became the "vehicles of choice"[59] among Western donors such as the World Bank, government aid agencies, and private foundations for distributing aid to civil society. Eager to bring aid to Egypt, Mubarak enthusiastically supported the establishment of organizations through which such aid was likely to flow. At the same time, development NGOs—aided by Egypt's new foundations, which themselves were a product of Mubarak-era policies—helped to pick up the slack as Mubarak downsized Egypt's public sector. Services previously provided by state agencies could be handed over to development NGOs, which operated on wider scales than their charitable NGO counterparts.

To the detriment of the NGO sector, however, the rapid rise of development NGOs and foundations resulted in a bloated and duplicitous group of organizations that struggled to define its collective identity. Having emerged as part of a top-down neoliberal development strategy rather than organically through grassroots participation, Egypt's development NGOs and philanthropic foundations wrestled with how to transition away from Egypt's culture of charity and to articulate and make salient the concept of development. Interviewees described the development sector as in its infancy, lacking strong, well-grounded, and accountable organizations, and poorly understood by the general public. Development NGOs and foundations adopted a common language that stressed sustainability, empowerment, and effectiveness, but their leaders were still trying to determine what these concepts actually meant and how they could be operationalized.

In addition, most Egyptians were unfamiliar with the concept of development. "Few people know anything about 'development,'" the leader of one NGO said. "They may know a few NGOs, but they don't know the sector.

They don't know its boundaries or what it does."[60] Compounding this general lack of knowledge was a public distrust of Egypt's new development NGOs. "NGOs are still not trusted," explained the director of one NGO. "Traditionally, charity took place around the mosques. For a long time, Western ideas were seen as suspicious."[61] Interviewees described a cynicism surrounding the development industry and suggested that "Egyptians are welcoming to people who help the poor and orphans" but suspicious of organizations that adopted the language and practice of development.[62] "Our character in Egypt is that we don't trust new things," said the leader of a development NGO in Upper Egypt. "We are afraid to try new things in development. People don't like change. It takes years to build confidence between ourselves and our beneficiaries."[63] Organizations worked to educate the public, but it was a slow process. "We are trying to change perceptions," explained the program officer of a community foundation. "We work with a small number of people, and it is successful. Philanthropy often means giving *zakat*. We have convinced some people to pay *zakat* to projects instead of directly to poor people."[64] The director of this foundation concurred. "It is difficult appealing to the brain but not the heart. We need a policy change. We need development, not charity."[65] But for the majority of Egyptians, charity remained the trusted norm.

Egypt's human rights organizations were even less trusted than development organizations. Funded almost entirely by Western donors, these organizations were seen as advancing foreign political agendas and, in doing so, shunning the local customs of charity. While I have argued that the growth of Egypt's NGO sector was directly connected to Egypt's evolving political economy—and thus inherently political—interviewees from both charity and development NGOs stressed that they did not discuss politics or advocate for public policies as part of their work. Doing so, I was told, was taboo not only because it broke the law but also because it made beneficiaries skeptical of the organization's aims. As human rights organizations pursued decidedly political aims, they were seen as being out of touch with local customs and disconnected from communities. "The problem with human rights organizations is that they are working from theory, not from the practical," explained the leader of an umbrella group of local foundations. "They are not connected to the people. The perception is that human rights organizations are full of graduates from the American University in Cairo and cannot relate to the people. The problem is that human rights organizations make democracy look foreign."[66] Another interviewee concurred, suggesting that advocacy NGOs were products of their donors, not of local support. "Human rights organizations didn't build a constituency," this development NGO leader said. "They remain weak because they don't have local support. They only have support of donors."[67]

Challenges posed by identity and trust issues were exacerbated by the fragmented and inefficient nature of the NGO sector. Interviewees described a sector crowded with many small organizations that duplicated each other's work and competed for scarce funding. "The problem is that many times we are doing the same thing, duplicating each other. There is no efficiency," lamented the director of one foundation.[68] Organization leaders explained that most NGOs were small and failed to coordinate their efforts or collaborate on joint initiatives. While some funders tried to encourage cooperative partnerships, most believed that such efforts were futile due to a legacy of fragmentation stoked by government repression of collaborative efforts. "Organizations see the risks of cooperating more than the benefits," asserted one observer of the NGO sector.[69] NGO leaders agreed with that assessment. "There is a problem in Egypt that people are not good at networking," said the leader of a private foundation. "They don't work together. Each organization has a sense of uniqueness. This is a barrier to maximizing impact. It is culturally embedded. People are struggling against it and recognize it as a weakness, but this is happening at the top levels of organizations. At the grassroots collaboration is still a problem."[70]

The bloated and fragmented nature of Egypt's NGO sector produced a culture of competition that played out at a variety of levels and pitted organizations against each other as they jockeyed for funds and prestige. As one foundation leader pointed out, Egypt "has [tens of thousands] of NGOs . . . but at the end of the day there are only a few foundations. There is an inequality between the supply of, and demand for, funds."[71] While the government and international donors also provided significant sources of financial support, there was never enough to underwrite the huge number of small NGOs vying for survival. As a result, organizations competed to be seen as the most effective and legitimate actors within the sector. This competition played out both between different types of organizations and among organizations of the same type.[72]

Competition between charitable and development organizations manifested primarily in disagreements over how to advance economic development. Leaders of development NGOs charged charity with being unsustainable. With charity, one foundation program officer said, "people are getting food and blankets but their lives aren't changing."[73] But charitable organizations had their own set of criticisms for development NGOs, which they saw as bureaucratic organizations that lacked connections to, and compassion for, those most in need. Indeed, leaders of development organizations conceded that small charitable NGOs—particularly those associated with mosques and churches—were important players in Egypt's poorest neighborhoods because they were deeply embedded in the communities they served and helped people to meet their immediate needs. Charities also relied heavily on financial donations from individuals, bolstering the notion that they were operated both by and for those they served.

Development and advocacy (or human rights) NGOs competed primarily over the best way to advance political reform. Leaders of both types of organizations espoused visions of a more democratic Egypt that respected individual civil liberties. But their views on how to transform that vision into reality diverged. Advocacy NGOs focused on national public policy reform and human rights defense, and their leaders believed that NGOs must take risks and engage openly with political issues to bring about reform. They criticized development organizations—including both NGOs and foundations—for being too cozy with the government and unwilling to take risks. Human rights NGO leaders noted that Egyptian foundations would not fund projects that challenged the government's philosophy and they accused development NGOs of being "not yet at a stage where they will be bold,"[74] insinuating that this caution stemmed from development organizations' friendly relations with the government.

Meanwhile, leaders of development organizations countered that they believed in the values of democracy and human rights but felt that "advocacy" was just a form of talk that failed to produce results. Development NGO leaders suggested that human rights NGOs' approach to reforming national public policies was exclusionary and out of touch with beneficiary populations. The director of a development NGO working with a Bedouin community in the South Sinai claimed that "people in the Sinai don't care about" human rights as marketed by advocacy organizations. "We do women's rights but we don't call it that. People need education and health. If you are hungry, do you care about politics?"[75]

Almost across the board, NGOs and foundations were secretive with their data, leery of sharing their financial status or internal operational mechanisms with other organizations. Instead, they competed to be perceived as the most effective and legitimate. Some groups tried to overcome this culture of secrecy and competition, and umbrella organizations worked especially hard to build a more collaborative environment. They struggled, however, against an ingrained culture of competition. "There are conferences," said one interviewee, "but what happens is everyone highlights their own agenda and successes. It becomes competitive. You end up getting attacked." Outside of structured networking events, this interviewee went on to say, "everyone works on their own in silence to get stuff done."[76]

Compounding these challenges of distrust, inefficiency, and competition that stemmed from the sector's bloating was a culture of fear imposed by government control and surveillance. "Civil society is coming from a culture of strict government control," explained the director of a community foundation. "It is scared. It thinks it is not free."[77] Organization leaders cited legal regulations and government surveillance as two of the biggest obstacles to increasing the sector's effectiveness. Egypt's NGO and foundation leaders were acutely aware that one misstep that either put them in violation of the law or attracted government suspicion could land them in jail and lead to the immediate dissolution of their organizations. With the exception of human rights organizations, which did take risks, Egypt's NGOs and foundations were, prior to the 2011 uprisings, exceedingly cautious and careful to situate themselves squarely on the side of the law and to maintain cooperative relations with the government. They stuck to safe projects in charitable and development realms and—again with the exception of human rights organizations—steered clear of activities that could be deemed political.

An NGO Sector Divided and Throttled, Impotent and Complicit

This chapter began with a vignette of charitable benevolence. It described a holiday of sacrifice and giving in which private, individual acts of charity were committed to express a love of God and care for mankind. This giving and receiving of meat on Eid al-Adha is part of a tradition of charity that runs deep throughout Egypt's history. While such extra-state forms of giving among individuals carry on in present-day Egypt, they constitute just a part of the country's contemporary philanthropic practices. Over the decades since Egypt's independence, an expanding sector of NGOs and philanthropic foundations has institutionalized charity. But Egypt's NGO sector growth was not an organic process driven by benevolent citizens. The state both promoted and tightly controlled Egypt's NGO sector expansion, encouraging many small, service-providing organizations to mushroom while cracking down on organizations that grew too large, attempted to coordinate their efforts, or waded into political waters.

Egypt's bloated NGO sector not only made it possible for the Mubarak regime to advance its neoliberal economic agenda; it also helped to prop up political autocracy. By encouraging organizations to proliferate but forcing them to remain small and compete with each other, the government both divided the NGO sector and throttled it,[78] ensuring that organization leaders would spend their time competing against each other to survive rather than banding together to fight for the rights of citizens. Egypt's large NGO sector also presented a guise of liberalization, exploiting the idea that more NGOs means more democracy to give the false impression that the state was on a path to greater political freedom. This masquerade was used not only to mollify local citizens but also to impress the international community.[79] While the regime's tolerance of human rights organizations was particularly savvy in this regard, the large field of development NGOs also brought in significant rents in the form of aid.

Finally, NGOs provided spaces in which activists could "blow off steam."[80] Interviewees noted that under Mubarak, people who wanted to advance change turned not to political parties—which were not only impotent but also played directly into the false idea that political representation was possible—but instead to NGOs. Describing political parties other than the NDP as "decoration,"[81] NGO leaders indicated that for decades their organizations provided refuge for activists. But as long as NGOs were powerless against the state, participation in them served as appeasement rather than empowerment.

Thus, Egypt's NGO sector, as it existed at the time of the January 25, 2011, uprisings, cannot be understood as a sphere of citizen empowerment. Rather, Egypt's NGOs and foundations were part of a corporatist system of governance in which the state and the NGO sector were mutually reinforcing. The state not only permitted but in fact propelled the expansion of a group of organizations that served as one of the country's few sanctuaries for would-be activists and dissidents. Faced with no other options for civic participation, Egypt's activists seized the space to create NGOs and foundations. But, constrained as they were by the vast regulatory regime governing the NGO sector, these organizations—however unwittingly—served to prop up both neoliberalism and political authoritarianism in Egypt.

2

The Widening and Narrowing of Egypt's Civic Space

The billboards were gone. Not the Koki Chicken or Juhayna Milk billboards, but the ones featuring Mubarak that had loomed over Cairo's streets. This change immediately confronted me when I returned to Egypt shortly after Mubarak was deposed from power as a result of the January 25, 2011, uprisings. The presidential portraits that had previously hung in every shop had also disappeared. Along with those constant reminders that an autocrat kept watch, the culture of fear and public self-censorship that prevailed under Mubarak's heavy-handed rule also vanished. In their place, revolutionary graffiti and a citizenry emboldened to openly discuss and debate politics appeared. A sense of euphoria filled Egypt's streets, shops, lunch tables, and cafés. A future determined not by a dictator but by the people seemed not only possible but unpreventable.

On January 25, 2011—Police Day, a national holiday in Egypt—tens of thousands of Egyptians took to the streets and squares across the country to protest police brutality. Galvanized by recent demonstrations in Tunisia that, on January 14, had ousted longtime president Zine el-Abidine Ben Ali, and organized by a Facebook page calling for citizens to march in solidarity against recent acts of violence by the Egyptian police, demonstrations in Cairo grew as protesters took over downtown Cairo's Tahrir Square. Undeterred even when Mubarak released camel-riding thugs to disperse the crowds, protesters remained for eighteen days, working across socioeconomic, religious, and political lines to guard the square and provide each other with food, water, and medical care. The Egyptian army arrived as well, but instead of dispersing protesters soldiers protected them from the police forces.[1] Soldiers helped to guard checkpoints around the square, and demonstrators began to fraternize with them.[2] On February 11, 2011, Hosni Mubarak stepped down and the SCAF was installed as a caretaker government.

This seemed to be an auspicious time for NGOs and foundations in Egypt. The organizations themselves did not participate in the January 25 uprising—those protests were loosely networked, and formal civil society organizations were conspicuously absent. After Mubarak's ouster, though, NGOs and foundations had an important role to play in marshaling Egyptians' enthusiasm for political reform. A swell of people young and old were eager to participate in rebuilding a more democratic Egypt. Some would join political parties and run for office. Others declined to participate in formal politics but still wanted to contribute to a political transformation. Civil society organizations stood to offer them that opportunity. With Mubarak gone, these organizations had the chance to take on previously banned activities related to political reform and provide spaces for civic engagement and activism.

But Egyptians' unbound exhilaration and the seemingly endless possibilities for reform were soon tempered by spikes in political turmoil and fluctuations in the economy. Signs of trouble emerged even in 2011, as the SCAF began to govern arbitrarily and opaquely. The generals in charge of Egypt's transition drafted new laws behind closed doors, issued decrees designed to secure and consolidate the army's power, and launched a smear campaign against Egypt's NGO sector. The 2012 presidential elections brought Mohammed Morsi, the Muslim Brotherhood's Freedom and Justice Party candidate, to power, and his government intensified the assault on civil society. Meanwhile, throughout 2012 and 2013, Egypt's economy spiraled downward as tourists and investors abandoned the country.

The political opportunity created by the January 25 uprisings was therefore one that civil society organizations would need to navigate carefully. Mubarak's departure did create an opening for democracy building. But non-democratic forces—many of which were more powerful than civil society groups—also stepped into that opening. The SCAF and Islamist groups, both of which posed threats to civil society's reform goals, moved particularly quickly to secure influence and power. This chapter traces the opportunities and threats that donors and NGOs faced in the early years after the 2011 uprisings and concludes with a brief overview of how two different groups—Western aid agencies and Egyptian philanthropic foundations—responded in those early years.

The Uprisings' Origins

In the years following the Arab Spring uprisings, scholars sought to explain their causes and consequences. Political scientists had spent years developing theories to explain the durable authoritarianism that had settled over the Arab region.[3] But as autocrats were toppled one after another—Ben Ali of Tunisia and Mubarak of Egypt were followed by Libya's Muammar Gaddafi and Yemen's Ali Abdullah Saleh—it became clear that the region's rulers were just as breakable as the fear that had forced their citizens into submission. Analysts studied the role of social and other forms of media in providing inspiration and organizational capacity to protest participants,[4] deployed social movement theories to understand the outbreak and growth of the protests,[5] and investigated the structural factors that led some autocrats to fall while others remained securely in place.[6]

Observers have consistently framed the Arab uprisings as movements for democratic political reform, and analyses have been undergirded by questions of democratization and durable authoritarianism.[7] But economic grievances were also salient for many of the protesters.[8] At the macro level, the structural adjustment reforms that Mubarak had implemented in the 1980s under pressure from the IMF and World Bank paid off. In exchange for privatizing and liberalizing its economy, the United States relieved Egypt of billions of dollars of debt in the 1990s.[9] Over the two decades prior to the uprisings, per capita income rose,[10] foreign direct investment increased,[11] and the country's GDP growth rate averaged an impressive 4.5 percent.[12] But the benefits of Egypt's economic growth were not widely or equally distributed. Elite insiders who were connected to the regime fared well. These "fat cats"—as businesspeople who prospered under structural adjustment were sometimes called—enjoyed priority access to contracts, monopoly rights, and financing, and saw their businesses flourish.[13] At the same time, access to government jobs dwindled and social service quality fell as Egypt scaled back its administrative bureaucracy and welfare state.[14] The number of jobs created in the private sector could not keep pace with a rise in skilled labor.[15] As prices rose and subsidies were cut, Egyptians were increasingly forced into poverty and the rate of people living below the poverty line rose from 16.7 percent in 2000 to 22 percent in 2008.[16] The authoritarian bargain that had helped to prop up Nasser, Sadat, and Mubarak—in which the regime provided access to jobs and generous welfare services in exchange for tolerance of political repression—fell apart.

And so political authoritarianism, along with a widespread perception of increased inequality, less access to economic opportunity, and the government's abandonment of a commitment to distributive justice, conspired to bring people to the streets.[17] One of the protesters' chants, "*Al-sha'b yurīd isqāt al-nizām*," or "The people want the fall of the regime," had clear political references. The protesters' calls for bread, freedom, social justice, and human dignity highlighted the fact that economic and political injustices—which were tightly interwoven in many Egyptians' minds—contributed to the uprisings.

Origin stories for Egypt's 2011 uprisings vary. Some framed the protests as spontaneous, sparked by a Facebook page highlighting Egyptian police brutality and by a Tunisian vendor who set himself on fire after police shut down his fruit and vegetable stand, triggering a wave of uprisings that overthrew Ben Ali.[18] This account rightly highlights the mobilizing role played by Facebook organizing and the inspiration that Egyptians drew from Tunisians' quick success in ousting their own dictatorial president. But while the size and scale of the January 25 uprisings took nearly everyone by surprise, and were spontaneous in that they lacked extensive forethought and planning, the uprisings did not come out of nowhere.[19] Rather, the 2011 wave of protests can best be seen as a particularly momentous episode in a much larger struggle for justice—what Maha Abdelrahman refers to as a "long revolutionary process"—in which various groups played a role in normalizing a culture of protest in Egypt.[20]

While small, episodic protests have taken place in Egypt since the early days of the country's independence in the 1950s, most scholars highlight the larger, more sustained forms of collective action that have occurred since the year 2000. These began with demonstrations in support of the Palestinian people, who struggled under Israel's occupation. Such protests had periodically broken out for decades but became particularly salient in 2000 when a wave of demonstrations celebrated the second Palestinian *intifada* (uprising). Activism over the Palestinians' plight intensified with the US invasion of Iraq in 2003, and by March of that year protesters began to openly express dissatisfaction with the regime's failure to support the Palestinians.[21] In September, demonstrations commemorating the third anniversary of the *intifada* morphed into antigovernment protests, marking an important shift in how protesters framed their demands.[22]

In the aftermath of the Iraq invasion, a group of university faculty formed the March 9 Movement for Academic Freedom to challenge draconian measures of regime control over Egypt's universities and the scholars they employed.[23] Members of the government reserved the right to monitor student union elections and to vet faculty members' research agendas, guest lecturers, and staff appointments. The March 9 group organized petitions, sit-ins, and public statements to highlight the government's attempts to curtail academic freedom. Group members also spoke out in support of students who had been detained by the regime and railed against cuts to university budgets.

Another major wave of protests emerged in 2004 with the founding of the group Kefaya ("enough").[24] Unlike previous resistance movements, Kefaya was expressly anti-regime, with the group's founding documents calling for democracy and political reform. Specifically, Kefaya aimed to bring an end to government repression and prevent the Mubarak family from extending its rule—a response to rumors that Gamal Mubarak, Hosni Mubarak's son, was being groomed to take over from his father.[25] Kefaya brought together intellectuals, politicians, and youth activists from across the political spectrum and deployed a variety of tactics, including petitions, sit-ins, public demonstrations, stay-at-home protests, and mass broom sweeps to symbolize the cleaning up of Egyptian politics. With its explicitly anti-government messaging, Kefaya broke the taboo of speaking out against the Mubarak regime.[26]

Kefaya's success cannot be attributed to the member activists' work alone. They were abetted by at least two unlikely suspects. One was Omar Suleiman, Mubarak's intelligence chief, who was rumored to have facilitated the licensing of *al-Masry al-Youm*, a progressive daily independent newspaper established in 2004 that featured an opposition editorial section.[27] The second was former US president George W. Bush, whose "Freedom Agenda" served as one of the United States' most strident calls for democracy in Egypt. Like his predecessors and successors, Bush regarded Mubarak as a "friendly tyrant"[28] whose support for Israel and fight against terrorism would be rewarded with strategic cooperation and generous military aid.[29] But when Bush backed up his strong rhetoric in support of Arab democracy by creating democracy aid funding mechanisms such as The U.S.-Middle East Partnership Initiative (MEPI) and sending his top officials to the region to reiterate the administration's commitment to democratization, he compelled Mubarak to, however unconvincingly, position himself as a reformer.[30] With notes of opposition now appearing in the press and Mubarak forced to turn a blind eye to at least some forms of resistance, Kefaya and other opposition groups had more room to maneuver.

A separate wave of protests called attention to economic injustices. The Egyptian workers' movement constituted one of the largest and most sustained protest movements prior to the 2011 uprisings, with as many as two to four million workers taking part in three to four thousand episodes of collective action between 1998 and 2010.[31] One of the "largest and most politically significant"[32] of the workers' protest events occurred in December 2006 at the Misr Spinning and Weaving Company, also known as Ghazl al-Mahalla, in Mahalla al-Kubra.[33] Twenty-four thousand of the company's twenty-seven thousand workers participated in a three-day strike to protest the government's failure to deliver promised worker bonuses. The strike closed the factory and halted production, forcing the government to not only concede to the bonus but also submit to additional demands such as transportation allowances, medical and day care, and investigations into corruption charges. Despite these concessions, tensions between workers, the regime, and the Egyptian Trade Union Federation (ETUF) continued to mount, and the annual number of acts of contentious action increased dramatically, jumping from 222 in 2006 to 692 in 2007 and then hovering between 440 and 550 over the next three years.[34] Protests took place across the country and included workers from a variety of fields including textiles, cement, transportation, engineering, garbage collection, and civil service. Tactics comprised factory strikes, demonstrations, occupations, sit-ins, and hunger strikes.[35]

The April 6 Youth Movement emerged in 2008 to act in solidarity with the workers. The group grew out of a Facebook page calling for nationwide protests on April 6, 2008, to support the Ghazl al-Mahalla workers. The Facebook page drew somewhere between 65,000 and 67,000 followers, but the group's online popularity failed to translate in the streets, with protest events drawing only a few dozen to a few hundred participants.[36] Still, the movement introduced Egypt's youth to "Facebook politics" and provided a platform through which youth could remain attuned to protest culture.[37]

One of the final protest waves leading up to the January 25 uprisings was, like Kefaya, expressly political in its aims. In August 2009, activists created a Facebook page calling for Mohammed el-Baradei—Nobel Peace Prize laureate and former Director General of the International Atomic Energy Agency (IAEA)—to run for president in Egypt's 2011 elections. El-Baradei seemed to be a viable alternative to Mubarak, and his potential candidacy drew supporters from across the political spectrum. When el-Baradei returned to Egypt from abroad in February 2010, more than one thousand supporters welcomed him with flags, banners, and patriotic songs, despite warnings by the security forces to stay away.[38] The Facebook page attracted over 240,000 followers, and a seven-point Manifesto for Change penned by el-Baradei garnered one million signatures.[39]

On June 6, 2010, a young Egyptian man named Khaled Said was pulled out of an internet café and beaten to death by the police. The episode was broadcast widely across social media, and a Facebook page created by Wael Ghonim, titled "We Are All Khaled Said," emphasized that Said could have been any middle-class youth. Thousands attended a series of vigils to commemorate Said while others staged protests to demand justice. Ghonim's Facebook page is credited with being one of the major—and final—catalysts of the January 25 uprisings.[40] When Mohammed Bouazizi, the Tunisian fruit and vegetable vendor, self-immolated out of economic desperation generated and exacerbated by government corruption, the spark in Egypt was lit.[41]

A Political Opportunity for Egyptian Civil Society

By the time the 2011 uprisings broke out, then, Egypt had experienced at least a handful of major protest waves over the previous decade. While the mass mobilization that occurred between January 25 and February 11 took virtually everyone by surprise, protest was well known to, and practiced by, Egyptians.[42] However, no part of this history of pre-2011 activism showcases NGOs as influential actors. While in some cases professional syndicates served as sites of mobilization, by and large the protest waves operated outside of formal organizational structures. More loosely networked, atomized collective action is common in autocratic states where rulers tightly constrain organizations.[43] That registered NGOs in Egypt were not prominent actors in that country's protest activities makes sense in light of the Mubarak regime's control tactics previously outlined.

Yet as the January 25 uprisings unfolded, narratives began to emerge that claimed that NGOs not only had a hand in, but in fact fomented, the upheaval. One such account came from the Mubarak regime itself, which claimed that the Egyptian NGOs that partnered with or received funding from US democracy promotion agencies were behind the disorder and that their efforts reflected foreign attempts to destabilize Egypt.[44] A competing account celebrated NGOs' alleged role in the uprisings. This telling, propagated by US journalists, suggested that the Western civil society promotion programs that funded Egyptian NGOs had "nurtured young democrats" in

Egypt and that the trainings that US-backed NGOs had offered to Egyptian activists had inspired their leadership of the mass peaceful protests.[45]

Since the 1990s Western donors had, in fact, channeled funds to Egypt's NGO sector as part of their democracy building programs. USAID earmarked around $20 million per year for democracy building in Egypt, and while those funds were spread across projects aimed at legislative, electoral, judicial, and civic reforms, the bulk of the grants were awarded to NGOs that in turn carried out the reform projects.[46] The EU, too, considered civil society organizations to be key partners in democracy building, particularly for their roles in advocating for and monitoring reforms.[47] Increasing the capacity of Egypt's NGO sector was a core component of strengthening civil society, implemented in part through an NGO Service Center that provided institutional support and small grants to local organizations. But NGOs were also charged with carrying out projects designed to provide research and training to cultivate liberal democratic reforms across the legislative, judicial, and civic spheres and to bring to light instances of corruption.

In fact, however, no Egyptian NGO leader I spoke with credited their organization with inciting the uprisings. Instead, these NGO leaders described themselves and their peers as having been taken completely by surprise by the protests. Furthermore, they criticized themselves for failing to motivate the mass revolts. "These organizations weren't related to the uprisings, instigating social revolt or revolution," said one development NGO director.[48] Another described NGO leaders as "hypocrites," going on to say, "We supported Mubarak and played by the system. If we were really principled, we would have admitted that we wouldn't have success at the national level."[49] Organization leaders also stressed that their organizations were not formally represented in Tahrir Square. Staff members of a variety of organizations—including human rights NGOs, development NGOs, and foundations—participated in the protests as individuals, but emphasized that they did not speak for their organizations while in the square.

Despite their NGOs' absence from Tahrir Square, Egypt's NGO and foundation leaders saw an opportunity to push forward democratic political reform in the weeks and months following Mubarak's ouster.

Conditions in Egypt during the year that followed were particularly favorable for Egypt's NGOs and foundations. Throughout the winter and spring of 2011, Egyptians were euphoric. The culture of fear that prevailed under Mubarak's reign had vanished, and in its place was not only optimism about the future but a firm belief that there had been a fundamental reconfiguration of the social contract. No longer would the people be at the mercy of an all-powerful ruler. Egyptians would be free to express their true beliefs and to participate meaningfully in civic and political life. Throughout the eighteen days of the uprisings, the people had claimed public spaces and the civic realm and asserted their authority to voice demands to the state. My interlocutors identified this euphoria as a sense of a new era from which there was no going back, one in which the people would be empowered to claim their social, economic, and political rights.

Leaders of NGOs and foundations noted four specific transformations that they believed could facilitate their leadership of democratic political reform. The first was a perceived weakening of the government apparatus. Not only did the army seem to side with the people when it refused to attack protesters during the uprisings but senior military officials who took over as part of the transitional government appeared ill prepared to govern. This created the impression of a power vacuum and gave organizations the freedom to flout the confines of Law 84 of 2002. "As NGOs, we used to be very careful about what we said," explained one NGO leader, speaking in early 2012 about the sense of liberation that organization leaders felt. "There had been self-censorship because of the security forces. There was a shift after the revolution, it was amazing. The trend after January 25 is toward advocacy and discussions regarding political systems. I think that will translate after January 25 with NGOs and foundations. I think even more that we will see new organizations that do human rights and advocacy."[50]

NGO leaders told me that they were inspired by the Egyptian people's eagerness to discuss and participate in political life, a second transformation that facilitated NGO leadership of reform. Whereas under Mubarak conversations about politics were strictly delimited, with support and praise for the regime being the only safe public display of political affiliation, after the uprisings everyone was talking openly about politics and discussing and debating different political viewpoints. "A new opportunity after the revolution is that people have the freedom to express their rights and different points of view," said one NGO leader. "The barrier of fear was broken [after Mubarak fell]," she went on. "People will express their rights now no matter what the cost."[51] And they would do so not only among friends but also in the most public of spaces. Another NGO director mused, "Do you know what's positive? The number of talk shows on television. They discuss the revolution, parties, the meaning of liberals and Islamic fundamentalism, the difference between the Muslim Brotherhood and Salafis. They offer public knowledge.

People are talking. There is a liberty to address these issues on television or in newspapers. I can say that this is positive. The liberty of talking."[52]

With this liberty of talking came a heightened political awareness, one that NGO and foundation leaders believed they should help to advance. "There is political awareness in post-revolution Egypt. Everyone in Egypt is talking politics and has awareness. Before the revolution there were very few [conversations about politics], because of fear and lack of education. The regime enforced this because they did not want change in Egypt," said one NGO staff member.[53] Organization leaders explained that there was now a need for NGOs to teach people about free and fair elections, what should be included in a constitution, and what their rights as citizens could and should be.

In a third transformation, activists created new organizations dedicated to advancing the aims of the uprisings. These grassroots organizations first emerged during the protests in the form of popular committees. On January 28 and 29, the Mubarak government unleashed an attack on demonstrators. Police were taken off the streets and "thugs" were hired to rob shops and homes and otherwise create fear and terror. The government allegedly hoped that protesters would be forced to leave the streets and return home to protect their property and families.[54] Instead of submitting to the attacks, citizens imposed their own order through *legan*, or popular committees, organized to secure local neighborhoods. Scholars read the formation of *legan* as an emergent form of organized grassroots collective action.[55] Whereas prior to the uprisings groups were forbidden from spontaneously organizing, and had to formally register as NGOs before operating, the creation of *legan* was thought to portend "tremendous promise for the emergence of genuine civil society activism in Egyptian localities."[56]

NGO and foundation leaders also recognized the value of *legan* as a new form of community organizing. "Popular committees have been securing the neighborhoods," said the director of an Egyptian community foundation. "They began to create a political movement. Now there are popular committees in every community. Egypt is a jewel under dust. The community spirit is there."[57] While some *legan* disbanded after security returned to the streets, others continued to operate and, in doing so, challenged the state's monopoly over both security and service provision. In addition to serving as neighborhood watch groups, many *legan* also became advocates for community development by organizing local residents to demand enhancements to, or even provision of, basic services such as gas lines, lighting, and health clinics.[58] Registered NGOs and foundations expressed interest in partnering with *legan*, thus creating the potential for more established organizations to align themselves with the grassroots activism inspired by the uprisings.

Directly after the uprisings, a number of young people created new organizations in order to institutionalize their reform efforts. Some worked explicitly on projects related to democratic political reform, while others focused on economic development. Regardless of their orientation, these groups sought to bring together revolutionary leaders with everyday citizens to galvanize change. Egyptian foundation leaders were enthusiastic about these new organizations and declared their intent to back them. "Since the revolution we have seen many new NGOs and initiatives. I don't know the exact number, and many are unregistered, but they have plans and want to do things. We are trying to find these initiatives, to support them and help them register," said one foundation director. "After the revolution more people want to do things but don't know how. Not just registered NGOs but also informal initiatives. We try to embrace this. We want and need to enlarge the pool of people to support informal organizations and initiatives."[59] Another foundation director described these new organizations as "very dynamic and enthusiastic and coming with the idea of change. They are scattered and disorganized, but when you guide them with funding they can have an impact and then we can discuss democracy."[60]

At the same time that foundations were faced with a new crop of organizations to support, NGOs were presented with additional manpower through volunteers eager to devote time and energy toward advancing change, a fourth transformation. During the uprisings and subsequent protests, people spontaneously took care of the streets and protest sites by picking up trash (as shown in Figure 2.1), serving at checkpoints where ID checks prevented thugs from entering, and setting up impromptu health clinics to tend to minor injuries. Many such volunteers sought out more organized forms of participation after the uprisings and turned to NGOs. NGO leaders remarked that they witnessed an increased number of people asking to help after the protests and suggested that these new volunteers would be a boon to their organizations' capacity. "Volunteers are a new approach to NGO work in Egypt. It is a new approach in our culture, since the revolution," said one NGO leader. "Traditionally there was no volunteer culture in Egypt, but there has been much more since the revolution."[61]

Figure 2.1. A volunteer collecting trash during a protest in Tahrir Square,
Cairo, May 27, 2011.
Source: Author's photo.

Thus, after Mubarak's fall, a confluence of factors created a unique opening
for Egypt's NGOs and foundations to shake off their own fear and cautious-
ness and initiate democratic political reform activities. But this opening was
in part predicated on the notion that the army, which came to power after
Mubarak's overthrow, would be receptive to democracy. Such an assumption
wasn't unreasonable, given that during the eighteen days of protests the army
appeared to side with the people. But it would turn out to be misguided.

Political Leadership at the Crossroads

The army first arrived on the scene of the 2011 uprisings on January 28, when
Mubarak dispatched troops to Tahrir Square.[62] That day was a bloody one,
with police firing tear gas, rubber bullets, and water cannons into the crowds

of protesters. As the army moved in, many of the protesters were wary due to rumors that the soldiers had been ordered to attack the protesters.[63] But the troops focused on restoring stability and helped to protect Tahrir Square from violent interlopers.[64] In turn, demonstrators began to fraternize with the solders and chanted what would become a famous refrain: "The army and the people are one hand."[65] By the time Mubarak stepped down on February 11, Egyptians had come to believe that the army was a friend of the revolutionaries.

Relatively early in the transition process, however, the army showed signs that it would not be such a friend. The SCAF—a council of army leaders convened in times of war or internal strife—assumed leadership of the transitional government on the evening of February 11 and pledged to hand over power to a civilian government within six months. This wasn't soon enough for some protesters, who declared that they would remain in Tahrir Square until a civilian-led government was installed and Egypt's thirty-year state of emergency was lifted.[66] They set up tents, settling in for a long standoff. But in an early show of force, soldiers cleared the square on March 9. Soldiers allegedly dragged some of the lingering demonstrators to the Egyptian Museum, which sits just beside the square, and tortured them.[67]

Meanwhile, army officials quietly began to institutionalize their governing power. In mid-February, the SCAF convened a panel of independent jurists to revise the country's constitution. The resulting constitutional declaration was put forth for a national referendum on March 19. The declaration laid out the powers of the different branches of government, specified the parliamentary and presidential election processes, and called for a parliamentary committee to draft a new constitution. Egypt's revolutionary youth and established liberals campaigned for a "no" vote, anticipating the Muslim Brotherhood's likely success in parliamentary elections and, as a result, their heavy hand in drafting a new constitution. Yet the referendum passed with 77 percent of votes in favor, and the Brotherhood began to turn their attention to electoral politics.[68] The "no" vote's heavy losses may have contributed to many revolutionary youths' decisions to avoid formal political processes and return to the streets.

Despite the timetable for a transfer of power laid out in the constitutional declaration, two articles in the declaration suggested that the SCAF wasn't yet ready to overturn Mubarak-era regulations or fully relinquish its power. Article 62 stipulated that all existing laws would remain in force, and Article 56 gave the SCAF full legislative authority.[69] The generals also kept on some

National Democratic Party (NDP) members and affiliates, maintaining Mubarak's cabinet and the judiciary, and appointing NDP loyalists to key ministerial posts.[70]

Protests over the SCAF's slow moves toward democracy continued to flare up throughout the summer and into August, when the army again emptied Tahrir Square. October 9 marked a particularly violent battle between soldiers and protesters, when military troops clashed at the Maspero television building with a group of Coptic Christians who were demonstrating against a recent church attack. The confrontation resulted in twenty-eight deaths and more than two hundred injuries.[71] Just days later, SCAF representatives announced that they would extend their power beyond the November parliamentary elections and retain full control over the government until a president was elected. The move meant that the legislature would remain subservient to the generals, who charged themselves with appointing the prime minister and cabinet and presiding over drafting a new constitution.[72] In November, the SCAF officially issued a set of supra-constitutional principles to cement their control over the constitutional process. The principles gave the SCAF the jurisdiction to control selection of the constitution drafters and veto any provision that "contradicts the basic tenets of Egyptian state and society and the general rights and freedoms confirmed in successive Egyptian constitutions."[73]

As NGO leaders took note of the SCAF's aggression and its moves to consolidate power, they sensed that the counterrevolution they had feared was beginning to take shape. "They are playing the same old tricks played by the old regime," said one NGO leader. "They have certain agendas but there is no transparency. It's the same old game. You can't assume that there has been much change between January 25 and today. Yes, the president is gone. But you can't see much fundamental change in how the country is ruled."[74]

It was the same old game, but with a twist. While the SCAF was clear that it would crack down on street-level protests, for months it remained unclear how it would treat formal civil society organizations. Law 84 was still in place, and NGO and foundation leaders wondered if and how the army would enforce it. Fearing retaliation for any efforts to promote political change, many organizations hesitated to act outside of the law's strictures. They described this state of ambiguity as one of the biggest challenges they faced in the early phase of the post-Mubarak era. "We lost time during the revolution," the director of one NGO told me in July 2011. "The situation is fluid. In most cases it's business as usual, but the interim administration is not taking decisions. We need to wait for a more established administration. Some areas of the government are ready to take decisions even though they are an interim government. Others are more cautious. But decision-making generally is slowing down."[75] "The major challenge is the lack of government policy," said the director of another NGO. "Since February 11 there is really no government, so it's hard for us to get new things moving except at the local level. At the national level it is impossible."[76]

By late 2011 it had become clear that the Islamists were the only opposition groups cohesive and organized enough to contest the SCAF. Many of the revolutionary youth resisted joining traditional political parties or organizing to push their political goals forward. But while the loose networks that the youth had created using social media and text messaging allowed them to elude repressive regime forces during the uprisings, their refusal to more formally organize in the ensuing months left them weak against well-established Islamist groups. The young revolutionaries' inclination to return to Tahrir rather than to align with existing political parties or create new ones disappointed my interviewees. "The youth are complaining," said one observer of the NGO sector, speaking to me in July. "It's very frustrating. They haven't rolled up their sleeves and gotten down to work. They are in danger of losing the leadership to the Muslim Brotherhood. They only have limited time. They haven't gotten into gear, they haven't stopped talking to themselves and gotten out to the people. They are not forming coalitions to compete on a party list. They will have seats in parliament, but they won't really compete in these elections."[77] NGO and foundation leaders accused the youth of being "in revolution mode, not work mode," and warned that in order to push their democratic agendas they would have to enter traditional party politics.

While the youth continued to protest, Islamist groups quickly turned to electoral politics. Two weeks after Mubarak's resignation, the Muslim Brotherhood announced that it had formed the Freedom and Justice Party to compete in future elections. Unlike the youth, members of Islamist groups had experience in electoral campaigning. Even though it was impossible for opposition groups to win a parliamentary majority in Mubarak's Egypt, elections offered a way for Islamist groups to organize, broadcast their platforms, and establish themselves as viable opposition candidates.[78] Knowing that the Brotherhood and other Islamist groups were disciplined and experienced, Egyptians widely expected Islamists to fare well in both parliamentary and presidential elections. This troubled my interviewees, who feared that Islamist policies would be unfriendly to civil society organizations.

Egypt's parliamentary elections took place from November 28, 2011, to January 11, 2012, and were considered the country's first free and fair elections. Islamist parties dominated, over and above what most Egyptians had anticipated.[79] The Muslim Brotherhood's Freedom and Justice Party won 47 percent of seats in the People's Assembly—the lower house of Egypt's two-tiered parliament—and the ultra-conservative Salafist al-Nour Party secured 24 percent. Combined, liberal and secular parties managed to win less than 30 percent of seats.[80] Many NGO and foundation leaders were alarmed. These secularists envisioned Egypt as a "civil state," governed by administrative laws and democratic practices.[81] Believing that Islamist groups were in favor of a theocratic state, they were skeptical that an Islamist-dominated government would allow NGOs any greater freedom to advance political reforms than Mubarak had. In fact, many feared that their opportunities to promote liberal democracy would be even more restricted under Islamist rule.

The Government's Crackdown on NGOs

If the political uncertainty of 2011 made NGO leaders leery, a government crackdown on Egypt's NGO sector that commenced that year and has escalated through the time of this writing downright scared them. The government's campaign against the NGO sector became apparent in July 2011, when Minister of Planning and International Cooperation Fayza Abou el-Naga announced the formation of a fact-finding committee to investigate illegal foreign funding of, and activities among, NGOs. The committee was commissioned by the Minister of Justice and headed by former state security prosecutors. While Justice Minister Mohammed al-Guindy had been brought into the transitional government's cabinet as part of an effort to remove Mubarak's old guard, Abou el-Naga was a holdover from the Mubarak regime and longtime skeptic of Western democracy promotion initiatives.[82] The committee went to work, and on September 26 al-Fagr, a weekly independent newspaper, published a leaked summary of the committee's report.

The al-Fagr article reported that thirty-nine Egyptian and foreign organizations were operating while unregistered, twenty-eight Egyptian NGOs were receiving foreign funds illegally, and several foreign NGOs were participating in the types of political activities banned by Law 84 of 2002.[83] Akhbar *al-Youm*, another weekly newspaper, released additional details from the report, disclosing the amount of funds that Egyptian NGOs received from Gulf-based foundations and the US government.[84] In early December, the Justice Ministry officially revealed that four hundred NGOs in Egypt had received foreign funding over the past six years, and on December 24 *al-Masry al-Youm* released leaked data that NGOs "and some famous Egyptian figures" received nearly 1.7 billion Egyptian pounds, or around $285 million, in foreign funds since June of 2010 alone.[85] Receiving foreign funds was not illegal so long as the funds were approved by the government; however, these announcements generated suspicion that Egypt's NGO sector might be serving as an instrument of foreign interests.

The government's investigation turned from innuendos of treason into a full-fledged crackdown on December 29, when state security forces raided the offices of seventeen Egyptian and international NGOs that were participating in democracy promotion activities. Security forces confiscated the organizations' computers, paper files, and cash, and temporarily detained employees while conducting their sweeps.[86] A judge in the investigation declared that the raided organizations were conducting "unlicensed and illegal activities without the knowledge of the Egyptian people." The NGOs were framed as carrying out clandestine foreign agendas that would destabilize Egypt, with reports indicating that the fact-finding committee "discovered that five foreign NGOs received secret money transactions from abroad" and found "a map showing Egypt divided into four parts: Upper Egypt, the Delta, Greater Cairo and the Canal provinces."[87] The map was cited as evidence of foreign espionage and plans to divide the country.

Two of the US-headquartered NGOs that had been raided—the National Democratic Institute (NDI) and the International Republican Institute (IRI)—were informed in late January that several of their employees had been banned from leaving the country.[88] The US embassy took the unprecedented step of sheltering the employees with US citizenship in the embassy compound out of fear that they might otherwise be detained by the Egyptian authorities.[89] Charges in the case were filed soon thereafter. On February 5, the Ministry of Justice announced that it had recommended that forty-three employees of the raided NGOs face trial before a criminal court for illegally accepting funds from international organizations and pursuing unlawful activities.[90] In March, after intense pressure from US officials and the posting of about $4 million in bail, the Egyptian government lifted the travel ban on the foreign employees and allowed them to flee Egypt. Late at night on March

1, the Americans left the country on a US military plane. [91] On March 3, the front page of *al-Masry al-Youm,* shown in Figure 2.2, featured a large photograph of an airplane along with smaller snapshots of the US citizens arriving at Cairo International Airport to board the flight.

The message of the photos was clear: the Americans were escaping justice. While Egyptian staffers would appear in the defendants' cage in criminal court, the Americans would watch the trial from the safety of the United States. The incident spawned local indignation and stoked suspicions that NGOs—both those implicated in the investigation and others throughout the sector—were operating as agents of foreign powers. The episode was particularly damning in light of a heightened sense of pride and nationalism in Egypt. Individuals or organizations perceived as disloyal to the country were ostracized, and the Ministry of International Cooperation did its best to paint NGOs as meddlers in Egypt's affairs. "There are development partners that have for some time now been pushing the democracy and human rights agenda," said Talaat Abdel Malek, an advisor to the Ministry of International Cooperation, "And I understand that, and I understand the need for it, but

Figure 2.2. Front cover of *al-Masry al-Youm,* March 3, 2012.
Source: Author's photo.

there comes a point when there is something that is called national sovereignty that has to be respected."[92]

While the NGO trial targeted international NGOs promoting democracy in Egypt,[93] fallout from the case reverberated throughout Egypt's NGO sector. First, it became dangerous, or in some cases impossible, to accept grants from foreign donors. Merely receiving donations from abroad put organizations at risk of being labeled by competitors and beneficiaries as foreign agents. Some organizations felt so threatened that they returned grants to international funders. Others waited to hear the results of the NGO trial before accepting foreign funds. "No NGO will dare take funds [from us] before the results of the trial," said a program officer at one major international aid agency. "If the NGO staff [charged in the case] are found innocent maybe things will get back to normal . . . [but] if the trial results are negative there will be challenges."[94] Foreign donors heard from their NGO grantees that they were alienating beneficiaries by accepting foreign funds. People began refusing the services of foreign-funded NGOs because they believed that the organization might have a secret agenda.

In addition to worrying about the reputational effects of accepting foreign funding, NGOs that accepted grants from abroad were faced with drawn-out approval times. According to the law, the government had sixty days to approve grants from international donors. After those sixty days, the organization was theoretically free to use the funds if approval had not been denied. In reality, projects were regularly postponed when the government failed to issue an approval, either because the organization's leaders were scared to proceed without permission or because the bank through which the grant passed refused to release the funds. NGO leaders indicated that the Ministry of Social Solidarity (MOSS) was holding up approvals for eight to twelve months, and then refusing some projects that had stood in limbo. Sometimes it was not MOSS but state security officials who informed organization leaders that their projects had been rejected. In addition, it became increasingly common for state security officials to show up on their premises or to phone them and remind them that they were being watched. It was clear that the government planned to use all tools at its disposal to intimidate and control the NGO sector.

It wasn't just human rights NGOs that faced problems. The government also stalled its approval of foreign-funded economic development projects. Organizations that steered clear of politics and human rights and focused on government-friendly areas such as jobs and education saw their projects held up or blocked if they were foreign-funded. When organization leaders inquired about the delays, they received no answers. To mitigate the risk of committing to foreign-funded projects when the funds might not ultimately flow through, NGO leaders built clauses into funding contracts stating that a project officially began not when the funds left the donor but rather when they were released by the Egyptian bank to the grantee. That way, organizations couldn't be held liable by foreign donors for projects that were never granted government approval.

The Egyptian state media appeared to collude with the government in its campaign against the NGO sector, widening the scope of public suspicion beyond those with a more intimate knowledge of the sector. A development NGO leader explained, "We feel sad and sorry because with the recent crisis the media dealt with it in a very bad way. They accused NGOs generally of being not faithful, spies, destroying Egypt's dignity, and interfering in politics. That's really bad, to use the media to attack NGOs."[95] A prominent revolutionary who created a development NGO after the uprisings to improve living conditions and spur resilience, economic opportunity, and citizen participation in a Cairo-area shanty town told me about the challenges his organization had in gaining trust after the media's campaign. Thanks to media propaganda, the activist claimed, rumors spread that he had been part of the April 6 Youth Movement, and people in the shanty town began to assume that his NGO had a clandestine political agenda. He and his staff spent much of the organization's startup time just talking with the slum residents in order to combat rumors and build trust.

No organization was immune from the crackdown, including small, grassroots NGOs. The director of one such organization that worked with the Bedouin community in Egypt's South Sinai explained that her organization had received a letter from the government explicitly instructing it not to do any work related to democracy. The letter also requested monthly (as opposed to quarterly) bank statements, along with narratives of how funds were spent. The director of this organization, which operated out of a tiny office on a shoestring budget, was so worried about government surveillance that she requested that all of our communications apart from face-to-face conversations take place via phone calls and text messages to circumvent what she believed was widespread email surveillance. Even in this phone correspondence, the information shared was kept to a minimum. By 2012, the window of opportunity that the January 25, 2011, uprisings had created for civil society to promote democracy was being muscled shut.

Great Expectations for Democratic Elections

Thus far, the story of Egypt's transition has progressed through early 2012. Over the course of a single year, the space for civil society activism and democratic political reform that was created by the January 25 uprisings was gradually constricted by the SCAF. But a common refrain among my interviewees during that year was that everyone in the sector was waiting for the presidential elections, slated to take place in the spring of 2012. Presumably, the elections would bring an end to the uncertainty and allow organizations to move forward with reforms that fit within the parameters of the new president's agenda.

Egyptians went to the polls on May 23 and 24 for the first round of voting. Spirits were high, with voters proudly displaying their purple fingers indicating that they had cast a ballot in Egypt's first free and fair presidential elections. Ahmed Shafiq, the last prime minister to serve under Mubarak, and Mohammed Morsi, the Freedom and Justice Party's candidate, emerged as the top two vote-getters and thus earned the chance to face each other in a runoff in June. On June 14, just two days before the second round of voting was to take place, the military dissolved the parliament and granted itself wide-ranging new powers, including control over the national budget and the right to issue new laws.[96] Presidential election voting moved forward on June 16 and 17, and Morsi emerged as the winner. Once again, however, the SCAF intervened. Minutes after the polls closed, the state media announced a new constitutional declaration issued by the SCAF. This updated the March 2011 declaration with eight new amendments designed to give the SCAF almost total autonomy in overseeing military matters and de facto veto power over the drafting of a new constitution. One human rights activist declared that "Egypt had 'completed its full transition into a military dictatorship.'"[97]

Nevertheless, Morsi took the oath of office on June 30, 2012. He waited less than two months before clashing with the SCAF and alienating liberal groups. On August 12, Morsi ordered the retirement of the top Mubarak-era military leadership, including Field Marshal Mohammed Hussein Tantawi, who had led the transitional government, and stripped the military of its role in drafting laws and the constitution. Meanwhile, Morsi appointed a cabinet consisting of outgoing government officials, technocrats, and Islamists. Liberal and secular groups were excluded. Morsi granted himself even greater powers in November, issuing declarations that gave his decisions immunity from judicial review and barred the courts from dissolving Egypt's Constituent Assembly or parliament. As protests erupted over these moves to consolidate power, the Constituent Assembly, dominated by Islamists, rushed to draft a new constitution. On December 15, the draft constitution was approved with 63.8 percent voting in favor.[98]

The new constitution did not bring calm. On the contrary, hundreds of thousands marched on January 25, 2013, the second anniversary of the 2011 uprisings, to protest Morsi's rule. Throughout the winter, as protests continued, Morsi increasingly distanced himself from both the military and the people. In April, a group of liberal reformers calling themselves Tamarrod (meaning "rebellion") circulated a petition calling for a new presidential election. Tamarrod claimed to represent revolutionary values and aims but was discredited as reports emerged that it received financial and logistical support from Egypt's military, Interior Ministry, and SSI, as well as funding from the United Arab Emirates.[99]

Meanwhile, the NGO trial lumbered on. The Egypt-based NGO staff members charged in the case appeared in court, sequestered together in a cage as their case was tried. The proceedings were slow and drawn out, impaired by judge recusals and multiple adjournments. Finally, after one and a half years, a decision was handed down on June 4, 2013. All forty-three employees charged in the case were convicted of operating organizations illegally and were sentenced to five years in prison.[100] Organizational leaders who had been waiting for the conclusion of the trial before making major changes to their strategies now had their answer: Egypt would be no more open to democracy promoting NGOs under Morsi's leadership than it had been under Mubarak's.

Donors' Responses to the January 25 Uprisings

The rupture of the January 25, 2011, uprisings created an unprecedented opportunity for civil society organizations in Egypt to contribute to a democratic political transition in Egypt. But that opportunity was accompanied by the threat of a slide back into authoritarianism. The political opportunity was immediately apparent. The threats emerged more gradually but revealed themselves even in the first year after the uprisings. Throughout 2012 and 2013 there was still a battle for democracy to be waged, but it was beset by roadblocks at a startling number of turns.

Donors to civil society organizations had an important role to play at the critical juncture of 2011, when the fight for Egypt's future was most pronounced and the field of actors contending for influence was most open. This was the moment when NGOs had the most freedom to take on new, or ramp up existing, democracy building initiatives—while Egyptians were still united in their enthusiasm for a more democratic future and while the SCAF was still too busy figuring out how to govern to be concerned about the actions of civil society groups. Two key sets of donors—Western aid agencies and Egyptian philanthropic foundations—recognized that NGOs would need additional funding in order to initiate or expand work on democratic political reform. Both sets of donors pledged to provide that funding, but only the Western aid agencies stepped in immediately with increased budgets for democracy promotion. The local foundations moved much more hesitantly.

Western donors—especially the United States and European Union— reacted to the uprisings rapidly, doubling down on their commitments to promoting democracy.[101] Some donors were new to the region, eager to help usher along what most at the time expected would be a major transformation in Egypt's political system. The Cairo office director of a US foundation that had a well-established presence in Egypt spoke of newfound interest in the Middle East among her foundation peers in the West. "There is huge interest [in Egypt among donors]. We will see hundreds of millions of more funds come into the country and region," she said, indicating that since the January 25 uprisings the foundation's local office had received a flood of calls from peers asking how they could get involved in promoting democracy in Egypt.[102] Government aid agencies also rushed to the region. The just-installed Egypt office director of one European aid agency that had previously not maintained a strong presence in the Middle East explained, "We moved into Egypt after the revolution. We set ourselves up remarkably fast. We probably responded faster to [the Arab] revolutions than to the [fall of the] Berlin Wall. That took one year, but in the Middle East things became clear on January 25, 2011, and [our Cairo office] opened in May."[103]

Western funders with established presences in Egypt also saw their democracy promotion budgets increase after the 2011 uprisings. "Immediately after the revolution we launched a request for proposals [related to political reform]. We received [additional funds] from headquarters. We were quick, reactive, and we did topics that were more sensitive—freedom of speech, anti-torture, etc.," explained the office director of a major Western government aid agency.[104] "We increased funding for democracy and good governance after the revolution," said the Egypt office director of another Western donor.[105] USAID raised its budget for democracy and good governance projects, from $15 million to $65 million in 2011.[106] This allowed the agency to nearly triple the number of democracy and good governance grants it awarded from ten in 2010 to twenty-seven in 2011.[107] The European Neighbourhood Policy Instrument increased democracy aid after the uprising from €39 million in 2007–2010 to €50 million in 2011–2013,[108] and in late 2011 the European Union established the European Endowment for Democracy in order to respond more rapidly to movements for democratization.[109]

Many international donors also expanded their budgets for socioeconomic development projects after the uprisings. In interviews, however, these grant makers stressed their work in the political arena and barely mentioned grants for socioeconomic development. Donor coordination meetings also focused on politics. Members of the Development Partners Group (DPG), a group convened by the UNDP and consisting mostly of Western government aid agency representatives, met regularly in the wake of the uprisings to discuss and strategize their responses. Most conversations focused on politics, according to DPG representatives. Coordination was also heightened through the Group of 8's new Deauville Partnership, a collaboration mechanism through which the international community was to galvanize around political transitions in the region.[110]

Western aid organizations granted their democracy promotion grants primarily to international NGOs and local human rights organizations—the two types of organizations that typically constitute the democracy promotion establishment. USAID was particularly notable for the preference it gave to international and human rights NGOs. Nearly 85 percent of its $65 million democracy and good governance budget was awarded, in grants, to US and international NGOs, with Egyptian organizations splitting the remaining $11 million.[111] In order to target those funds to human rights organizations, the agency abandoned its policy of funding only registered NGOs and began bypassing government ministries and funneling grants directly to both unregistered NGOs and human rights groups registered as civil companies.[112]

The rapid response of Western donors to the 2011 uprisings stands in stark contrast to a far more muted response by Egypt's philanthropic foundations. Before pushing ahead with grantmaking for democracy promotion, the foundations first had to extricate themselves from their past ties to Mubarak. "Are we going down with the regime?" foundation board members asked themselves in the wake of the uprisings.[113] Even before the SCAF's crusade against the NGO sector, foundation leaders worried about how the SCAF would treat them, their corporations, and their foundations. This can be attributed to the fact that most donors to, and leaders of, Egypt's foundations had close ties to the former Mubarak regime. In exchange for corporate contracts, monopoly rights, and other business favors, they used their foundations' philanthropy to help advance the government's development priorities. Some also served in Mubarak's cabinet or expressed political loyalty through membership in the NDP. "Foundations are the old regime," one foundation director declared bluntly. "They served as a tool for the former government to implement corruption. We all shared in the deterioration of the situation."[114] This left foundation leaders uncertain and, in many cases, scared after the old regime was ousted. They knew neither who the new regime would be nor how it would govern.

Connections to Mubarak, based on business perks, also left the foundations distrusted by the general public. In a 2011 survey conducted by the IRI, 69 percent of respondents said that they disapproved of Egypt's business community.[115] One of the central demands of the protesters was, after all, to eliminate corruption and create a more level economic playing field. Several of Egypt's most prominent foundations were led by corporate magnates who had prospered under Mubarak's economic liberalization and privatization strategies—Mohammed Mansour (Mansour Foundation for Development), the Sawiris family (Sawiris Foundation for Social Development), and Yasser el-Mallawany (EFG-Hermes Foundation) among them. A number of foundation leaders—especially Mansour and el-Mallawany—were now under fire for their ties to Mubarak. Foundation staff members felt the heat as they tried to reposition their foundations after the uprisings to be more responsive to "the people." They faced resistance from beneficiaries who were suspicious of foundations named for corporate moguls, and at the same time they couldn't move too quickly to change because they didn't know what the new regime would look like. So instead of putting all their energy into realignments with civil society, they operated "in standby mode, waiting to see where the power would lie."[116]

The SCAF's early moves to consolidate the military's power were problematic for Egypt's business community. The army had long maintained a fraught relationship with business people as the two groups vied for Mubarak regime patronage.[117] With Mubarak out of the picture, the SCAF flexed its muscles, launching investigations and pressing corruption charges against some of Egypt's most prominent corporate elites. In early 2011 Egypt's Central Auditing Organization announced that it would open more than a thousand corruption complaints that had been submitted to the government in recent years, which suggested that a witch hunt within the business community might be under way.[118] Later that year, the SCAF developed a blacklist of corruption suspects.[119]

But the SCAF developed no systematic approach to the investigations or indictments, showing no rhyme or reason for which business magnates were chosen for investigation and offering no clear signals of how it perceived the future role of the private sector.[120] This left members of the business community, including prominent philanthropists, "terrified," not knowing if or when they would be targeted.[121] Some fled the country, others watched their family members and business associates go behind bars, and others were themselves slapped with charges and barred from leaving the country.[122] Board members of at least two of Egypt's leading foundations faced investigations and charges,[123] and others wondered if they would be next. Facing such a precarious future, the leaders of Egypt's foundations were not inclined to draw further attention from the SCAF by funding or engaging in democracy promotion activities.

On top of this political uncertainty, foundations were confronted with economic challenges. Egypt's economy declined precipitously after Mubarak's resignation, as economic turmoil wrought by the uncertain political transition was magnified by a global political downturn.[124] A collapse in tourism, previously a major source of revenue, also contributed to the country's economic slowdown.[125] After ranging from 4 to 8 percent between 2008 and 2010, Egypt's GDP growth rate fell to negative 4 percent in the first quarter of 2011 and hovered around zero for the rest of that year. By 2012, it recovered to just over 5 percent.[126] Meanwhile, the country's unemployment rate jumped from around 9 percent, where it had hovered since 2008, to around 12 percent in 2011 and 2012. Inflation also spiked after the uprisings, jumping from 4.7 percent in 2012 to 11.7 percent in 2013.[127]

As the economy spiraled downward, the profits of Egyptian corporations were hit hard. This, in turn, affected Egyptian foundations' grantmaking budgets. Since so few had built up large endowments, most relied on a corporate parent or board members of a family business to supply their annual grantmaking budgets. As corporate profits were squeezed, foundations struggled simply to maintain their existing grant commitments. There were no extra funds for new political reform projects. At the same time, Egyptians were placing greater demands on NGOs for basic social services as economic stress led to job losses and price inflation. The situation created a form of double deficit: both NGOs and their local foundation donors were financially strapped.

Egypt's foundations did their best not to disappear. While one did temporarily close its doors directly after the uprisings, others found creative ways to honor their commitments to their grantees. Some managed to redirect budgets for administrative costs into grantmaking budgets. Others offered grant extensions to NGOs that had to cease work during and immediately after the uprisings as a result of security concerns. Foundations also tried to offer support beyond the grant check; for example, by helping NGOs partner with each other and identify other potential sources of funds. Such changes may seem minor. But in fact, they signaled a significant shift among foundations. These institutions could have backed down entirely. They certainly had political and economic excuses for doing so. Instead, most doubled down in their efforts to support NGOs working for change.

Foundation board and staff members alike described the 2011 uprisings as a major opportunity for their philanthropy. They were disarmingly frank about their organizations' complicity in perpetuating an unjust political economy under Mubarak and readily admitted to being on the wrong side of history when the uprisings broke out. But they were equally adamant about wanting to change—to extricate themselves from the Mubarak regime and to ally themselves with individuals and groups in civil society working for both political and economic reform.

Many indicated that they had been waiting and hoping for the freedoms that Mubarak's ouster so tantalizingly presented. One foundation donor, who described herself as a "kid" but was actually a successful businesswoman, said that of course she participated in the 2011 protests. "We young people were there [in Tahrir Square]. We pushed for change, for rights for the poor. Even rich kids related to the regime wanted change. We wanted social change. The social factor was the main factor [behind our involvement]." Others said that they believed that the opening of Egypt's political and economic space would, over the long term, be good for both business and philanthropy. Despite short-term economic declines, they envisioned a future of increased foreign investment, a more vibrant local economy with new startup businesses, new job opportunities that would raise living standards, and an end to the corruption that had sullied their corporate reputations. Foundation leaders also saw expanded opportunities for the types of corporate social responsibility initiatives that could help them prove to a skeptical public that they were, in fact, on the side of citizens.

Some foundation staff members were taken aback by the quick go-ahead they received from their boards to embrace the uprisings as an opportunity. For many years program staff had negotiated a tricky balance between advocating for citizens and respecting the interests of board members. They had relatively little room to maneuver on the advocacy front, given board members' close ties to Mubarak, and they anticipated that their boards would react cautiously in the aftermath of the uprisings. Instead, many found that their boards gave them more authority to steer grantmaking toward issues of social justice. One staff member expressed "shock" that her board responded this way,[128] but foundation staff members embraced the opportunity to "support the *shebab*" (people).[129] "Before, with the old regime, the last goal was the country and its people," one foundation staff member explained. "Now, it is the opposite, the people are first. We have to give back. It's a must now."[130]

But the SCAF's crackdown on both business and civil society, coupled with Egypt's struggling economy, placed very real constraints on the ability of foundations to put the people first and galvanize them for change. Despite viewing the 2011 uprisings as a major political opportunity, Egyptian foundations did not initiate new grants for democracy promotion. Instead, they redoubled their existing work in socioeconomic development realms.

Whither Democracy Building?

The early years after Egypt's uprisings marked a critical stage in the country's trajectory. With Mubarak gone, there was a unique opportunity to build a more democratic Egypt. The hundreds of thousands of protesters who participated in the eighteen days of uprisings showed that civil society *could*— through mobilizing and working together across divisions of class, religion, gender, and age—overcome decades of authoritarian rule. But removing Mubarak was only the first step. For democracy to take hold, civil society would need to maintain its momentum and organize to prevent a backslide into authoritarianism. NGOs stood to provide one avenue for such organization.

The path forward would be rocky. While the swell of Egyptians wanting to contribute to building a more democratic Egypt was a boon for NGOs, the moves by the SCAF and Islamist groups to consolidate their power posed threats to NGOs' autonomy and to their ability to take on democracy promotion initiatives. A deteriorating economy posed further challenges. However, in the early years after the uprisings, NGOs had a rare opportunity to join the struggle to build a more democratic Egypt. To do so, they would need financial backing.

The divergent responses of Western aid agencies and Egyptian philanthropic foundations are striking. Western donors reacted quickly and forcefully, channeling additional funds into democracy and good governance budgets and extending grants to international democracy promotion NGOs and Egyptian human rights organizations to ramp up their political reform activities. Local philanthropic foundations, by contrast, remained focused in the socioeconomic development realm. Yet both groups of donors insisted that the 2011 uprisings created an opening for them to work for democratic political reform. These donors espoused remarkably similar goals, yet differed quite dramatically in how they set about trying to achieve those goals. Why?

One plausible explanation is that the leaders of Egypt's foundations, for all their protestations, weren't truly interested in reform. The business people who created and governed the foundations had profited greatly from the status quo under Mubarak, and despite his removal it wasn't clear that the regime behind him had disappeared. Perhaps the foundation leaders were just biding their time, waiting to see if a fundamental transfiguration of Egypt's political system would transpire or whether, after the dust settled, Egypt would return to business as usual.

In fact, Egypt's foundations *did* move cautiously as a result of the political turmoil. But there is a second explanation as to why Western donors and Egyptian foundations responded differently to the uprisings: perhaps the two groups had fundamentally different opinions about how best to promote democratic political reform in Egypt given the prevailing political, economic, and cultural context. Allowing for this possibility opens up the tantalizing prospect of analyzing the democracy promotion strategies of two different groups more deeply—on the one hand, the Western aid agencies, international NGOs, and human rights NGOs that constitute the democracy promotion establishment; on the other, Egypt's philanthropic foundations and their development NGO grantees. With the benefit of hindsight, we now turn to the task of comparing the lessons learned from each group's approach.

3

The West's Democracy
Promotion Playbook

"I think that what we're doing is useless. No one predicted the revolution. The support we gave to civil society had nothing to do with what happened."[1] I was taken aback when I heard these words, uttered by the staff member responsible for democracy and good governance grants at a major Western aid agency. It was early 2012, and we were sitting and chatting over coffee in a gleaming office building overlooking downtown Cairo. This was not my first interview with a member of a Western aid organization, but it was the first one in which my interlocutor expressed such deep doubt over her organization's approach to democracy promotion in post-Mubarak Egypt. Sensing my bewilderment, the staff member went on to explain, "It is nice to think that NGOs influenced the revolution, but I don't believe it. I don't understand why the army is so worried about civil society. If you want proof, look at the election results"—here the staff member was referring to the recent parliamentary elections, which Islamist party candidates won in a landslide. "In [our funding for] civil society we try to export our values to people for whom it isn't their cup of tea. My colleagues in the Development Partners Group and at the embassies are very dedicated to a certain agenda but it is completely disconnected from the reality on the ground. The agenda wasn't asked for by the people."[2]

This view was not widely shared among staff members of Western aid agencies. Most believed that the 2011 uprisings validated the democracy promotion work they had been pursuing over the years and that such work should be expanded in order to support a full transition to democracy. Yet many scholars of foreign aid, along with a strikingly large number of Egyptian NGO leaders, would likely find merit in the agency staff member's skepticism. Scholars have faulted the West's democracy promotion strategies for lacking revolutionary potential. Meanwhile, staff members of Egypt's development NGOs regularly criticized Western democracy aid for imposing bureaucracy upon recipient organizations and for failing to resonate with diverse populations. Yet Western aid, no matter its drawbacks, often serves as a lifeline for NGOs promoting democracy in autocratic contexts.

The contradictions and contested roles of Western democracy aid were brought into sharp focus in the years after Egypt's 2011 uprisings, as Western democracy brokers described their organizations' efforts with various levels of confidence.[3] Many believed in their work. Some, like the staff member quoted earlier, raised concerns about its efficacy. Staff members of Egypt's NGOs condemned the arrogance and red tape that they believed accompanied it, yet they recognized that Western aid provided an important—and in some cases irresistible—source of financial support. After introducing how members of the democracy promotion establishment responded to the 2011 uprisings and situating that response in the West's standard democracy promotion playbook, this chapter analyzes how a variety of actors who intersect and interact with Western aid perceived its promises and pitfalls.

Western Aid to Egypt by the Book

While the specific strategies, tactics, and levels of democracy aid to Egypt in the wake of the 2011 uprisings varied by donor agency, Western donors' democracy promotion programs displayed several relatively uniform characteristics. Perhaps most conspicuously, funded projects focused primarily on aspects of procedural liberal democracy, including elections, rule of law, constitutional reform, youth participation, women's rights, government corruption, and transitional justice. Donors placed a heavy emphasis on reforming the *institutions* of democracy: elections, the legislature, the judiciary, political parties, and so forth. Much of their work aimed to make national political bodies more accountable, transparent, and effective. As a result, grants tended to flow to organizations that traded in information: think-tank style groups that could provide the technical know-how necessary to train new political leaders and improve government institutions.[4] These included international NGOs such as the NDI, IRI, Freedom House, and International Research & Exchange Board (IREX), as well local human rights organizations.

The outputs produced by Western democracy aid were highly technical. They included workshops and training sessions for politicians and activists, manuals and websites designed to educate citizens about liberal democracy, elections monitoring, independent media development, and legal representation for activists and dissidents. Implementing NGOs reported that they were "publishing many statements,"[5] "documenting the revolution, including military trials and martyrs,"[6] "conducting awareness campaigns,"[7] "monitoring the media,"[8] "conducting research and offering a legislative magazine,"[9] and "producing manuals."[10]

Trainings were especially popular. In a project funded by a US-based aid agency, one human rights organization created a Democracy Academy for youth. "We need to train people in a school of democracy. We need to teach people what democracy is in theory and in practice," the director of the program explained.[11] The academy hosted thirty participants over fourteen days. Instruction relied first on texts, teaching participants about the philosophy and history of democracy. The academy then took a "practical" approach, in which participants wrote essays about their visions for a democratic Egypt. To spread the academy's reach, organization staff members created a "democracy game" software application to be used by young people in other Arab states that had experienced uprisings. Trainings were also popular with European donors. The European Neighbourhood and Partnership Instrument's (ENPI) project to empower women in Egypt gave over one thousand women "training and awareness sessions to raise their self-confidence, knowledge, leadership, and negotiation skills,"[12] while the Westminster Foundation for Democracy hosted induction training sessions for new Members of Parliament and Germany's Konrad Adenauer Stiftung offered political seminars for Egyptian youth.[13]

Voter education and elections monitoring were also favored projects and often involved the use of internet technology. One human rights organization created an election simulation website. Offered in both Arabic and English, the software asked the user questions about his or her political and economic preferences and then matched them to a political party. The program also offered information on the candidates running for office. This same organization also proposed to have international bloggers paired with local election monitors in order to have "international citizens" monitoring, and spreading information about, the elections.

In addition to funding local NGO leaders to carry out trainings and elections monitoring, Western donors and their international NGO grantees brought academic experts to Egypt to consult with political and party leaders, policy researchers, and think tank and NGO staffers. One such workshop was hosted in partnership with the AUC, and featured a panel that included two scholars of electoral laws and was moderated by a renowned

Egyptian dissident. As I signed the guest book for the event, I took note of the affiliations of the audience members who are pictured in Figure 3.1. Most were from AUC, USAID, and various international NGOs. During the event, the panelists delivered remarks, in English, on the pros and cons of various electoral law configurations.[14] The floor was then opened for questions. When asked how the information presented in the panel would be delivered more widely, outside the rarified circles of the educated elite, the two panelists looked at each other baffled. One finally responded that they had not thought about that. "Perhaps we should go to the mosques?" he asked with a shrug.

I offer this anecdote not to undermine the panelists, who have helped to guide countless other transitioning states in reforming their electoral laws and whose expertise stood to offer equally valuable counsel to Egyptian reformers. But the nature of the workshop itself—targeting a highly educated stratum of Egyptians and expats, conducted in English, and situated within the ivory tower of the AUC—typified the technical, professional approach of Western democracy brokers. Democracy aid in Egypt circulated

Figure 3.1. Audience members at a seminar on electoral laws held at AUC's Tahrir Campus, Cairo, June 2011

Source: John D. Gerhart Center for Philanthropy and Civic Engagement at the American University in Cairo.

among a milieu of like-minded professionals who were both well versed in and committed to the language, concepts, and values of liberal democracy. Through their trainings, workshops, manuals, and websites, Western democracy promoters, along with their grant recipients, injected their conceptualizations of democracy, and the tools presumably needed to attain and maintain it, into Egyptian society.

These donors were following what could be termed the democracy promotion playbook, a set of strategies that characterize much of the democracy aid granted by Western agencies. The West's effort to promote democracy throughout the world began to take shape in the early 1980s and was buoyed by the fall of the Soviet Union at the end of that decade. Since the 1990s, Western governments—including the United States, European Union, individual European states, Australia, Japan, Canada, and others—have provided democracy aid as a specific element of their foreign assistance packages. Democracy aid has, as its name suggests, the explicitly political goal of promoting democracy—either by nudging authoritarian governments to democratize or by consolidating democratic governments in recently transitioned states. It is administered and implemented by a variety of organizations, including bilateral and multilateral aid agencies (e.g., USAID, the United Nations, ENPI), foundations specifically designed to promote democracy (e.g., the United States' National Endowment for Democracy and the German Konrad Adenauer Stiftung), quasi-governmental NGOs (e.g., the NDI, the IRI), and advocacy, human rights, research, and legal aid organizations in the target country. Democracy aid is a distinct form of aid targeting political reform. It is separate from foreign aid for socioeconomic development, humanitarian support, and other categories of foreign assistance.[15]

While each organization in the democracy promotion field operates by certain specific principles, strategies, and tactics, most democracy aid organizations—no matter what the source—display certain characteristics. At the strategic level, Western democracy aid attempts to spread liberal democracy through a top-down approach. Projects primarily target the reform of national political institutions such as legislatures, judiciaries, and constitutions.[16] Goals include the establishment of free and fair elections, legislatures consisting of multiple political parties and lawmakers representing citizens' interests, independent courts, a transparent legal and regulatory environment, the eradication of corruption, and the establishment of a democratic culture within civil society. These priorities are established by the country providing the aid and projects are carried out by a coterie of organizations specifically devoted to building democracy.

At the tactical level, democracy aid supports technical projects implemented by trained professionals. Typical activities include publishing research and reports on policy issues, hosting trainings and workshops for citizen activists and political leaders, monitoring elections, and consulting with legislative and judicial bodies.[17] Grants are consistently awarded to a cadre of international NGOs and to a handful of well-established, well-known, and well-connected human rights organizations in the target country.[18] Employees of these organizations are highly educated, conversant in the donor's language, and skilled in navigating grant application processes, managing projects, and reporting results.[19]

Applicants for, and recipients of, democracy aid propose, carry out, and report on projects with measurable and directly observable results. Application forms ask organizations to lay out strategic plans, budgets, logic models, timelines, and anticipated results. Throughout the life of a grant—which is generally short term, often two to three years at most—organizations must report back to the donor on progress made. At the termination of the grant, organizations must provide a detailed report on the results of the project. In order to demonstrate progress, organizations typically implement projects with quantifiable outputs; for example, the number of women in parliament, the number of human rights violations tried in court, or the number of workshops conducted and research reports released. Projects funded by democracy aid are rarely revolutionary in their aims or potential. Instead of confronting dictators or galvanizing collective action among citizens, the projects funded by democracy aid target specific, technical reforms of governing institutions.[20]

A Backlash against Foreign Funds in Post-Mubarak Egypt

On the ground in Egypt, local NGOs met Western democracy aid with ambivalence. On the one hand, the increased funding for democracy promotion projects was tantalizing for organizations desperate for additional financial support. On the other hand, NGO leaders widely believed that the West's democracy aid came with strings attached. Scholars have noted that foreign aid—whether for political reform or economic development—tends to produce and reinforce relationships in which NGO grant recipients become upwardly accountable to their donors and increasingly removed from their local constituents.[21] Noting this upward accountability that foreign aid demands, Egyptians believed that Western aid agencies used their grants to advance their own agendas. "The biggest funder [of NGOs in Egypt] is USAID," explained one NGO director. "But the US government supports dictators and Israel. There is suspicion of anything from outside, including NGO funding from outside. And the US money goes to human rights and [combatting] female genital mutilation, which are things that people don't want [funding for]."[22] NGOs were thus caught in a bind: if they accepted foreign democracy assistance, they could be charged with serving as tools of the West; if they declined foreign aid, they struggled to survive.

After the 2011 uprisings, accepting democracy aid from abroad became even more perilous amid a heightened sense of national pride and suspicion of foreigners trying to meddle with Egypt's political transition. Just as freedom from autocratic rule was a core demand of the Tahrir Square protesters, so too did Egyptians expect autonomy from foreign powers as they negotiated their country's post-Mubarak trajectory. Egyptians were determined to "shape future policy in [their] own image rather than Washington's."[23] Many of my interlocutors were critical of Western donors' rush to fund democracy promoting activities in the wake of the uprisings. "USAID is now coming in massively," said one Egyptian foundation director. "They use money to buy implementers of their vision. They give money to democracy and human rights so now everyone wants to work on these issues even if they weren't involved with these issues before."[24]

Some NGOs refused to accept democracy funds from USAID in particular because of the stigma of carrying a US agenda that such grants held. The director of one human rights organization explained, "We have no American funders since 2005 because they are not approved by the board of trustees. The board fears imperialism that results from American funding." Even though this organization relied exclusively on foreign aid for its survival, it forwent the potentially lucrative grants proffered by USAID. The NGO leader suspected that in the wake of the uprisings other organizations would also boycott aid from the US. "Many NGOs probably won't apply for American grants [now]. Many NGOs fear being hated by the Egyptian people because of American policies in the Middle East."[25]

Organization leaders were also affronted that USAID broke the law after the uprisings when it bypassed the MOSS and gave funds directly to NGOs. Describing the agency as "arrogant," one development NGO leader charged,

"They didn't respect the laws of Egypt. They gave money directly to human rights NGOs and not through the Ministry of Social Solidarity." Citing human rights NGOs' dependency on foreign donors and the upward accountability that instills, this NGO leader went on to claim, "Human rights organizations didn't build a constituency. They remain weak because they don't have local support. They only have support of donors." The European Union did not escape criticism. This same NGO director said that he believed that NGOs had an important role to play in building democracy in Egypt, but that "our weakness is state policy and EU policy. The EU is trying to force people to adopt their beliefs. NGOs can't agree to do programs that will get them into trouble with the government."[26]

In addition to tainting the reputations of grantee organizations in the eyes of many Egyptians, Western democracy aid imposed bureaucratic hurdles on grant applicants and recipients. Interviewees worried that when tempted with new opportunities for funding, Egyptian organizations desperate for donations would create new projects, hire new staff members, professionalize their operations in order to apply for grants, and then be left with unsustainable projects, employees they could no longer afford to pay, and useless technologies after the grant duration ended and the donor moved on. Many organization leaders recognized that their organizations did not have the necessary capacity to apply for and manage democracy grants from Western donors. The NGO leaders who did apply complained that jumping though the required hoops to win the grants took time and resources away from their work. Other groups were completely ineligible. The complex application procedures for democracy aid cut out important populations. Tribal leaders and village elders, for example, who were intimately familiar with their communities' needs and could facilitate collective projects, often lacked the language skills and industry-specific knowledge needed to fill out application and reporting forms. Staff of small, grassroots organizations often faced similar limitations.

Local NGO leaders believed that the imposition of bureaucratic practices and development jargon not only was a nuisance but actually hindered progress toward the very democratic values that Western donors claimed to be promoting. By channeling most democracy aid to elite organizations that work on reforming national political institutions, Western donors often ignored cultural nuances and overlooked local resources that could be mobilized to build a more democratic culture in society. One NGO leader contended that by disregarding such local resources, imposing their own vocabulary, and requiring local NGOs to professionalize their work, foreign donors "slowed down the march toward freedom and democracy. They diluted energy toward values. They were claiming to fight for democracy and freedom while actually delaying its rise."[27] Organizations that refused to apply for Western democracy aid in order to stay true to their own ways of working not only passed up lucrative grants but also struggled to attract staff who were wooed by the higher salaries that aid recipients could offer. "We can't recruit," explained one foundation leader, "because everyone wants USAID salaries and we cannot afford that."[28]

While relatively few members of Western aid agencies critiqued their organizations' approaches to democracy aid, some did acknowledge the distortions that their funding created. Like the staff member quoted in the opening of this chapter, they declined to take credit for the uprisings, and they noted that the Egyptian human rights organizations they bankrolled lacked popular support. The director of one European aid agency's Egypt office mused, "Human rights organizations would not exist without foreign funding. Is that okay? Or human rights organizations would still exist, but they might not have multi-colored reports, tea boys, etc. In a way we have created standards by which NGOs must have offices, staff, and be professional. This is a Western vision. It can be done less expensively by the community. You don't need a fancy logo in order to have a good NGO."[29]

And yet it was the professional organizations with the right logos and vocabulary that seemed to be winning democracy aid. As he thought about the democracy aid flowing to Egypt, the director was "at a loss in reading which grants were extended." He speculated that many organizations received funds because they had "the right literature and proposals," but he wasn't convinced that the organizations had a great impact.

Democracy Brokers' Criticisms of Egyptian Foundations

In light of the hazards that accepting foreign aid posed to Egyptian NGOs, I wondered not only if local foundations might offer alternative sources of support but also if Western donors consulted with local funders about how to design their aid to be most effective in the Egyptian context. When I asked this question, most staff members of Western aid organizations gave me a quizzical look. Clearly, my query seemed ridiculous. Staff members went on to tell me that, so far as they could tell, local foundations weren't interested in democracy building. "The local foundations are more into development and charity," said the Egypt office director of one Western aid organization, voicing an assumption that was widely held by her peers. "We work at the level of political rights."[30]

Foreign donors were well aware of local foundations' close ties to the Mubarak regime. In 2010, the Egypt office director of one donor organization told me, "Very few Arab foundations are social justice philanthropies. Most of the money is from corporate donors. The foundations are closely linked to the government, so they are not radical regarding the re-organization of society." Noting what she perceived to be positive trends in the growth of local philanthropy, the director went on, "There is huge wealth here and people do feel charitable. It is encouraging that philanthropy is institutionalizing. This is a good starting point. But," she cautioned, "it is not based upon a critique of the government. There is a decline in Egypt and people in the elite are concerned. But they are not willing to go toe-to-toe with the government."[31]

After the uprisings, this same office director indicated that she perceived Egypt's foundations as being much less active and less visible compared with before the revolution. "What happens when there is an uprising and the head of the family [who governs the foundation] is eyed with suspicion or thrown in jail, or business is bad because the economy has slowed down?"[32] she asked, picking up on very real challenges that local foundation leaders faced. Across the board, staff members of Western aid organizations indicated that they had never considered partnering, collaborating, or even meeting with local foundations because of a perceived divergence of interests.[33] One interlocutor was so convinced that Egypt's foundations were opposed to engaging with issues of democratic political reform that he believed that if members of local foundations were to attend meetings of the Development Partners Group, where Western donors met to discuss their strategies in Egypt, nobody would feel free to have "frank discussions."

Staff members of human rights organizations, who relied heavily on Western aid for their survival, criticized local foundations for being too scared to support their work. "Egyptian funders won't fund human rights," said the director of one human rights NGO. "They just build buildings. They are afraid of the government, scared of the government."[34] A particularly frustrated staff member of another human rights organization lamented:

At the local level there are no local grant makers for human rights organizations. Businessmen won't pay the cost for our work. The cost is too high.

That funding would be against the government and the government would put restrictions on his work and investments. Local funders are funding only economic development. This is a big issue. There is a huge problem in development NGOs and foundations—they have very strong relations with the government. The government will make their work easier. This is a huge problem.[35]

Time and again, human rights NGO staff members railed against Egypt's foundations. Rightly noting the close connections between most foundations' founding donors and the Mubarak regime, human rights staffers opined that local foundations structured their economic development work around the government's priorities and embraced Mubarak's philosophy that economic development must come before the country could be ready for democracy. One human rights NGO staff member said bluntly, "The idea that economics must come first is the official argument of the Mubarak regime. These people [who lead foundations] don't know democracy."[36]

The Contradictions of Western Democracy Aid

Early in my fieldwork, I assumed that the democracy aid provided by Western agencies was the essence of democracy promotion. I believed that it was the model I should use to judge Egyptian foundations. Relatively quickly, I learned that, on the ground, Western democracy aid was highly contested. But was there an alternative for NGOs wanting to do the work of democracy building? At first, I believed not. Egypt's foundations did not issue new grants for democracy promotion after Mubarak's fall. They continued to dwell in the field of socioeconomic development. Meanwhile, even the staff members who criticized the standard democracy promotion playbook seemed hamstrung. They weren't setting strategies; they were implementing strategies that reflected the priorities and beliefs of government bureaucrats in their home countries. Thus, despite the criticisms lobbed at it, the West's democracy promotion playbook seemed like the only game in town. Then, in early 2012, I went camping on the Red Sea. Over coffee and cigarettes on the beach, I learned of an intriguing alternative.

4

All You Need Is Tea

An Alternative Democracy Promotion Playbook

Egypt in 2012 was inhospitable to Western researchers, particularly those studying civil society. The government's crackdown on NGOs was in full swing and the SCAF was actively stoking suspicions of foreigners. I was planning to cut my fieldwork in Egypt short early in the year and return to the United States. A television advertisement in rotation at the time featured a Westerner—portrayed as a spy—meeting with unsuspecting Egyptians in a café. As the Egyptians discussed the national security situation, the Westerner listened intently, probing his companions for additional information. The spot concluded by urging Egyptians to be careful of what they said, warning that every word came with a price.[1] Over and above concerns for my own safety, I didn't want to endanger any NGO staff members who agreed to meet with me. Besides, I thought I already had enough data to answer my original research question, which focused on the roles of Egypt's philanthropic foundations in promoting democratic political reform. Up to that point, I had spoken primarily with the leaders of local foundations and with staffers of international donor agencies, international NGOs, and Egyptian human rights NGOs. The foundations had not fundamentally changed their strategies, despite vowing to take on democratic political reform when they convened at the 2011 Arab Foundations Forum conference. Meanwhile, the Western democracy brokers and human rights activists who were working overtime on democracy building activities were not surprised that the foundations declined to take part. I therefore concluded that Egyptian foundations were, just like their NGO counterparts, co-opted by the government and unlikely champions of democracy.

Before leaving Egypt, I wanted to swim in the Red Sea. A daily swimmer, I seek out new swimming holes wherever I travel. A friend told me about a camp in the South Sinai, so I booked a long weekend there and prepared for a few days of relaxation and decompression. The owner and director of the camp, it turned out, used the profits from tourism to fund an NGO that he had created to undertake development projects in collaboration with the local Bedouin community. One evening after dinner I told the camp director, Bassem,[2] about my project. Bassem listened patiently as I spoke about the research and my conclusions. When I finished, he paused for a moment, smiled, and replied, "Katie, I don't need money to build democracy."[3] I was puzzled and curious. Bassem explained that he needed money for his economic development projects: to build a school and outfit it with instructional materials, teachers, and technology; to set up a recycling facility; and to build a health clinic and pay its doctors. But he did not need money to build democracy. All he needed was tea, Bassem told me. I was even more puzzled. How was tea going to build democracy?

Bassem smiled again and explained that with tea, he could bring together the men from the local Bedouin community. As they enjoyed the tea, they would discuss their problems, debate their priorities, and develop solutions that they would enact collectively. Discussion, debate, agenda setting, and problem solving was, in the context of an autocracy, the real stuff of democracy. The Bedouins with whom Bassem worked didn't practice democracy by going to the polls; not only were Egyptian elections historically rigged but Bedouins were largely disenfranchised.[4] Instead, they did so by creating a participatory public sphere around cups of tea.

Bassem's story made me realize that I had been approaching my project with Western biases, regarding both the meaning of democracy and what the protesters in Tahrir Square were demanding in the first place. The demonstrators were not calling for a Western-style liberal democracy. They were calling for economic and social justice, freedom, and human dignity. In asking whether Egyptian foundations had restructured their grantmaking to fund democracy promotion—which I assumed to include elections, legislative and judicial reform, and public policy advocacy—I was fundamentally asking the wrong question.

I was not alone in my biases. As outlined in chapter 3, Western donors read the uprisings as an opportunity to inject into Egypt the form of liberal democracy they had at home and that they believed should be spread throughout the rest of the world. For decades they had been conducting a delicate dance with the Mubarak regime as they funded democracy and good governance programs designed to restructure Egypt's electoral laws, legislature, and judiciary, to build its civil society, and to free its media. Donors' heavy focus on national democratic institutions was in line with institutional or procedural understandings of democracy. In the words of political scientist Nathan Brown, "democracy understood as a political system in which senior positions of authority and major policy directions are determined as a result of competitive elections with widespread suffrage."[5]

If one understands democracy this way, then seminars on electoral law reform and academies that teach the fundamentals of democratic governance systems make sense. But Egyptians didn't want to be schooled in this form of liberal democracy. They wanted to define and build democracy on their terms, not according to the rules laid down by Western democracy brokers. They conceptualized democracy as encompassing much more than contested elections—what political scientist Lisa Wedeen refers to as the "stripped-down notion of democracy"[6]—and understood that for democracy to take hold in Egypt it must allow citizens to participate actively and meaningfully in public life writ large and to claim not only their political rights but also their social, economic, and—indeed—human rights.

Equipped with this new perspective, I wondered if in fact I had perceived a nonresponse to the uprisings because I assumed that the protesters aimed to bring institutions of procedural democracy to Egypt. If that assumption is relaxed, and the uprisings are understood more broadly as calls for human dignity—including but not limited to social and economic justice, an end to corruption, and greater rights and freedoms for Egyptian citizens—one is forced to ask not why Egyptian philanthropic foundations and development NGOs did not take certain actions in response to the uprisings but instead what their responses can teach us about understanding and promoting democratic political reform in Egypt and other authoritarian states.

Both national surveys and my own interviewees suggest that most Egyptians believe that "democracy" is the best form of governance for Egypt.[7] But how do Egyptians understand the concept? What components of democracy are most relevant in post-Mubarak Egypt? How does democracy fit in and intersect with social and economic concerns? Finally, how do local civil society organizations attempt to cultivate democracy in the face of government repression and economic decay? As I swam my laps in the Red Sea, I realized that these were the questions I should have been asking. I decided to remain in Egypt and ask them.

Democracy by Public Deliberation

The form of democracy that Bassem described reminded me of the form of democracy that Wedeen found in another Middle East country. In Yemen, *qāt* chews occur daily, in which people gather, often for hours on end, to chew the leafy stimulant.[8] During the *qāt* chews, participants discuss affairs ranging from current events to public policies to family gossip. Happening as they do in public, the deliberations that transpire in *qāt* chews constitute, Wedeen argues, a form of substantive democracy. First, Wedeen suggests, "the very activity of deliberating in public contributes to the formation of democratic persons."[9] Participants vibrantly discussing and debating current events and public affairs embodies the essence of democracy as it was originally conceived.[10] Writing in 1938, Thomas Mann warned of the shortcomings of a democracy "confined to the technical-political aspects" of majority rule, calling instead for a democracy "which is inspired above every other with the feeling and consciousness of the dignity of man."[11] Elections in authoritarian contexts—when they occur at all—do not bolster but rather undermine citizens' dignity, since they are rarely free or fair. Public discussions not only allow participants to voice their opinions on public affairs in a more dignified manner, they also encourage citizens to develop norms of tolerance, inclusion, and social solidarity that are discouraged in autocracies.[12] The very acts of disagreeing with a strongman ruler and of debating alternatives as a group of diverse individuals both constitute manifestations of democracy and fundamentally challenge the culture of fragmentation, fear, and silence that upholds autocracy.

Public deliberations also constitute a form of democracy to the extent that they encourage participants to be aware of current events and to hold government officials accountable. Wedeen notes that when we narrow the definition of democracy to include only the occurrence of contested elections, issues of actual governance are left unaddressed. "Once elected," Wedeen points out, "representatives can act as they wish."[13] Unless mechanisms are in place to hold politicians accountable to the general public, and particularly to society's poor and marginalized, they may very well end up creating policies and engaging in practices that benefit only themselves and the elites from whom they derive favors. In Yemen's *qāt* chews, government officials often sat and chewed along with everyday citizens and were challenged to defend or alter the policies they put in place. Even in public discussions from which government officials are absent, participants can generate the will and courage to make claims on the government. By recognizing shared grievances, citizens can more readily act collectively to claim their rights and demand greater accountability and responsiveness from government officials.

Whereas in Yemen *qāt* chews were sanctioned by the state, in Mubarak's autocracy discussions in the public sphere and collective problem-solving were discouraged and suppressed. The secret police infiltrated all forms of public gatherings, listening for conversations that criticized the Mubarak regime or expressed potentially rebellious forms of citizen agency. As a result, people feared discussing unsafe topics. One Egyptian foundation leader asserted, "People don't know how to disagree and to discuss. People have their opinions and can't see any other opinion as legitimate. There is not a culture of discussing and debating."[14] An NGO leader observed that in addition to fearing discussion, many Egyptians were wary of gathering publicly. "People don't gather except around religion, for example Friday prayers." As a result, people rarely organized to demand their rights. "Here in Upper Egypt," the NGO director explained, "people are marginalized because they are not organized, so they don't reach for their rights."[15]

Not only were habits of organization absent in Egyptian society, so too were norms of participation in public life. Citizens were taught to rely on the state or on private charity to provide services and to keep their communities operating. "Participation is a major dilemma," noted one NGO leader back in 2010. "We must shift the power structure from the top to people on the ground. [People] have the right to analyze their own problems and develop solutions."[16] This was not to suggest that the state should be absolved of responsibility for citizens' well-being but rather that citizens should enjoy some level of self-determination and have some influence over the quality of life in their collective communities. As political scientist Sheila Carapico found in Yemen, where taxes were collected without services being provided in return, "local initiatives to ameliorate the situation were seen as brazen acts of insubordination. Community projects constituted political mobilization."[17] Citizens asserting their own agency to improve their lives can, Carapico notes, fundamentally challenge the regime and its control over everyday life.

On the Red Sea, Bassem told me about bringing Bedouin men together around cups of tea. He also convened the women of the local Bedouin community. Like the men, they took part in the types of deliberations that Wedeen observed in the *qāt* chews, and that Brown refers to as "democracy as discussion," over the challenges they faced and their priorities for the future.[18] Bassem told me that the women concluded that one of their main concerns, one that they wanted to address proactively, was weight gain.[19] As the Bedouins led less nomadic and increasingly sedentary lives, the women found themselves adding kilos. Understanding the negative health consequences of weight gain, they devised a scheme to slim down. Namely, they decided to create and administer aerobics classes for themselves. They secured second-hand stereo equipment, learned aerobics techniques, and led classes. Bassem pointed out that one might question the link between aerobics and democracy, but he argued that the acts of meeting together outside of the home, discussing their problems, and implementing solutions to improve their livelihoods were, in the Bedouin women's lived experiences, the very essence of democracy.[20] The regimes of Mubarak, Sadat, and Nasser had marginalized Egypt's Bedouin community, denying its members basic public service provision.[21] By working collectively to improve their quality of life, the Bedouin women who created the aerobics classes fundamentally challenged the idea that they were resigned to be helpless and dependent.

Projects that convened members of a community to deliberate and problem solve were common in post-Mubarak Egypt. The NGOs and foundations at the helm worked not only with Bedouins but also with handicraft producers, widows, and residents of shanty towns. The input from the organizations themselves was small, but the resulting practice of public deliberation was significant. The leader of a foundation that focused on women described the conversations they convened this way: "It is a peer-to-peer approach. The women do the core work—they assess problems and set plans. It is locally driven and self-sustaining. We are allocating money but it's peanuts—mainly the cost of the soda. The costs are for small meetings and the women drink Coca-Cola. It doesn't cost anything."[22] But he went on to say that the process of meeting, identifying their problems, and working together to find solutions gave these women a sense of agency that they had hitherto lacked. Political theorist Ali Aslam describes such processes as "micro-practices" of citizen sovereignty, or collective acts that "produce alternative forms of associational life and mutual attachment among citizens than those currently available through hegemonic articulations of state power."[23]

These micro-practices link everyday life and politics. In Aslam's words, they politicize "the habits of acquiescence and idleness that reinforce [the state by] deepening popular political disengagement" and "pick up on desires for community and agency that had been diverted toward areas outside of politics by presenting politics as more than state actions, beginning instead with the day-to-day concerns of ordinary citizens."[24] The Mubarak regime strove to atomize its citizens and make them dependent on an all-powerful state. By coming together to recognize their mutual interests and take collective action, however small, to improve the quality of their lives, the Egyptians just described were enacting what sociologist Asef Bayat refers to as "life as politics."[25] They rejected the notion that the government held a monopoly on their sovereignty, their agency, and their ability to form community and act collectively. In doing so, they were fundamentally challenging the legitimacy of authoritarian forms of rule and acting as democratic persons.

Often in authoritarian contexts, such micro-practices of sovereignty take place outside of NGOs due to invasive state surveillance of formal organizations.[26] In Egypt, formal, registered NGOs played a role by giving encouragement and helping to create spaces for deliberation and problem-solving among their beneficiary populations. But citizens themselves led discussions and used their own agency to improve their lives. This not only ensured that whatever initiatives that emerged from the discussions were built from the ground up; it also provided a level of cover for the NGOs which, when the citizens began calling on government officials to claim their rights, could not afford to be seen as the instigators.[27]

The Everyday Politics of Economic Development

Understanding Egyptian NGOs' and foundations' democracy building work requires us to take seriously the priorities of everyday Egyptians. What kind of democracy do Egyptians want for themselves? What fundamentals of a democratic political system—for example, freedom, justice, equality of opportunity, government responsiveness, and human dignity—resonate most forcefully with citizens? Without first acknowledging Egyptians' desired outcomes, it is impossible to appreciate local foundations' and NGOs' democracy building strategies, and it is impossible for Western aid to create more effective interventions.

Recall a rallying cry of protesters in Tahrir Square: "bread, freedom, and social justice." It was not a faltering economy per se that spurred Egyptians to take to the streets; the perception of widening inequality and a feeling of social and economic exclusion among all but the most elite Egyptians were at least as motivating.[28] As the Mubarak regime pursued neoliberal economic policies and brought the business elite into its political fold through crony capitalism, Egypt's poor became poorer and the middle class felt increasingly squeezed. Even those who had enjoyed some fruits of economic privatization—those who could afford to shop in Egypt's malls and drink cappuccinos at its new cafés—watched nervously as jobs disappeared and as their neighborhoods suffered from government neglect. One woman told me that she knew some sort of revolt was inevitable after she returned home from extended travel and saw that trash had piled up in the streets of her neighborhood. This woman lived in Maadi, a leafy suburb of nice homes and villas populated by well-off Egyptians and expatriates. To see piles of rubbish even in this upper-middle-class enclave was an indication of government neglect that extended beyond traditionally poor and marginalized groups.[29]

The widespread sense of economic injustice that prompted many Egyptians to join the protests was attributed to Mubarak-era policies. "The economy was growing at perhaps 6 percent?" one NGO leader speculated, pointing out that Egypt's economy was not, as a whole, floundering. "But the economic growth wasn't leading the population to have a better life. The economy gave more to a few, who had all of the opportunities to increase their wealth and power."[30] As the blame was placed squarely on the government, efforts to combat economic marginalization became increasingly political. NGO leaders maintained that by working with underserved populations— to ensure that "the poorest of the poor" were afforded these basic rights— they were helping to advance the aims of the uprisings.[31] "Our foundation is staying with the same thing, jobs and unemployment," said the program officer of one Egyptian foundation. "These issues caused the revolution."[32]

After the uprisings, Egypt's economy declined as tourism and foreign investment ground nearly to a halt. The poor were disproportionately affected, as the government lifted subsidies and the supply of commodities shrank. "So many lives have been disrupted by the revolution," said one NGO director. "It even affects men who sell water and cigarettes."[33] Workers in the tourism industry struggled to make ends meet as people who had once flocked to see Egypt's pyramids and other cultural and archaeological wonders worried that the country had become too volatile for safe sightseeing. Men who led camel rides and hawked trinkets at the pyramids competed for the lone traveler undeterred by the political turmoil, while hospitality staff at resort hotels folded napkins and set tables for guests they knew would not arrive. The SCAF tried to use the economic crisis to its political advantage, claiming that the uprisings had worsened, not improved, Egyptians' lives. Its message was that before the uprisings, everything was better. Now there was no petrol, no affordable food, and no tourists. This rhetoric paved the way for subsequent government officials to try to seize for themselves the same form of authoritarian power that Mubarak had enjoyed.

In suggesting that the collective citizen action and demands for civic freedoms that were at the heart of the uprisings were responsible for Egypt's economic problems, the SCAF made a clear link between the economic and the political. NGO and foundation leaders also linked the economic and the political, but to a different purpose. They suggested that economic justice was critical to, and went hand in hand with, the advancement of democratic political reforms. Organization leaders argued that their beneficiaries could not concern themselves with democracy if they could not feed themselves and their families—"You can't empower people politically if they can't eat," one foundation director said bluntly.[34]

For many poor Egyptians, everyday struggles to put food on the table trumped aspirations for political democracy. Surveys have consistently shown that the number-one concern of Egyptians in the years following the 2011 uprisings was economic security, and in fact one conducted just after the uprisings found that 82 percent of respondents considered the economy one of the country's two most important challenges.[35] Conveying a commitment to economic justice would thus be critical for groups hoping to influence the country's trajectory. Those who prioritized democracy and put economic development on the back burner were unlikely to earn widespread legitimacy and support.

Political scientist Tarek Masoud argues that the Islamist parties dominated Egypt's first set of post-uprising parliamentary and presidential elections because they managed to convince voters that they would pursue redistributionist policies.[36] Deploying a vast charitable network to get goods and services to the poor while simultaneously broadcasting their economic promises through religious sermons, Islamist groups made the case that they would redesign Egypt's economic system to work for the poor, by redistributing wealth and strengthening the welfare state.[37] This focus on economic justice paid off at the ballot box as Islamist candidates dominated parliamentary elections and ultimately won the presidency.

NGO and foundation leaders regularly cited the influence of the Muslim Brotherhood's charity when describing how their own economic development projects advanced wider goals of democratic political reform. The director of one development NGO said, "The reason the Islamist parties won is because of the civil society they do, including charity in food, health, and education. Do you consider this political? Of course it is. It is very clear. You can't deny that the Muslim Brotherhood is doing [charitable] work and they use it politically. Advocacy and talk doesn't do anything. Working with people on the ground makes a difference, and this is politics."[38] Access to food, healthcare, education, and jobs was what people needed from the country's leaders. The political and the economic were tightly intertwined, and only groups that understood this would have a credible voice in building Egypt's future. "Islamist groups were the only ones with an economic agenda," declared one interlocutor, "and they were the only ones who looked serious."[39]

Some activists involved in the 2011 protests gravitated to economic development work to further the uprisings' aims. One, who created an operating foundation, explained, "We were founded by youth in the revolution. I was shot [during the protests]. It took me twelve hours to get an operation. I saw others who were injured and received no medical care. Even during the operation I could hear, 'If you don't pay you won't receive an operation.'"[40] Understanding that the injustice he experienced after being shot reflected wider societal disparities in access to human services, this activist decided to establish an organization to improve the quality of life in Cairo's shanty town communities. "We realized that there were people working on the political side so we said, 'Let's go on the ground and help people in need.' Slums account for eighty percent of the population. Eighty percent of employment in the slums depends on construction and handicrafts, but these industries are gone."[41]

The organization developed projects to build employment opportunities but also to address education and healthcare needs. Pointing out that the uprisings did not yield immediate benefits for shanty town residents, the foundation director related that he and his organization originally had to overcome skepticism and distrust among beneficiaries. " 'Tell me how the revolution will help,' the people said. The majority in the revolution were not [middle-class] people like us. We directed, but the rest were not like us. We leaders needed to show the others we are there for them." The foundation recruited volunteers to work directly with the shanty town dwellers to devise life-enhancing programs. The objective was to show that collective action by diverse citizens could, in fact, lead to better outcomes than relying on the government and being resigned to the low-quality services it provided. "You can't be pro-regime if you are working on development," the foundation director concluded.[42]

The idea that all Egyptians had a right to employment, healthcare, education, housing, and safe and secure communities fundamentally challenged the neoliberal philosophy that only the strongest competitors deserve decent standards of living. In this context, economic development was a decidedly political act for multiple reasons. First, since economic injustice served as a key driver of the 2011 uprisings, organizations' efforts not just to ameliorate the pain of inequality but to work with Egypt's most economically marginalized and help them claim their basic rights was one way to advance the uprisings' goals. Second, for Egypt to create an inclusive democracy, it would need to ensure that the poor and marginalized were granted the human security necessary to allow them to care about questions of politics. Third, until the poor had the power to claim their economic rights and believe in their own agency to bring about change, they would be swayed to vote for the party that provided the best handouts rather than the party that offered the best vision for Egypt's future.

Yet leaders of human rights organizations widely criticized Egyptian foundations and development NGOs for being too focused on economic development at the expense of democracy. Human rights activists seized on the idea that economic justice was a precursor to a viable democracy and argued that this was the justification used by the Mubarak regime to discourage organizations from taking on democracy promotion. Human rights NGO leaders faulted development organizations for treating democracy as a luxury and stated that they did not seek funding from local foundations because they perceived these funders as being uninterested in human rights.

Leaders of Egypt's development NGOs and foundations were absolutely interested in human rights. But unlike staffers of both human rights organizations and Western aid agencies, who focused primarily on political and expressive rights, leaders of development organizations placed social and economic rights and distributive justice on the same plane. They rejected a tendency among Western donors to consider economic and political development as separate and distinct categories and guided their work not by the notion that bread should come before politics but rather that bread and politics were inseparable.[43] "We can't just do 'awareness,'" said the director of an NGO that worked with Bedouins in the South Sinai. "It's all connected." He explained that as part of its education programming, the organization built an internet technology space filled with computers and a projector. "We do education and awareness there," he said. "We show films that interest the Bedouins and then we discuss them. We build awareness through films and discussion. Awareness is connected to education, health, and the environment."[44] The uprisings paved the way for many organizations' forays into political work. But politics was always woven into, and often masked by, economic development projects. On the surface, the projects were about jobs, education, and healthcare. Embedded within them, however, were efforts to educate beneficiaries about their rights as citizens and empower them to claim their rights from the government, as well as a commitment to the idea that true freedom could be attained only through political *and* economic justice.

Some local NGOs found creative ways to integrate grants from Western donors that came with separate democracy promotion and economic development components. The work of one small, Egyptian organization operating in the South Sinai exemplifies how. This organization received such a grant with two components: one for economic development and another for political reform. The political reform component provided funds for the organization to lead a voter education and registration drive. But the organization's leaders did not take the typical top-down approach of simply educating beneficiaries about democracy and explaining the importance of voting. Instead, they recruited Bedouin volunteers to host community meetings to ask participants about their priorities and discuss how changes resulting from the uprisings could help them. "In meetings, we say that the purpose of the meetings is to find out about the priorities of the community," the organization's director said. "I can say, of course, that in some cases we talked about democracy."[45]

The director's reasons for framing the meetings as priority identification and agenda setting were twofold. First, the organization did not want to appear to instruct the Bedouin community on how to behave as democratic citizens or paint democracy in an unambiguously good light. The director explained,

> The history of the Sinai is that people go in and make promises but don't deliver. The Bedouins have their own way of doing things. They don't want to stop being a Bedouin even though they want the fruits of modernization. We recognize the centrality and importance of being a Bedouin. It doesn't work when people sit in Cairo and decide what people want. We go in and sit and drink tea and listen to what people want.[46]

Second, the director wanted to avoid sanctions on her organization, which had already received messages from the government warning that it was illegal to work on democracy promotion. The director feared that if government officials saw increased voter participation among the Bedouins they would become suspicious. Community meetings could be framed not as democracy education but rather as steps to identify local priorities and address them.

As such, the information gleaned from the meetings that were hosted under the political reform component of the grant fed directly into the economic development component. The organization's director explained,

> Economics is the second part of our project. The idea is to get communities to debate priorities and establish consensus. To get people to work together to make things happen. But we were preempted. This information has come out in meetings [held for the democracy component of the grant] already. They need everything. The communities are utterly undeveloped. The donor will ask, "How is it that all these people are asking for wells and hand-icraft materials?" The priorities are simple, but there is no simple solution.[47]

There was no simple solution because engaging in economic development with the Sinai's Bedouin communities necessarily entailed confronting the longstanding marginalization that the Bedouins faced. Not only were the Bedouins excluded from basic government services but they were also perceived by many Egyptians to be "other," unskilled and uncivilized people.[48] To secure their rights to education, jobs, and healthcare, along with community infrastructure such as wells, olive presses, and looms that would allow the Bedouins to use the skills that they most certainly possessed, was a form of freedom. "The notion of freedom is incredibly important to Bedouins. Permanently living in the presence of an occupying force leads to psychological problems. They are permanently reminded that they are second-class citizens. We want to facilitate Bedouins having a voice, if we can do that," said the director.[49] Having a voice entailed not only exercising their right to vote but also securing the services and infrastructural capacities that might lead to economic justice and, above all, freedom.

This scrappy, grassroots organization thus managed to creatively fuse what the donor conceived as two separate grant components: one political, one economic.[50] The meetings they coordinated did lead to a swell of Bedouins registering to vote and voting. But they also identified a variety of basic needs that, while simple, had been unaddressed for decades by the Mubarak regime. Fulfilling these needs was an important step in progress toward the freedom and dignity that constituted the core aims of the 2011 uprisings. It was a decidedly political act.

Egyptian Conceptions of Political Reform

While the organization just described managed to secure some of the Western democracy aid that flowed to Egypt in 2011 and reframe it in a way that resonated locally, other organizations were frustrated by Western donors' narrow understandings of what constituted "political." They felt left out of contention for those lucrative grants. Leaders of Egypt's development NGOs saw that Western democracy brokers conceptualized citizenship first and foremost as an act of voting and that this mindset led funders to prioritize projects related to elections and similarly formal routines of political engagement, such as establishing political parties and running for office. For Egyptians, though, citizenship was rooted not in voting but in active, collective engagement in and contribution to community and country. Attuned to Egyptians' desire for this more substantive form of democracy, NGO and foundation leaders structured their projects in ways that built spaces for cooperative participation, free expression, cultivation of solidarity, and claiming of rights. On the surface, the programming did not appear to have a political objective; initiatives in education, arts and culture, youth development, and community infrastructure building could fit squarely into any template of socioeconomic development programming. But the aims were all part and parcel of efforts to cultivate democratic citizens.

When NGO and foundation leaders gathered citizens around cups of tea for deliberation, they were educating participants in the ways of democratic personhood. This form of education was markedly different from the democracy education programs sponsored by Western donors. Whereas the former aimed to foster critical thinking, negotiation, and problem-solving skills in an effort to build collective agency, the latter schooled participants in the technicalities of liberal democratic governance. Recall from chapter 3 the democracy academy that one human rights organization hosted through a grant from a major Western donor. Academy leaders lectured to participants about the theory and practice of liberal democracy and then had students write essays about their visions for Egypt's future. The academy also created a software package to spread lessons about democracy more widely. Like many programs funded by Western donor agencies and implemented by human rights organizations, this academy was technical to the point of requiring students to have well-developed literacy skills and access to computers.

By contrast, the target populations of development NGOs and foundations were often illiterate and lacked access to computers and other expensive technology devices. They were also poor, and as such most were more concerned about securing their basic needs than with voting in a liberal democratic system. On top of this, they were the most likely to consider themselves helpless to change Egypt's future. So instead of offering seminars, workshops, and academies that taught the nuts and bolts of democratic governance, NGOs and foundations targeted the fundamentals of basic education—such as literacy, math, and science—and wove lessons about civic rights and techniques of civic engagement into the academic programs. The goal was to educate critical thinkers, problem solvers, and active citizens.

Jordanian diplomat and scholar Marwan Muasher faults education systems throughout the Arab world, and in Egypt in particular, for creating docile and obedient citizens who have learned to accept and believe the information handed down to them.[51] Curricula designed around memorizing facts and classroom cultures that prohibit students from challenging the material or questioning their teachers have, Muasher argues, left citizens unskilled in dissent, resistant to diversity of thought, and unlikely to question the prevailing—even if unjust—status quo. NGO and foundation leaders noted these curricular and pedagogical weaknesses, and blamed Egyptians' failure to come together after the uprisings and build a shared vision for the future in part on this crisis of education. They felt that Egypt's poor education system contributed to the messiness of the country's transition, suggesting that the reason strong democratic leadership did not emerge was because of the lack of attention to civic values in public education.

It was the values of discussion, debate, and respect for diversity that NGOs and foundations worked to cultivate, both in informal gatherings around tea and in the formal education programs they administered. The 2011 uprisings gave these organizations not just the opportunity but the mandate to stress pluralistic values through educational programming and directly connect those values to citizenship. Organizations did not scrap their development programs after the uprisings but instead realigned the content of those programs with democratic aims. One foundation director explained,

Our mandate [after the uprisings] is still education and health. In education we go more in depth, with civic education and engagement—not just scholarships and new schools. We have to focus on curriculum and teacher skills. The rationale is to teach students to be good citizens. Not just someone who protests but also someone who keeps the neighborhood clean and maintains Egypt's identity of co-existence between Muslims, Christians, and Jews. We are Arabs, yes, but not 100 percent Arabs. We are African, Mediterranean, Bedouin, Nubians. We must revive this feeling about our roots. We need confidence in our skills and our ability to change. . . . We are focusing on kids aged five through fourteen, helping them to be aware of who we are, what we have achieved, and what we want in the future. We focus on values that translate into daily habits of good citizens.[52]

At all levels of education programming, from early childhood through adult classes, organizations connected learning to democratic citizenship. Literacy programs were particularly popular, and organization leaders pointed out that such a large portion of Egypt's population was illiterate that every candidate for public office was assigned a symbol beside his or her name on the ballot so that those who couldn't read could still vote.[53] By increasing literacy rates, the hope was that more people would not only be able to read ballots but would also seek out newspapers, candidate informational flyers, draft legislation, and other documents relevant to the country's governance. Combine this critical reading and thinking with economic justice, the reasoning went, and Egyptians would be less susceptible to vote buying.

But while Egyptian NGO and foundation leaders saw direct links between education and democratic development, they found their education programs ineligible for Western donors' new democracy and good governance grants after the uprisings. One NGO leader expressed particularly strong frustrations about this:

When we had the 2011 uprisings, the European Union had a bid meeting. There was a request for proposals for democracy building. It was a big meeting of about two hundred people representing different organizations and I was asked to explain my proposal. There were two rooms, one for English speakers and one for Arabic speakers. "The most important thing is democracy," they said. I said, "I am coming for education." I talked to [an EU representative] during the break. Education is the basis for democracy. How can people do democracy if they are illiterate? I asked if they have grants for education. "No, just for democracy," he replied. That is narrow thinking. They spent so much money. I laugh at our attitude. We push women to vote, but in the elections they choose the Muslim Brotherhood who is against women. The most important thing isn't voting but how to choose, why to choose. There is a lot of work to do. It is not political action that will change society but social involvement. People must feel that they own their future, that they are not dependent on others. Poor people think, "We are just poor and need to wait for the authority to change." We teach people that they must ask for the change they want and that they must contribute and participate.[54]

It was spaces for contribution and participation—often far away from ballot boxes, legislative halls, and even formal NGO offices—that organizations tried to create.

When I arrived to visit a small Egyptian organization on the outskirts of Cairo back in 2010, the headquarters were so unorthodox I wondered if I was at the correct location. Instead of traditional offices, I walked into a large room filled with paint-splattered tables strewn with paintbrushes, paints, and smocks; the walls, shown in Figure 4.1, were covered in children's artwork. The director of the NGO told me that the organization hosted art classes for local children as a revenue-generating activity. The fees—charged only to those families who could afford to pay—funded the organization's grantmaking and charitable activities. When I returned to the organization in 2011, the director explained that the art had begun to serve additional purposes.[55] The art students were painting scenes that depicted democratic political processes, such as voting, that were distributed to the community's illiterate population in order to help them understand their rights as citizens of the new Egypt. In addition, the art distracted attention from the organization's riskier activities. Paintings of sailboats, flowers, and animals concealed the NGO's less benign work of mobilizing community members around democratic political reform.

The NGO had long been a space for the community, where residents discussed their challenges and priorities. It offered grants and planned activities to address the priorities identified. After the uprisings, the organization transformed itself into a gathering place of citizen activists and facilitated discussions among local residents about their priorities in post-Mubarak Egypt. In the early days after the uprisings, the NGO and its constituents focused on the rights of local residents who had been killed protesting in Tahrir Square. First, the organization held a public funeral for these "martyrs." The director told me, "[We were] the first to calculate the martyrs in the area. Not the human rights organizations. We sent invitations to all [residents of the

Figure 4.1 Children's paintings on the walls of an Egyptian NGO, February 2010.
Source: Author's photo.

community]."[56] The NGO led the funeral procession in prominent areas of the community. It convinced local government officials and religious leaders to attend, thus raising the funeral's profile and generating public discussion. "[After the funeral] we held meetings for the martyrs' families, lawyers, and human rights organizations," the director said. "We took information on the martyrs to the attorney general and held a big demonstration. It was the first

Egyptian demonstration for the martyrs."[57] The NGO helped residents form a pressure group to advocate on behalf of the martyrs. This group confronted government authorities to demand that the martyrs' deaths be treated as a collective case against their murderers—namely, government security forces who opened fire on Tahrir Square demonstrators.

The NGO's decision to hold a public funeral represented an attempt by citizens to reclaim public space. Such claims were common after the uprisings and reflected a spirit of public ownership that was sparked when protesters initially took over Tahrir Square in the early days of the protests. Prior to the uprisings, public space was governed by the state. "Previously if you tried to do an event and gather people you couldn't," explained one NGO director. "You couldn't gather groups with the same interests together. Now we are organizing groups and events and media."[58] Often, such activism was marked by art. Egypt's streets were lined with graffiti after the uprisings, with the art conveying political messages, challenges of daily life, and celebrations of Egypt's heritage. One piece, pictured in Figure 4.2, depicted young men

Figure 4.2 Young men who lost their lives in the protests. Graffiti, Cairo, April 2012.
Source: Author's photo.

Figure 4.3 Economic impacts—women carrying gas canisters bought on the black market. Graffiti, Cairo, April 2012.
Source: Author's photo.

who lost their lives in the protests. Another, shown in Figure 4.3, pictured a group of women carrying gas canisters—at the time, there was a black market for gas and long lines for canister refills. Another, shown in Figure 4.4, illustrated social media's influence on the uprisings, with signs for Facebook, Twitter, and al Jazeera surrounding the word 7ORYA,[59] the transliteration of "freedom." When the government built a stone wall to block passage through Mohammed Mahmoud Street to Tahrir Square, graffiti artists painted it to

Figure 4.4 Depicting the influence of social media on the uprisings. Graffiti, Cairo, April 2012.
Source: Author's photo.

depict the other side of the street, making it seem as if the wall didn't exist (Figure 4.5). On a wall next to the blockade, one artist painted a street sign, shown in Figure 4.6, with the name "Street with No Walls."

Artistic expression in public spaces was not always so direct in its political messages. A group of independent artists launched a festival called al-Fan Midan, or "Art is a Square," in the spring of 2011. The organizers chose the festival's name to "emphasize that art is everybody's right," and the group aimed to reclaim the streets as public spaces for free, uncensored expression.[60] Featuring theater, music, poetry, literature, and film, al-Fan Midan began in Cairo but was rolled out in nineteen additional governorates in order to combat Cairo centralization. Admission was free and the festival aimed to present art as not a luxury for the rich but a right for all citizens. In addition to reclaiming the streets, festivals like al-Fan Midan exposed attendees to a range of ideas and viewpoints.

The director of an Egyptian foundation that began supporting street festivals after the 2011 uprisings saw the celebrations as a way to showcase

Figure 4.5 A wall obliterated by a painting. Graffiti, Cairo, April 2012.
Source: Author's photo.

diversity and open spaces for the expression of new ideas. Speaking about
al-Fan Midan, she remarked, "It brings people from everywhere to attend.
People sing, there are awareness sessions, and people see that no matter
what our religious backgrounds we are all Egyptians."[61] Arts and cultural
performances were widely considered to be sustaining momentum for
change. Suggesting that change would take time—ten years at least—the director of a regional foundation said, "We have been living in backwards societies but now they are opening with possibilities for change. We don't have
change yet, we have the possibility for change. We want to share the ways
people incorporate the possibility of change into cultural production."[62]

Art in post-Mubarak Egypt was not simply a vehicle through which citizens could reclaim public spaces and express their creative talents. It was
more broadly a vehicle for social inclusion and collective visioning, amplifying the voices of some of Egypt's most marginalized people to ensure that
their perspectives entered the public realm. Arts and culture served as a tab-
leau on which Egyptians could paint their visions for a more free, just, and
inclusive Egypt. Through a variety of artistic performances, people across

Figure 4.6 Street sign painted on a wall. Graffiti, Cairo, April 2012.
Source: Author's photo.

classes, religions, and political persuasions presented, negotiated, and amal-
gamated their hopes for change. In some cases, formal NGOs provided the
space and resources for such performances. In others, art was produced by
individuals and informal, voluntary groups who claimed the streets as their
theater. In both instances, local and regional foundations sought creative
ways to support the groups. Traditional grants sometimes posed a problem,
given the informal nature of much of the post-uprising cultural production.
But foundations recognized their importance in advancing the uprisings'
aims. "After the revolution more people want to do things. . . . Not just registered NGOs but also informal initiatives. We try to embrace this. We want
and need to enlarge the pool of people to support informal organizations and
initiatives."[63]

Enlarging the pool of people with a say in Egypt's future was a key goal of
participants in the 2011 Arab Foundations Forum conference. Foundation
leaders stressed the importance of working with populations far from the
centers of power who had traditionally been given no voice in determining

Egypt's future. One declared, "We need to begin where ordinary Arabs stand. The center versus the periphery will be an issue [and we need to] take our work to the periphery and out of the center. . . . Foundations need to learn to work with informal and less established groups. New initiatives are coming up every day. We need to be listening, to have our ears to the ground."[64] The notion that change must be propelled by everyday Egyptians—and by *all* Egyptians, regardless of class, religion, or geography—was a strongly held conviction among leaders of Egypt's foundations and development NGOs and a theme that came out forcefully in conversations. "Egypt is full of energy," said one development NGO director. "There is fear that if the force in the center collapses, everything will collapse. But with central force, there is dishonesty. Philanthropy is about working at the periphery; for example, about giving people the freedom to build a park."[65]

Here again we see the political nature of collective agency, expressed in the NGO director's belief that citizens should not need to rely on the state to build their park. Comments like these were made not in support of neoliberalism, which also would prefer to have people building their own park rather than depending on the state for it. Rather, they suggested that the idea that atomized citizens had to rely on an all-powerful ruler for their quality of life had no place in post-Mubarak Egypt. Analyzing the collective action of the popular committees that formed during the 2011 uprisings to protect neighborhoods, scholar Jennifer Bremer points out that "genuine grassroots civil society and collective action at the local level" are "key component[s] of a pluralistic democracy that [have] heretofore been lacking in Egypt." The idea that people could build their own park suggested that, in Bremer's words, "neighbors have the capability to govern themselves," which was "a transformative idea in a society that historically looked always to the leaders at the top of the pyramid to solve their problems and had been sharply punished whenever another approach was tried."[66]

But unless acts of collective agency brought together people from across religious, class, and geographic divides, they would not be sufficient to cultivate the mutual trust and cooperation necessary for a truly pluralistic democracy. Recall from chapter 2 that one of the main impediments to reform in the year after the uprisings was disunity among Egyptians. Decades of Mubarak-era efforts to divide Egyptians had fragmented the population and instilled distrust of the "other." While neighbors joining forces to secure their homes and demand better government support for community infrastructure was itself a transformative idea in post-Mubarak Egypt, NGO and foundation leaders emphasized that for a full transformation to take place groups taking collective actions would need to grow increasingly heterogeneous. "We need to have people care about fellow humans, not just similar humans," insisted one NGO leader.[67]

Organization leaders proactively built diversity into their programs after the uprisings. A youth camp program created in the wake of the uprisings taught people aged sixteen to twenty-four about "citizenship, rights, responsibilities, participation, activism, and understanding the state-society landscape."[68] Originally, the NGO behind the camp used workshops, similar to those held by human rights NGOs, to instruct participants about civic values. But after a month, the organization's staff reflected on what made their work different from the other workshops that were created for budding Egyptian democrats, and they concluded that workshops would not change lives. So, thinking back to their own formative experiences participating in camps, they decided to abandon the workshop model and experiment with seeding citizenship through camps. Their goal was "life-changing impact" that promoted freedom and decision-making among youth. Inclusion and respect for diversity was built into all camp programming. "The big thing [for the campers] is to learn to work together with diverse people," the director told me. At first, he admitted, relations between religious and secular campers were tense. But by the end of the camp, those youth were working hand in hand as teammates. This cooperation resulted not from trainings on the importance of diversity but from everyday interaction and cooperation within the camp's activities such as theater productions and activity planning. "We avoid preaching," the director said. "In our programs we embed values in a context that interests youth."[69]

Despite working to nurture values of citizenship, freedom, and respect for diversity among the campers, the NGO did not claim to be involved in politics per se. "From citizenship," the director explained, "we can embed values without formal political education. We don't have a political agenda or promote a political ideology."[70] The goal was to bring together young people from diverse backgrounds and provide a space in which they could practice the cooperation and build the trust expected from democratic citizens. But in Egypt, this was an inherently political act. And just as trust and respect had to be built across religious lines, so too did it have to be built across divisions of class. By 2011, neoliberalism and authoritarianism had succeeded in creating fierce competition for economic success among the middle and upper classes and in resigning the poor to not just a lifetime but in fact generations of poverty. This combination contributed to horizontal relationships marked by rivalry and vertical relationships built upon dependency. Collective agency was practiced as infrequently among the rich as it was between the rich and poor.

But within the uprisings themselves and in the months following, many economically privileged Egyptians began to fight more forcefully for the rights and dignity of the poor. Key to organizations' efforts to secure rights for the poor was a commitment to bottom-up, collaborative efforts. These organizations believed that top-down interventions would fail because they would reproduce systems of dependency—the same types of systems autocratic rulers relied on to keep citizens attached to them. Organization leaders insisted that projects run by "people who sit in Cairo and decide what people want" were doomed to fail.[71] Instead, interventions could succeed only when NGOs took the time to deeply understand the challenges of the poor and facilitated, rather than directed, efforts to claim their rights and improve their lives.

Speaking about his organization's work with poor and marginalized communities, one NGO director explained, "Our broad strategy is to work on the ground, to understand the reality, to understand how they live, to provide them with the tools" to improve their lives as they envisioned.[72] This organization, and others like it, did not want to provide the tools for the poor to become pawns in the corrupt neoliberal status quo. Rather, their leaders expressed a commitment to basic values of equity and justice that were not yet within reach of many of Egypt's poor. "There is a struggle to give credit to people's thoughts, ideas, and expression no matter what their social status," an NGO director said. "There is a problem that policymakers and academics see themselves as authors of strategies and policies, and as the authority."[73]

Bottom-up efforts to build collective agency across formerly divided groups were, more subtly, acts of defiance against the state's power to divide and exclude. In fostering relationships built on equality, respect, and trust across fragmented groups, Egypt's NGOs and foundations were upholding the values of solidarity on display in Tahrir Square in 2011, when rich and poor provided each other with food and medical care and when Copts and Muslims protected each other's peaceful prayers and stood together in symbolic displays of unity, as shown in Figure 4.7. Their work emphasized that all Egyptians had the "right to have rights" and that by working together, Egyptians had the agency to build a more plural and democratic Egypt.[74]

Citizen solidarity and collective agency, while essential components of a healthy democracy, can take a country only so far. Widespread, consistent provision of basic services that fulfill human needs is also necessary to cultivate human dignity and deliver the promise of a just society. One role of Egypt's NGOs and foundations was to provide basic services when the government either was absent or offered substandard levels of quality and care. But coaching beneficiaries to demand more equitable and respectable services from government agencies—everything from food and housing to quality education, healthcare, and safe streets—took on heightened urgency and salience after the uprisings. "These are issues that sometimes you think should be easy to solve, but they're not," said the director of one foundation. "The major underlying problem is a lack of services."[75] He went on to tell me about the plight of widowed women:

Figure 4.7 Show of solidarity across religions at a protest in Tahrir Square, Cairo, May 2011.
Source: Author's photo.

Let me tell you about widows in Egypt. If a husband dies, his money is taken and given to his family, not his wife. Many widows are very poor. They have medical and other debts that they cannot pay. In a male-dominated society, men are responsible for the finances of the household. Women don't have money. When they are widowed, they find themselves with a big problem: they are helpless. There is also a social stigma, especially in conservative areas. A woman living on her own is seen as having no rights. People talk about her. In general, female heads of households in Egypt endure much gossip. It makes their lives difficult.

The foundation director explained that his organization brought together widows in various villages in peer-to-peer communities. In one such community, the women identified fourteen problems that stemmed from substandard provision of basic government services. For instance, skyrocketing prices of gas and bread had led to black markets for both. In order to secure gas at an affordable rate, women were forced to queue for hours and carry heavy gas canisters on long walks back to their homes. Latrines were also problematic. Poor upkeep led to unsanitary conditions and the spread of diseases among community members. Foundation staff worked with the women to help them learn their rights to these basic services and to make collective claims on local government officials for them. "Women are empowered to talk on their own behalf rather than have us talk for them. This fits with the Egyptian culture, especially in Upper Egypt. Grassroots change works better. Lobbying doesn't work here. Maybe in the US it works but not here."[76]

One organization built a set of libraries in villages throughout the country to serve as spaces of civic awareness and activism. The NGO had an active literacy program, which the libraries supported. Ostensibly, the library construction was undertaken to provide resources and spaces for literacy training. But the libraries also served another purpose: they were spaces for deliberating local problems and strategizing ways to solve them. In the libraries, NGO staff worked with village women as they identified, and organized to solve, local problems, such as installing basic shelters at village bus stops.

The women's collective problem-solving was complemented by rights-claiming activities. For example, one of the problems identified in a village outside of Alexandria was a community-wide rat infestation. Women used a library as a home base to strategize how they would eliminate the rodents.

They went as a group to the local pesticide office, where officials provided the women with poison and showed them how to use it. The poison worked, and the women were so happy to be finished with the rats that they began a campaign to exterminate them in neighboring villages. The women hosted meetings where government officials were called on to provide poison and explain its use. Rat extermination expanded as a result.

While in the case of rat extermination government officials supported citizen-led initiatives, in other cases library members called for direct government action. In one village, motorists regularly sped past the local school and community members feared for the students' safety. A group of villagers organized in a library and then went to the local traffic office every couple of days to demand speed bumps and crosswalks at the intersections around the school. Ultimately, the traffic officials installed the safety features that the women demanded. "This never would have happened without the women's requests," the NGO staff member responsible for the libraries insisted. Not only did government services improve but the women also "had a feeling of being citizens, of doing something for the village."[77]

Instead of being idle consumers of whatever the government chose to provide, the women featured in these stories acted as citizens who worked collectively to demand their rights and improve their lives and their communities. Collective action to solve problems and improve communities was a form of defiance against government neglect. "The strategy of the ruling regime has been to not allow much to take place," said one NGO staff member in 2011. "They are not encouraging proactive people or organizations to take on roles. There is a widening gap between the SCAF and the people. The SCAF is curtailing efforts to move things."[78] In the years following the 2011 protests, successive transitional governments cracked down on civil society in an effort to silence dissent and obstruct civic movements for reform. Through their development work, Egypt's NGOs and foundations sought to foster solidarity and a belief that as a group of citizens Egyptians possessed both control over their lives and the power to hold the state accountable. Tying citizen solidarity to collective agency, organization leaders drew attention to government failures and insisted that by working together people could demand better.

Never did foundation or development NGO leaders publicly claim to be promoting democracy. Doing so would draw government scrutiny and result in repression. Yet in private conversations, organization leaders fluently connected their work to democratic political reform. "Everything we do is related to democracy at the end," said one foundation director, "but it is called 'sustainable development.' If 'democracy' makes the government upset we won't say 'democracy.' Let's be smart. You have a mission, you don't need to say your ideology in addressing issues. We must think outside the box."[79] Some organization leaders confided that they had been working on "democracy" long before the uprisings, but avoided referring to the work as democracy promotion. "We began projects related to citizen participation and public decision-making in 2005," said one NGO director. "This was before talk of 'democracy.'"[80] The director went on to tell me about the tension that arose when trying to obtain funds for "citizen participation and public decision-making" from Western donors and simultaneously avoiding the term democracy promotion so as not to attract the government's attention.

> We work on how to organize people to be strong. I believe NGOs have a strong role regarding democracy. Our weakness is state policy and European Union policy. The EU is trying to force people to adopt their beliefs. NGOs can't agree to do programs that will get them into trouble with the government. It is a mistake for the EU to present a program that has aspects that prevent the government from accepting it. You need to present the program in an intelligent way to avoid government scrutiny. We look innocent by talking about supporting local initiatives. But it's not innocent because I do citizen participation. Be smart. Adopt a language to do something comprehensive.[81]

Organization leaders maintained, time and again, that they didn't "do politics." They did education, job training, healthcare, and other types of economic development projects that did not carry the political sensitivity—and downright danger—of "democracy." But in the same breath, they spoke of promoting human rights, participation, and the freedom to choose. "There are many grant opportunities in democracy, human rights [after the uprisings], but this is not our area," insisted one.[82] However, he went on to say that his organization did, in fact, integrate human rights into its development work.

> We do human rights in two areas: children's rights and participation, and women's rights and participation. It is very important that people share in the decision making of the country. I don't mean in Cairo. Cairo is not Egypt. In rural areas people aren't taking decisions. They are being deceived

by religious and political slogans. [Participation in decision making] is a kind of democracy, a kind of human rights.[83]

It just wasn't the kind of democracy or human rights that Western democracy brokers were interested in funding.

From Subjects to Citizens

When I began conducting fieldwork in 2010, leaders of Egypt's philanthropic foundations highlighted their efforts to shift philanthropy in Egypt from charity to development. If their strategies worked as envisioned, beneficiaries of development aid would cease to rely on handouts and begin to use their own individual and community resources to improve their lives. They would gain independence and dignity. This logic fit neatly into the Mubarak regime's neoliberal scheme of economic privatization and welfare state rollback. But neoliberalism failed to work out as advertised, and led not to independence and dignity but rather, for many Egyptians, to despair. Coupled with political authoritarianism, it created a system in which wealth and power was concentrated among a small set of political and business elites who were tied together in webs of loyalty and corruption. Unwilling to continue to acquiesce to such a system, Egyptians took to the streets on January 25, 2011, to demand freedom, justice, and dignity.

The foundation and development NGO leaders with whom I spoke saw the uprisings as an opportunity to cultivate not only independence and dignity among their beneficiaries but also active citizenship.[84] It was a citizenship performed not just by voting in elections but by reclaiming a public sphere for deliberation and expression, by practicing collective agency to improve communities, and by making claims on the government for human rights—to food, jobs, healthcare, education, and community infrastructure. It demanded a new social contract: one in which the Egyptian people were not subjects of a dictator but rather citizens with the freedom to live their lives as they saw fit *and* the entitlement to demand and receive responsiveness and accountability from their government.

Egyptian foundations and development NGOs fully recognized and celebrated the inherently political nature of their projects. Yet in order to maintain local trust and avoid government repression, they couched the political nature of their work in terms of "safe" socioeconomic development programs.[85] Their aim was democratic political reform, which for them entailed freedom, agency, and justice for all Egyptians. Rather than a politics of state institutions, it was a politics of citizenship.[86] It was democracy promotion, but by another name.

These foundations and NGOs were promoting democracy, but they were not following the West's democracy promotion playbook. Their focus was not on elections, constitutions, or national government institutions. Their focus was on freedom and justice at grassroots levels, and particularly among Egyptians who had long been made to feel that they had no voice in their country's future. The foundations and NGOs served not as leaders of democracy building but as facilitators. Instead of creating and imposing their own reform initiatives, they worked closely with grassroots communities to cultivate democracy on citizens' terms. Responding to beneficiaries' foremost desire for economic justice, foundation and NGO leaders wove democratic concepts of participation, claiming rights, and free expression into socioeconomic development programs. This approach was both culturally resonant and politically smart. These foundations and NGOs largely escaped the government's crackdown on organizations seen as doing democracy and human rights work. Yet their approach was decidedly political. It fundamentally challenged patterns of exclusion and hierarchies of privilege while promoting a new social order in which all citizens were endowed with voices and rights.

Egypt's foundations and development NGOs were, in essence, creating a new democracy promotion playbook. But it was one for which success would be nearly impossible to measure. In his study of development aid in Lesotho, anthropologist James Ferguson found that aid from Western donors for technical development projects was ineffective because it failed to recognize and take into account the underlying political consequences of the development interventions.[87] Western democracy aid to Egypt and to other countries more generally is notoriously technical and, counterintuitively, apolitical. It avoids addressing the knotty political issues inherent in citizen mobilization, collective agency, or economic injustice. With funding directed to programs that can demonstrate measurable, quantifiable results, it overlooks programs aimed at cultivating citizens' agency, freedom, and even happiness.[88] It ignores democracy by discussion and the civic value of deliberation and collective problem solving in the public sphere.

Increased voter participation, diverse representation in government positions, prosecution of human rights abuse trials, and constitutional reforms are all measurable outcomes. Feelings and expressions of agency, justice, and happiness are not. But the track record of Western democracy aid is notoriously weak, failing to truly confront dictators or to work with all citizens to envision and participate in radical change.[89] Egyptian foundations' and development NGOs' democracy promotion playbook offers an alternative approach, one that takes seriously the radical notions of freedom, justice, and active citizenship for all. And one that costs little more than a cup of tea.

5

Promoting Democracy in the Face of Autocracy

In the summer of 2014, I found myself wandering the streets of a Cairo neighborhood. I was trying to find an international NGO that had removed its sign from the building due to the government's intensifying assault against civil society. The snaking, crisscrossing streets of that particular neighborhood are confusing enough *with* signs. Without them, I was lost. Finally, I called the director of the NGO to ask for directions. After he described some landmarks to guide me, I reached the building. The NGO director instructed me to climb the stairs to the door of the organization's office. There was no sign there, either.

I entered what seemed like a shell of an office. There were chairs and desks, a kitchenette filled with coffee cups, and ashtrays. There were no computers or printers. There was very little paper. As he handed me a coffee, the NGO director explained that he and his staff expected their office to be raided by the government, then led by President Abdel Fattah al-Sisi; they had removed signage in order to make the organization slightly less conspicuous and done away with printers, web servers, and other technologies that could provide evidence to be used in a court trial against them or their local partners. The headquarters office in Europe was under alert that any day the NGO might lose its outpost in Egypt.

After a year away, I had returned to Egypt in 2014 to learn how the NGO sector was faring. The state of this office foreshadowed what I would find: namely, that the government's targeting of civil society had forced most NGOs to adopt low profiles and to be incredibly cautious in their actions.

The Rise of President Sisi and the Threat to Civil Society

About one year earlier, in June of 2013, the opposition group had called Tamarrod called for mass protests against then-president Mohammed

Morsi.[1] The Muslim Brotherhood responded by recruiting its own supporters to the streets in Morsi's defense. Millions demonstrated, with one group calling for Morsi to step down and the other rallying to support him. On July 3, the military, now led by General Sisi, ousted Morsi, suspended the constitution, and imposed an interim government. While civilian politicians were appointed to lead the interim government,[2] speeches given by Sisi aimed at shoring up a public "mandate" for the military to confront terrorism and provide security.[3] Once again, Egypt was officially under military rule.

Sisi's SCAF laid out an ambitious timetable for a transition to civilian rule—it planned to draft a new constitution and hold parliamentary and presidential elections within six months—but governed harshly. In the months following the coup, members and supporters of the Muslim Brotherhood took to the streets in protest. The military responded with force. A particularly violent confrontation came on August 14, when security forces crushed a sit-in taking place in Rab'a al-Adawiya Square in the Nasr City district of Cairo. According to Human Rights Watch, over a thousand demonstrators were killed.[4] An Egyptian court dissolved the Muslim Brotherhood and confiscated all of its assets on September 23, effectively reneging on its promise to include Islamist groups in democratic political processes.[5] The military junta was no more open to secular protesters than it was to Islamists and their sympathizers. In November the government issued a new law that effectively banned all street protests by requiring gatherings of more than ten people to obtain advance government approval. Those who moved ahead without such approval faced heavy fines or prison. The free assembly and free speech the 2011 revolutionaries had fought for had been quashed by a new authoritarian government.

The leader of that transitional authoritarian regime would soon gain full presidential powers. From May 26–28, 2014, Egyptians again went to the polls in a presidential election. This time, the contest was between General Sisi and Hamdeen Sabahi, a veteran workers' activist. Sisi emerged victorious with 97 percent of the vote, ensuring that once again the military would enjoy a leading role in the governance of Egypt. Sisi's policies toward Egypt's NGO sector were no more lenient than those of Field Marshall Tantawi's SCAF, which had launched the initial attack on NGOs back in late 2011. Throughout 2013, the government had worked to draft a new law to replace Law 84, the repressive NGO law of 2002. During the summer of 2014, shortly after Sisi took the oath of office, the government publicly circulated the latest draft.

I asked the director of the international NGO with the barebones office about the draft. He became animated and angry, explaining,

> We spent one and one half years lobbying on the NGO law. We had a nice draft before Morsi. Under Morsi the parliament created worse drafts. After the IRI/NDI debacle [the trial of the employees of the seventeen NGOs that the SCAF raided in late 2011] we formed a group of international NGOs— human rights and development organizations—plus the Development Partners Group to put pressure on the government. This was around seven or eight months after the revolution. As a collective force—EU member states, the US, local human rights organizations and international NGOs— we put enough pressure on the government to shelve the draft. Now it is much worse, like North Korea.[6]

I asked the director what elements of the draft law were so troubling. He picked up one of the few pieces of paper on his desk and launched into a list of restrictions laid out in the draft law:

> There will be a coordinating committee enforcing the law—government bodies, the Ministry of Interior, and the security apparatus is responsible for it. Foreign funding is forbidden without approval and reasons for objection are open. Punishment [for accepting foreign funds without approval] is prison. All entities—including law firms and companies—[that are acting as NGOs] must register as NGOs or they will be dissolved and their employees will be sent to prison. MOSS may enter an organization at any time. Assisting an international NGO without permission leads to prison or a fine. Conducting field research leads to prison. International NGOs may only work for society's needs and the development priorities of the government. International NGOs need approval to buy or rent office premises.

He looked up and took a breath before concluding, "It will be the death of civil society if they can enforce the current draft law."[7]

Leaders of Egypt's foundations and development NGOs also said that they felt strained as government surveillance and control over civil society escalated. One foundation leader told me, "We are all under surveillance, watched by the government and the intelligence services. You don't know who is watching who."[8] And yet most of these organizational leaders remained optimistic and energetic. Shortly after Mubarak was deposed in 2011, I was regularly told that a barrier of fear that had kept Egyptians from fighting for change had been broken. Foundation and development NGO leaders repeated that message in 2014. Despite the military coup and despite the fact that all signs pointed to continued government repression in the years ahead, most organization leaders were still resolved to push for democratic change.

Since the government remained hostile to organizations working on issues of political reform, foundations and development NGOs continued to "serve tea," cultivating democratic values and practices among beneficiaries in the most careful and subtle of ways. Egypt's NGO sector did not have the collective strength to go head-to-head with the government or advocate for national reforms. Organizations therefore continued to incubate democracy at the grassroots. They ran summer camps, created arts and culture programs, developed organic farms, led literacy programs, and conducted other development-type activities designed to shore up Egyptians' resolute aspirations for freedom and lay the groundwork for a more democratic and just future. Organization leaders continued to tie their initiatives directly to the emancipatory aims of the 2011 uprisings while prudently marketing their development interventions in public-facing communications.

Throughout 2014, the draft NGO law wound its way through the approval process. In the meantime, the Sisi regime took additional measures to strangle Egypt's NGO sector. The trouble began in September 2014, when President Sisi amended Article 78 of Egypt's penal code. Now, penalties of life in prison and steep fines of no less than 500,000 Egyptian pounds awaited anyone found guilty of receiving funding or other support from a foreign source deemed to threaten national interest, unity, or the public peace or breach national security. Previous punishment for accepting such funds was imprisonment and a fine of no less than 1,000 Egyptian pounds.[9] Sisi's amendments to the code posed a particular threat to Egypt's human rights organizations, which relied on foreign donations to finance their efforts to promote democratic political reform and bring to light government policies that threatened human rights. Many of these organizations had registered as law firms and civil corporations to avoid the restrictions of Egypt's NGO law, but this amendment to the penal code applied regardless of an organization's registration. The amendment also spoke to the level of personal repression the Sisi regime was willing to undertake as it moved to stifle dissent. Not only were organizations at risk; so, too, were the livelihoods of the people working in those organizations.

Soon, all organizations operating in the capacity of NGOs would have to register under Law 84. In July of 2014, MOSS released a statement in the state newspaper *al-Ahram* ordering all "entities working in the field of civic associations" to register within forty-five days. The deadline was extended to November 10 after the published directive was met with a national and international outcry.[10] Organizations that did not register by the November deadline could face investigation and prosecution. The registration requirement put Egypt's human rights organizations in a difficult predicament. By registering as law firms and civil companies, they had avoided many of the constraints imposed by Law 84 and thus managed to lead advocacy campaigns critical of the government. Registering under the law would make it "impossible," according to the director of one human rights NGO, to continue their work as usual.[11]

With the registration requirement, the Sisi regime was effectively throttling the sliver of Egypt's NGO sector engaged in open opposition and dissent. The director of the international NGO featured in the opening vignette of this chapter explained that the government's attack on human rights organizations was so intense that employees of the human rights organizations his NGO partnered with had "bought prison clothes packed in prison bags so that when they are dragged to prison they won't have to wear bug-infested prison uniforms."[12] Anticipating this fate, a number of organizations shuttered their Egypt offices. These included al-Mawred al-Thaqafy, which supported regional arts and culture; the Arab Penal Reform Organization, a regional human rights NGO; and the Carter Center, an international institution promoting peace, human rights, and democracy.[13] Human rights NGO Cairo Institute for Human Rights Studies (CIHRS), meanwhile, announced that it would move all regional and international programming outside of the country.[14]

Following through on its threats to investigate NGOs' registration and activities, the Sisi regime began raiding offices, issuing travel bans to NGO employees, and freezing the assets of several high-profile NGO leaders and human rights activists. In the spring of 2015, the government placed travel bans on employees of the Egyptian Democratic Academy even though the organization had filed registration papers before the November 10 deadline.[15] In June, Mohammed Lotfy, the executive director of the Egyptian Commission for Rights and Freedoms (ECRF), was prevented from traveling to Germany to participate in a conference on human rights.[16] Also in 2015, four ECRF staff members were arrested while conducting field research on housing conditions in greater Cairo. In July, government officials visited CIHRS's office and demanded to see documents regarding the organization's founding, registration, budgets, accounts, and funding contracts. Bahey Hassan, the director, reportedly received death threats.[17] Egypt's human rights NGOs, along with their leaders, were under full-scale attack.

In early 2015, the government began dissolving NGOs alleged to be affiliated with the Muslim Brotherhood, which in 2013 had been designated a terrorist group and banned from operating.[18] By the end of February MOSS had closed 169 such organizations. On March 1 it dissolved 112 more, and on March 18 it shut down 99 more, for a total of 380 Brotherhood-affiliated organizations shut down in the first few months of 2015.[19] A year later, in March 2016, MOSS announced the opening of a special unit charged with observing and assessing the work of foreign NGOs operating in Egypt. While ministry representatives insisted that the purpose of the unit was to help foreign NGOs work more effectively, leaders of human rights organizations that worked closely with foreign organizations were skeptical and felt that the unit was a thinly veiled attempt to increase surveillance.[20]

It wasn't just new laws and tactics that the Sisi regime would use against NGOs; the regime restored old investigations as well. In March 2016, the government reopened Case 173, under which forty-three NGO employees were convicted in 2013 of operating organizations illegally. Whereas the first segment of the case focused on foreign organizations, this part targeted Egyptian NGOs. A report published in *al-Shorouk* identified forty-one local NGOs that were under investigation for receiving foreign funding, including the Arabic Network for Human Rights Information, the Egyptian Institute of Democracy, the Egyptian Initiative for Personal Rights, Nazra for Feminist Studies, CIHRS, the Egyptian Democratic Academy, the Hicham Mubarak Law Center, and Nadeem Center for Rehabilitation of Victims of Violence and Torture.[21] Throughout the year, a number of NGO leaders were banned from travel and had their personal and organizational assets frozen while the case was under investigation. They included prominent figures in Egypt's human rights community, such as Hossam Bahgat, founder of the Egyptian Initiative for Personal Rights, and Gamal Eid, executive director of the Arab Network for Human Rights Information.[22] Shortly after the case reopened, the investigative judge issued a gag order prohibiting all media outlets from publishing anything about it other than official statements issued by the presiding judges.[23] Later that year, in August 2016, MOSS reportedly sent a letter to a number of NGOs outlining a new regulation that would require organizations to announce all planned activities to the Social Affairs Directorate's security department.[24]

Meanwhile, the latest draft NGO law was moving toward approval in a process that lacked transparency and did not include consultation with civil society leaders. The draft was approved by the Cabinet in September and then moved to the State Council and Parliament, where it was hastily approved in November "without any substantial debate or dialogue."[25] President Sisi ratified the law the following May, putting into place what the International Center for Not-for-Profit Law termed "the most repressive law affecting civil society organizations seen yet in Egypt."[26] Like Law 84, Law 70 of 2017 places draconian constraints on the creation, operation, funding, and autonomy of organizations, requiring any that do "civil work" to re-register within one year, no matter their legal form or name. To register, organizations must have ten founding members and physical premises and pay registration fees of up to 10,000 Egyptian pounds (around $550; Article 8). MOSS is given the authority to halt registration during any part of the process.

Organizations that manage to register under the law are circumscribed in the activities they can undertake: they must pursue development and social welfare objectives and act in accordance with the state's development plan, needs, and priorities. They cannot do "any work of a political nature" or that which "may cause harm to the national security, law and order, public morals or public health" (Article 13). Organizations are also prohibited from conducting opinion polls, and to undertake field research they must first gain government approval (Article 14). Like its predecessor, Law 70 grants the government extensive surveillance capabilities. MOSS officials may enter an organization's offices at any time to inspect its records (Article 27). Organizations registered under the law that fail to report a change of premises, receive foreign funds without approval, or misuse public funds could have their boards of directors dismissed and replaced by a government-appointed temporary board (Article 42). Government officials also have the right to review any new board members proposed by the organization and can disqualify any that it deems inappropriate (Article 34).

Law 70 created a new agency to monitor foreign organizations operating in Egypt and foreign funds dispersed to Egyptian organizations. The National Agency to Regulate the Work of Foreign Non-Governmental

Organizations (the Agency) comprises representatives from different government ministries as well as security and intelligence officials. Egyptian NGOs seeking funds from abroad must obtain prior approval from the Agency before accepting donations or grants from outside Egypt (Article 24). The Agency has sixty days to approve requests; a lack of approval is considered a denial (Articles 24 and 70). Organizations that receive foreign funds must publish this information on their websites and with MOSS (Article 25). Organizations that accept funds without permission are subject to dissolution (Article 43). Under Law 70, permission is now needed not only to use foreign funds but also to spend donations from local sources. NGOs receiving funds from Egyptian sources must notify MOSS thirty days before receiving such funds and must receive ministry approval before spending them (Article 23).

Foreign organizations seeking to operate in Egypt are required to gain prior approval from the Agency (Article 59) and pay up to 300,000 Egyptian pounds (approximately US$16,500) for a three-year permit. Like their local counterparts, foreign organizations may only undertake activities that align with the government's development priorities; political activities are banned, as are activities that "may cause harm to the national security, public order, public morals or public health" (Article 62). MOSS has the authority to halt foreign organizations' activities at any time or cancel the organization's permit if it violates the law or for reasons "related to any threats to national security, public safety, public order, or in accordance with the principle of reciprocity" (Article 68). Local NGOs wishing to collaborate with a foreign organization or hire a foreign employee must gain prior approval from MOSS (Articles 19 and 66). As a whole, these articles made Egypt a downright hostile environment for foreign NGOs.

Shortly before Sisi ratified the law, a group of NGOs, political parties, and public leaders called on the president to veto it and return it to Parliament for "substantial changes that would bring it in line with the Egyptian constitution."[27] Arguing that the law "disavow[ed] the letter and spirit of the constitution and Egypt's international legal obligations under multilateral UN conventions and bilateral treaties with the EU," they stated that the law would also constrain development NGOs' capacity to deliver the social services that were desperately needed as Egypt's economy continued to decline. Ignoring these arguments, Sisi signed the law on May 29, 2017.[28] The question remained: would the law indeed dismantle Egyptian civil society?

Perseverance under Pressure

I returned to Cairo in October 2017 to investigate. Unsurprisingly, NGO leaders expressed great frustration with the new law. At a conference of NGO and foundation leaders, one development NGO staff member described it as unconstitutional. "It is counter to collective actions. It has created grayness. It is badly written. It creates conflict between MOSS and the coordinating committee. The coordinating committee is not open or transparent. The law has no calendar for responding [to NGOs' requests for registration and funding]. And no response equals rejection."[29] Another said, "We are operating within a state framework in which the government doesn't distinguish between regulation and control. Philanthropy will lose the chance to grow and develop if this continues. Legislations governing civil society organizations will put us in a straitjacket. If there is over-regulation, things will stop."[30] The director of an international private foundation agreed with his local colleagues, suggesting that the sector needed the government to provide an enabling regulatory environment that would allow organizations to experiment in new fields.

Instead, the government was restricting experimentation. Not only did it limit the activities that organizations could pursue, it also restricted their ability to carry out the types of research needed to develop and evaluate the success of new programs. While the results of many initiatives, particularly those related to citizen empowerment, were difficult or impossible to measure (as chapter 4 notes), organization leaders were trying to measure other development outcomes. They stressed that their ability to do so was threatened by the new law: "The entire research environment will be affected."[31] The feasibility of gathering data itself became a question, but NGO leaders were determined to try. The problem with the law, I was told many times, is that it is impossible to evaluate impact without research. "I worry about the fact that research is being subcontracted to consultants outside of NGOs," an NGO leader said. "And research is being undermined by the security services."[32] These NGO staff members yearned for fair, straightforward legal structures instead of the bureaucratic red tape and mountains of paperwork necessary simply to gain the authority to do research on their own programs and focus areas.

Other NGO leaders pointed out that Law 70, like its predecessor, pressured organizations to adopt government priorities while preventing them from engaging in advocacy or activism. "It's not difficult to work with the government if you work on government priorities and follow the rules of the game. It is different if you try to influence policy," said one.[33] Activism was further curtailed at the individual level through the 2013 Protest Law, which required groups and individuals to provide the government a three-day notification before protesting and gave the Ministry of the Interior the right to cancel, postpone, or move the protest if it believed that protesters would break the law. "Demonstrations are forbidden," I was told. "People want to demonstrate but can't do so if it doesn't match what the government wants and will approve."[34] This NGO staff member went on to lament, "Now it is forbidden to have three people together in the street. Cafés have closed, they don't want youth together."[35]

And yet, this NGO staff member insisted, "The dream is still alive. The youth were willing to lose an eye, to be killed in the revolution. They still dream. Demonstrations are not allowed, but . . ." she trailed off, suggesting that government regulations were unlikely to completely stifle social activism.[36] But NGO leaders also stressed that protests should not be the only venues through which Egyptians could have their voices heard. Organization leaders emphasized their own roles in amplifying citizens' voices. They were careful to note that it was their role to serve as a platform from which citizens could themselves be heard. "Philanthropy can't 'represent' voices," said one foundation leader. "We must bring voices in through giving marginalized groups the authority to speak."[37] An NGO leader concurred, saying, "We have been carrying the flag of participation for decades. Often in communities, those who are better off participate more. This is a paradox of participation. Philanthropy should open new space for citizens to have their voice and to speak of their own interests."[38]

After the uprisings, voices were raised to demand basic services from the government. The same held true in 2017. One NGO leader said, "We need to create a platform for people to represent themselves. Often services aren't provided." He gave an example of a health program the NGO was undertaking in Sohag, a governorate in Upper Egypt. "First, we listen to the people. How are they receiving services? The government is spending money but the services are not there. There is a gap between the central government in Cairo and the services in the villages."[39] The NGO leader went on to say that a "complete solution" was needed and that such a solution necessarily entailed local citizens demanding service provision by the government. For the NGO to simply provide services would lead neither to citizen empowerment nor to government accountability. Just as they did in 2014, my interlocutors stressed the political nature of economic rights and equality and argued that their efforts to help citizens claim their basic rights were part and parcel of political reform.

NGOs continued to integrate lessons about rights and freedoms into arts and culture programs. In an arts education project that aimed to help young people express themselves and learn about various rights-based values, the programming targeted youth who were working to provide for their families. "Many children in our area begin working at nine years old," a staff member explained. "During their days off, we provide art classes; for example, song, theater, and drawing. Through the classes we seek to impart the following values: accept others, the right for girls to play, the right for girls and boys to play together, respect for others, and to know the truth by themselves. We are trying to help children to understand their rights using simple ways to explain. This is your right, for example to speak up and have your voice heard."[40] She told me that NGOs like hers, which were working at grassroots levels and in underserved communities, had a critical role to play in educating people about their rights. She had little faith in formal political groups playing this role. "Party heads don't reach the people," she said. But arts and culture were channels through which NGO activists could both educate beneficiaries about their rights and provide the space for beneficiaries to express themselves and claim their rights.

Practicing democratic values internally became an important paradigm-shifting function of Egyptian NGOs and foundations. One NGO, which was working to change family law to respect the rights of all family members, not only men, was also working to ensure that women were awarded equal status within the organization. "Seventy percent of our organization is composed of women employees," explained the NGO's director. "The goal is to make women feel capable to do the job, to make them feel that they have the chance and the competence." He said that women are often stronger employees than men because they feel that they have to prove themselves in a society that always presumes men are smarter. "If a man and woman are next to each other, the attention is given to the man and what he says. In our organization, men must compete. Promotions are based upon merit, not on tenure or gender."[41]

Facing an increasingly opaque regime, development NGO and foundation leaders also highlighted the importance of their own transparency. Mubarak-era repression had created a climate of fear and secrecy: organizations were required to share their information with MOSS, but they were reticent to divulge details about their operations or financials with peers or the public. In post-uprising Egypt, NGO and foundation leaders agreed that secrecy was no longer acceptable. "We need to push for increased transparency and reporting," said one foundation director. Noting that many organizations were slow to change, she added, "It is shocking that our foundations [in Egypt] do not release financials. The rest of the world does."[42]

Rather than being demoralized or crippled by Egypt's new NGO law and the government crackdowns that accompanied it, Egypt's development NGOs and foundations displayed fortitude and ingenuity as they continued to press for change. One organization that had relied on grants from a small international grantmaking organization for basic operating support had been forced to de-register. Under Law 70, the organization could no longer receive aid from abroad. Yet it persevered. After noting that it would be interesting to watch how organizations adapted to the law's new restrictions, the NGO's founder told me, "For ourselves, despite having been de-registered, we seem to be doing more work than ever. The less funding we have, the more our team's role consists of attracting practical support and resources from local people and internal donors mainly in Cairo. Virtually all the practical work we do is supported that way now. . . . So I'm trying to keep the usual balls in the air, keeping the work going on the ground . . . while keeping all of us out of trouble."[43]

NGOs increasingly looked to local volunteers to run programs and to individual donors to contribute small donations for both capital and operating costs. Many also turned to revenue-generating activities. Eco-tourism continued to grow in popularity; some organizations developed eco-villages to generate tourism and promote local trades while using profits to fund organizational activities. Meanwhile, many youth established social enterprises as a way to promote social change outside the confines of the NGO structure. While on the one hand such organizations could be perceived as playing into President Sisi's economic privatization agenda—and indeed, Sisi looked kindly upon social enterprises—they were instead described to me as venues for building momentum for change in ways that were sustainable regardless of the supply of foreign aid, immune from the agendas imposed by foreign aid, and unrestrained by the confines of Egypt's NGO law. "We don't want grants," said one NGO director who was working with a local social enterprise incubator to develop revenue generation strategies. "It puts you under government scrutiny in an era of paternalism."[44] The director of an organization that promoted social enterprise pointed out that social enterprise aligned well with Egyptians' renewed appetite for risk taking after the uprisings. "There is a new wave of people willing to take risks," she said. "The immunity to fear went up. Everyone is out of their comfort zone and taking risks. Entrepreneurship is all about taking risks. There is a huge wave of very good ideas." She went on to say that part of this engagement with risk entailed pressing for political and policy change, and that social enterprise leaders were trying to make headway. Expressing a view common among NGO leaders, she added, "Change must come from the bottom up. It doesn't matter who is in power. We need a social movement on the ground to lobby for high-level political change."[45]

Building Citizens under Authoritarianism

During my 2017 visit to Egypt, I was struck by the number of billboards advertising new neighborhoods in metropolitan Cairo that were home to budding businesses and luxury villas, such as those shown in Figure 5.1. In downtown Cairo there were flashy new hotels, new streetscapes, and new restaurants that served hamburgers and sushi. Plans for a new administrative capital were under way. A government propaganda video entitled "We Can Do More, We Work Together" was being circulated. It featured "success stories all over Egypt," including the new Suez Canal, new cities and social housing projects, the development of shanty towns, and progress on agriculture and gas mega-projects. Aired on state-run Nile TV, the video portrayed the central role of the armed services in protecting Egypt's national security and included impressive shots of roaring fighter jets, massive ships, and lookout towers. The video also projected modernization and suggested that Egypt was regaining its leading role regionally and internationally, supporting women's empowerment,[46] and engaging youth in building Egypt's future. "Together," the video assured viewers, "we can make change."[47]

Outward signs of progress were a thin façade covering up economic hardships and pervasive government repression. Prices for staples such as petrol, sugar, bread, and gas were climbing while job opportunities were shrinking. Middle-class friends told me that they had tightened their personal budgets and couldn't imagine how the poor could afford groceries. Meanwhile, the Sisi government attacked any individual or organization that called attention to creeping authoritarianism or advocated for democratic

Figure 5.1 Billboard advertising new luxury apartments, Cairo, October 2017.
Source: Author's photo.

political change. Its assault on civil society was, by most accounts, the worst
Egypt had ever experienced.

But the government was not the only group in Egypt to deploy veneers
to its advantage. Development NGOs and philanthropic foundations also
used them as a survival strategy. When I returned to Cairo in 2017 I expected to hear about dashed dreams of freedom and about NGOs' slashed
programs, hamstrung budgets, and reined-in goals. To be sure, a number

of organizations—particularly those openly dedicated to human rights and democracy promotion—had been shuttered by the government. But leaders of the organizations that survived showed remarkable mettle and expressed hope that their work would ultimately help to bring about economic justice and citizen sovereignty. They were not deterred by Law 70 or by government raids of human rights NGOs. Instead they redoubled their efforts to create spaces for citizens to articulate their voices and claim their rights, but carefully couched this work in both the language and practice of government-sanctioned socioeconomic development.

Even under authoritarianism, it is still possible to cultivate an active citizenry, a citizenry, Asef Bayat suggests, that is "endowed with the 'art of presence' . . . that possess the courage and creativity to assert collective will in spite of all odds by circumventing constraints, utilizing what is possible, and discovering new spaces within which to make themselves heard, seen, felt, and realized."[48] Since the heady days of the 2011 uprisings, Egypt's development NGOs and foundations have been working to cultivate just this type of active citizenry. Even under the harsh laws implemented under President Sisi, there has been no death of civil society in Egypt. It has not been possible to extinguish organizations' determination to push for democratic change and a new social order using whatever ways they can muster. Instead, by creating spaces in which citizens can envision and articulate alternative futures, the development NGOs and foundations featured in this book keep Egyptians steeped in civic virtue and prepare them for future mobilizations for change.

Conclusion

When the Egyptian uprisings broke out on January 25, 2011, and concluded with the overthrow of President Hosni Mubarak eighteen days later, Egypt's future looked bright. It appeared that the country would be part of a wave of political change sweeping the Arab region. Tunisia's former leader, Zine el-Abidine Ben Ali, had already fallen, while Yemen's Ali Abdullah Saleh and Libya's Muammar Gaddafi would soon follow. As these events unfolded, Western democracy brokers rushed to the region with aid and technical assistance designed to speed along transitions to liberal democracy. Meanwhile, political scientists gathered at conferences focused on democratic transitions and published articles and books analyzing the causes of the uprisings and overwriting a decade of literature that sought to explain authoritarian resilience.[1] From the perspective of many observers (largely Westerners), it appeared that democracy would soon settle on the Arab world.

Within the next couple of years, however, governments cracked down on civil society activists while cohesion between different religious and ideological groups fizzled out. Two groups many considered antidemocratic—the army and the Islamists—emerged as the only factions capable of mobilizing popular support and gaining power. Meanwhile, economic decline diverted citizens' attention from democratic political reform toward meeting their basic needs. As the Arab Spring turned to winter, Western donors slashed their democracy promotion budgets and researchers went back to their desks to explain why the uprisings failed.[2] One particularly stinging assessment described a "bitter litany of failed uprisings, brutal crackdowns, flawed elections, and endemic violence" throughout the region and foresaw a "doleful outlook for Egypt"[3] in particular.

Such doomsday chronicles are not wholly unfounded but reflect a short-sighted understanding of the uprisings as make-or-break moments for the advent of liberal democracy in the Arab world. Clearly the uprisings did not bring about swift transitions to democracy. While Tunisia continues along a rocky transition, Egypt has fallen deeper into authoritarianism and Syria, Yemen, and Libya have descended into devastating civil wars. But while the protesters were calling for the overthrow of corrupt dictators and an end to political authoritarianism, they were not calling specifically for liberal democratic institutions and procedures that are the typical measures of democracy. Instead, they were calling more fundamentally for freedom, dignity, self-determination, and a new social compact predicated on a shift in power relations between rulers and citizens. They were demanding to be heard, and to be granted political liberation, distributive justice, and the protection of human rights broadly conceived. They understood democracy in a substantive sense: a form of governance in which citizens are granted rights, freedoms, and the power to exercise collective agency over their future.

Understood in this light, the Arab uprisings—which unleashed citizens' pent-up desires for sovereignty and broke barriers of fear that had been entrenched over decades—can be read not as a one-off opportunity for democracy to take hold but rather as a turning point in a larger revolutionary struggle that has not been squandered. During 2011, citizens managed to cross ideological divides and call with a collective voice for freedom, dignity, and social justice. Struggles for these values continue to this day even as autocratic regimes do their best to repress them. Often, such struggles are manifested not in public spectacles but through group discussions and debates, collective problem solving, artistic production, and the claiming of basic rights. Whereas such pursuits are seen in established democracies as everyday, unremarkable acts, they can be "brazen acts of insubordination" in autocracies where citizens are discouraged from thinking, acting, and mobilizing of their own free will.[4]

The spectacular displays of solidarity among the protesters in Tahrir Square gradually faded to memory over the course of 2011, as Egyptians failed to coalesce around a shared vision for the future.[5] Old fissures re-emerged as different groups sought to advance their own unique interests. While perhaps disappointing for those who hoped to see a swift transition to democracy, these divides and differences should come as no surprise given the Mubarak regime's decades-long campaign to fracture society. It should also, then, come as no surprise that the West's attempt to export its version of democracy to Egypt was met with resistance and resentment. This was not the time for one group to impose its will on the collective whole. Rather, it was a time for multivocality and the negotiation of competing ideas. It was a time for transformational change, built from the ground up.

And this is where the Egyptian development NGOs and grantmaking foundations that are the focus of this book come into the picture. These organizations did not foment the uprisings, but they did seize upon the opportunity presented by the overthrow of Mubarak to reposition themselves as facilitators of collective visioning and as advocates of political, economic, and social justice. Unlike most Western donors, who moved in to Egypt with increased budgets for democracy promotion that were then rendered virtually illegal by the government, local organizations moved slowly, carefully, and covertly. First, they engaged in a period of self-introspection in which they acknowledged their own complicity in the authoritarian status quo. Most Egyptian NGOs and foundations were caught up in co-optive or controlled relationships with the Mubarak regime and, as a result, held back from truly challenging the regime's dominance. Recognizing that the 2011 uprisings gave them the chance to realign with citizens, they vowed to make that shift and support grassroots civil society in its struggle for a new social contract. But organization leaders also realized that the power of the Mubarak regime ran deep and were circumspect about the leeway they would have to pursue radical political reform—particularly when working as formal organizations. As we saw, the SCAF confirmed these trepidations as it launched a widespread assault on the NGO sector less than a year after Mubarak's removal.

While Egypt's development NGOs and foundations did not develop new democracy promotion projects or redirect grants to the human rights organizations engaged in such programming—typical signs of democracy building work—they cultivated democratic political reform in other ways. They recognized that economic justice was both high on their beneficiaries' agendas and an inherently political quest. Mubarak's pursuit of economic privatization through corrupt tactics served as a form of governance that, while promoting self-help and entrepreneurialism, absolved the state of its responsibility to provide a strong social safety net and led to inflation, unemployment, and heightened income inequality.[6] As select political and corporate elites—often one and the same—prospered, the working class saw its access to employment, affordable food, and quality education, housing, and health care dissolve. NGOs' efforts to help citizens reclaim those basic rights were decidedly political acts.

Egypt's development NGOs and foundations also supported a democratic culture by creating spaces for citizens to discuss, debate, collectively problem solve, and express themselves freely. These democratic acts had been discouraged by the Mubarak regime, which preferred to silence citizens or pit them against each other while safeguarding its monopoly over the national dialogue and its sole right to determine the country's future. By creating the space for open dialogue, in which participants identified their own priorities and visions, Egypt's development NGOs and foundations were helping their beneficiaries adopt new identities as citizens with collective agency over their individual and communal lives. These organizations supported the kind of collective visioning that could undergird a more sustained civic revolution— one that might ultimately result in a more transparent, accountable government that granted citizens the freedom, justice, and rights they demanded in Tahrir Square in 2011. All the while, though, the NGOs and foundations were careful to weave these efforts to cultivate democratic values and governance into their existing socioeconomic development programs. This strategy recognized the intertwined nature of politics and economics in Egypt and allowed these organizations to evade the repression faced by others that more overtly promoted democracy.

While Egypt remains under autocratic rule at the time of this writing, the ongoing democracy building work of local development NGOs and foundations offers important lessons for both theory and US foreign policy. Theories rightly argue that NGOs in semi-autocratic states tend to be weak vis-à-vis the government. The research presented here confirms that prior to the 2011 uprisings, Mubarak's control strategies worked. Few Egyptian NGOs or foundations held adversarial positions against the state or had a goal of democratic political reform. But in the wake of the protests, many NGOs and their local foundation donors adopted creative strategies to build momentum for democratic change that allowed them to circumvent the government's repressive tactics. Their agility suggests that NGOs and foundations operating in autocratic and semi-autocratic states can help support incremental progress toward democracy in ways that existing theories overlook.

Political scientists and scholars of democracy aid have criticized US democracy promotion for failing to nurture locally rooted, change-oriented civil societies; instead, it supports professional NGOs that are well versed in the language of democracy but out of touch with on-the-ground realities.[7] The examples provided by local Egyptian civil society organizations offer lessons for how US foreign policy officials and the authors of the United States' democracy promotion strategies could construct a more citizen-oriented, bottom-up approach to democracy aid. Egypt's NGO sector has not failed—rather, the prevailing aid paradigm has obscured real opportunities to nurture civic activism.

NGOs as Organs of Democracy Building

Throughout the 1980s and 1990s, scholars hailed NGOs as part of civil society and, as such, key agents in citizen-led development and democratization.[8] Celebrated as less bureaucratic and nimbler than government agencies, NGOs were deemed more effective than governments at delivering development solutions. NGO sectors ballooned as Western agencies poured development aid into these organizations throughout the Global South.[9] They became key strategic partners of Western funders seeking to export democracy. As democracy aid increasingly flowed to civil society groups, NGOs responded by creating new programs targeting human rights, public policy advocacy, and legal assistance.

While aid to NGOs continues apace, the organizations that receive grants have come under fire for serving as agents of their donors rather than representatives of local citizens. In order to win lucrative grants, organizations are compelled to professionalize and adopt the priorities and languages of their funders at the expense of social embeddedness in, and connections to, local communities.[10] In both socioeconomic development and democracy promotion, NGOs bankrolled by foreign aid carry out top-down projects designed to impress donors and ensure future funding streams.[11] But projects that fit neatly into theory-based logic models and produce timely and measurable results rarely succeed in mobilizing citizens for transformative change. Instead, even when targeting political reform, such projects tend to be apolitical in their methods and ameliorate, rather than disrupt, the status quo.[12]

In addition to the pressures imposed by aid, NGOs in many parts of the Global South face government regulations that prevent them from pursuing radical change agendas. Formal laws delimit the goals and activities that they can pursue while informal harassment creates cultures of fear and distrust within NGO sectors.[13] As the case of Egypt has shown, organizations operating in such environments understand that they are being constantly monitored by the state. As a result, they find it prudent to keep a low profile and do work that is politically safe rather than joining to mobilize as a cohesive oppositional force.

Egypt's 2011 uprisings brought weaknesses of the country's NGO sector to light. NGOs did not instigate the uprisings or even participate in them as formal organizations. Instead, protesters were loosely networked; they connected, mobilized, and strategized through social media, text messaging, and word of mouth. Egyptians came together across religious, socioeconomic, and ideological divides to unite in calls for "bread, freedom, and social justice," and ultimately the fall of Mubarak, without the support of NGOs.

After Mubarak's deposal, the United States predictably poured money into traditional democracy promotion NGOs, with the majority going to local human rights organizations and international NGOs that had specific democracy promotion mandates. This strategy produced two sets of backlashes. One, as outlined in chapter 2, was from the SCAF, which shut down a number of these organizations, charged and convicted their employees for operating NGOs illegally, and drafted a new law that, when approved in 2017, became the most draconian set of regulations for NGOs in Egypt's history. The other came from scholars who recognized that human rights organizations and international NGOs had limited mobilizing potential, given their relatively tame tactics and detachment from everyday Egyptians.[14] The Arab uprisings demonstrated the power of local citizens to voice their objectives and demand change, and the democracy promotion establishment was (rightly) criticized for putting so much faith in a set of NGOs that were out of touch with local people and their priorities.

But to write off all NGOs as ineffective agents of democratic political reform risks distorting future democracy promotion policies and strategies. As this book has shown, NGOs *can* create spaces for dialogue, debate, and rights claiming—key components of any democratic society. Often, however, efforts to cultivate a culture of, and demand for, democracy are couched within and behind socioeconomic development programs. This approach can be far more culturally attuned than more overt forms of democracy promotion, as it addresses high-priority economic concerns while also acknowledging the intertwined nature of economics and politics in much of the so-called developing world. And, while inherently a decidedly political approach, it is safer than the "tame"—but undisguised—democracy promotion strategies favored by US democracy brokers. Ironically, while most projects bankrolled by US democracy aid lack revolutionary potential, they still antagonize repressive regimes. Meanwhile, projects woven into socioeconomic development programs that nurture democratic citizenship at grassroots levels are far less likely to be suppressed.

If we understand Egypt's 2011 uprisings not as a movement to bring liberal democracy to Egypt but rather as an articulation of multifaceted demands for freedom, dignity, and equality, we see that after Mubarak's overthrow many of the country's development NGOs and grantmaking foundations did align with civil society and created programs intended to advance revolutionary goals. And when we understand democracy in the substantive sense—as a system of power relations that "maximizes the opportunities for individuals to influence the conditions in which they live, to participate in and influence debates about the key decisions which affect society"[15]—it becomes clear that many of Egypt's development NGOs and foundations were in fact promoting democracy. But they were doing so on Egyptians' terms, not on the terms of US democracy brokers. Moreover, they managed to persist in their efforts throughout years of relentless government crackdowns on Egypt's NGO sector. Their agility suggests that we must give local NGOs, and their democracy building capacity, a second look.

Reforming US Democracy Aid

Scholars of US democracy aid have criticized it for its top-down, technical approach that fails to confront dictators head on.[16] The short-term outputs of reports, trainings, conferences, and similarly professional activities aimed at schooling recipient states in the values and the practices of liberal democracy are neat and measurable and their successful completion is generally sufficient to win future grants and secure the organization's place in the democracy promotion establishment.[17] Rarely, however, do these *outputs* bring about the desired *outcome*: democracy. Instead, they depoliticize the process of democratization by taking it out of the hands of everyday citizens and turning it into a technical, procedural enterprise administered by government bureaucrats and development specialists.

As democracy experts earn high salaries to carry out projects ostensibly designed to convince locals of the promise of democracy, they too often fail to involve or even interact with the vast majority of target country populations. Yet as the Arab Spring uprisings and other recent social movements have shown, people around the world don't need to be convinced. Aspirations of freedom, equality, and social justice are driving people to the streets to fight for these values.[18] Moreover, even after the most visible, contentious acts have quieted—due to either outright government repression or encroaching feelings of frustration and helplessness—local organizations can and do continue to mobilize citizens to demand democracy in subtle yet persistent ways. Many will never refer to their work as "democracy promotion." In quiet conversations, though, they will insist that their activities—in realms as diverse as literacy, healthcare, and arts and culture—prepare beneficiaries to exercise their voice, demand accountable representation, and engage as democratic citizens. Efforts to promote discussion and debate, collective problem solving, free expression, and rights claiming among everyday citizens are decidedly political, yet many of the projects into which these efforts are incorporated are ineligible for the lucrative democracy aid doled out by most Western agencies.

Some program officers I spoke with at US and other Western aid agencies recognized that their democracy promotion programs were out of touch with local citizens and many readily admitted that their work was not responsible for the 2011 uprisings. These program officers also despaired that while their budgets for democracy and good governance programs did increase after Mubarak was deposed, few changes were made to their grantmaking strategies to reflect the new environment.[19] Egyptians across the country were clearly ready to take responsibility for their country's future and work collectively to bring about a transition to democracy, and yet a mismatch remained between the targets of democracy aid and the priorities and practices of everyday citizens. Other program staff of Western aid organizations placed great faith in their democracy and good governance programs and were surprised that more Egyptian NGOs did not rush to apply for their funds.

Regardless, in-country staff rarely set policy; instead, they carry out the policies set in donor country capitals. Meanwhile, Western-based bureaucrats seldom spend significant time in the countries to which their aid flows, save for a few high-profile trips to capital cities where they meet with prominent politicians and intellectuals. Democracy aid policies are therefore based on the interests of the grantmaking country and on conversations with target-country residents who are fluent in the democracy promotion lexicon and whose organizations carry out programs that fit with the standard democracy promotion playbook. As a result, democracy aid strategies remain relatively stagnant and self-perpetuating.

Experts on democracy building have for years been calling for democracy aid to be reformed in ways that make it less bureaucratic and more in touch with ordinary citizens and local contexts.[20] So far, the United States' democracy aid strategy has remained stubbornly resistant to major change, but recent events should give foreign policy makers reason to consider a fundamental revision. First, countries are updating foreign funding laws to more tightly restrict the flow of international donations to local NGOs. From Ethiopia to India, Zimbabwe, Ukraine, China, Ecuador, Bolivia, Hungary, Russia, and many others, countries around the world are making it more difficult for funders to support foreign NGO sectors.[21] While the proliferation of such laws poses broad threats to the future of foreign funding for NGOs, most regulations place the strictest conditions and constraints on grants to human rights and advocacy NGOs. The United States will likely find its efforts to fund typical democracy promotion NGOs increasingly stymied, and will need to look for other channels through which to support democratic political reform.

Second, current US president Donald Trump has cut foreign aid budgets and reduced USAID staff.[22] This means that fewer resources need to be stretched more broadly, and maintaining distinct budgets for democracy and good governance initiatives requires both staff time and money. This reality, along with the fact that political and economic issues can rarely be neatly disentangled, calls for breaking down funding silos.

Third, recent social movements such as Occupy Wall Street and Black Lives Matter in the United States, the Colour Revolutions of the former Soviet and Balkan states, the Gezi Park protests in Turkey, and Idle No More in Canada show that there is no shortage of passion and desire for the core values of democracy. These citizen mobilizations also suggest that people are fed up with traditional institutions and solutions. The power elite are not delivering, and technology has allowed more people than ever to connect over shared grievances and rally to call for fundamental change. A continued focus on the national institutions of democracy, rather than on the foundational values of democracy at all levels of governance and civic life, risks ignoring the message of contemporary social movements.

In sum, the standard democracy promotion playbook is obsolete in today's climate of hyperconnected, citizen-driven activism. Aid agencies and the international NGOs that carry out projects on their behalf need to reform their democracy promotion strategies and practices if they wish to build legitimacy and become relevant players in future democratic transitions. The following set of recommendations, drawn from the lessons learned over my years of research in the Middle East and experience working in government and private philanthropic sectors, aspires to help US policymakers and aid practitioners build nimbler, citizen-oriented strategies for promoting democratic political reform.

De-Silo Grantmaking

Grant makers—including government aid agencies and private foundations—are siloed institutions. Narrowly defined areas of focus—such as education, arts and culture, health and human services, environment, economic growth, and democracy—are cordoned off into distinct programs. Program officers are assigned to particular areas in which they gain knowledge and through which they make grants to organizations carrying out projects that fall within the program area's focus.

Such silos are obsolete in today's world.[23] Transformative change happens not within neatly packaged sectors but through efforts of interconnected groups and organizations that transcend boundaries. Artistic production, for example, not only enhances culture but also creates economic opportunities and produces a space for the free expression that challenges the status quo and bolsters pluralism. Education leads to job opportunities, but it also provides the literacy and critical thinking skills necessary to act as a democratic citizen. Good health is a necessary precursor to civic and political engagement, just as it is necessary to stay in school or hold down a job. Moreover, free expression, high-quality education, and healthcare are all human rights; their protection upholds a free and democratic society.

Maintaining a program area for democracy and good governance separate from other areas of development not only disregards the marriage between economics and politics; it is also downright dangerous for both the grant maker and, even more importantly, the grantee. NGOs operating in autocracies cannot afford to win grants and conduct programs that will get them into trouble with the government, and "democracy promotion" grants will often do just that. The tag of "democracy" also opens organizations up to being accused by the general public of implementing foreign agendas. This presents a dilemma: many organizations need foreign funds in order to survive, yet accepting certain types of funds—especially grants for democracy building—threatens their legitimacy on the ground and attracts government harassment.

Aid organizations can eliminate specific democracy and good governance program areas without abandoning their commitment to funding democratic political reform. Grantmaking structured instead around broader themes and values, with political reform goals and political thinking underlying all programs and projects, might prove more relevant. Thematic areas might include:

- *Leveraging Local Resources.* Grants in this area would support initiatives developed through community-led collaborations. Priorities and solutions would be identified at the community level, and community members would be involved in all programmatic levels including planning, implementation, and evaluation. The overarching aim would be to support citizens' efforts to define and build their future by providing the space to practice collective visioning and civic action. Local ownership of the agenda would be key to success.
- *Community development and human dignity.* Grants in this area would support all facets of human rights, including education, healthcare, jobs, community infrastructure, and a clean environment. While grants would support socioeconomic development programs, the wider aim would be for citizens to understand their rights and exercise their agency to demand them from the government—all while nurturing and upholding the value of human dignity.
- *Information and expression.* Grants in this area would support all forms of free expression and access to information. Grants to education programs, arts and culture production, and independent media would aim to support a culture of idea exchange and debate, self-expression, critical thinking, and tolerance of competing viewpoints.

This type of integrated approach to grantmaking could be implemented comprehensively across geographic space. Currently, democracy aid tends to flow primarily to organizations in capital cities, while certain cities and villages further afield become darlings of economic development aid. Rural towns and villages also need to be included in visioning and building their country's future. Locally rooted, comprehensive aid programs whose overarching aims surround processes of exercising collective agency, expressing a variety of viewpoints, and claiming human rights could support widespread involvement and ownership.

An integrated approach would also promote collaboration and coalition building among grantees. Too often, aid fosters competition among grant seekers and hierarchies between those organizations that receive aid and those that do not. Instead, collaborations among organizations could be incentivized and supported throughout the grant cycle, from application to program implementation to evaluation. Collaborations may have to be structured creatively to avoid the types of government suppression described in chapter 1. However, the risk of government scrutiny need not deter aid organizations from promoting cross-sector collaboration. Instead, aid providers can work with grantees to structure smart collaborations and stand up to government opposition if and when it occurs.

Finally, any integrated, bottom-up approach to democracy promotion that addresses both political and economic grievances must grapple with the fact that the free market doctrine that guides many US economic development grants may be deeply unpopular among the people that aid purports to support. If foreign policy makers are truly committed to democratic values such as freedom, rights, dignity, and equality, then aid frameworks must better account for citizens' demands for new social contracts that demand political *and* distributive economic justice. Policies that shield the state from responsibility for the welfare of its citizens will remain out of touch with local priorities and risk derailing momentum for democratic change.

Seek Out New Types of Grantees

In order to adopt a more citizen-oriented approach to democracy aid, donors can look beyond the usual suspects as grantees and seek a wider range of views and insights from people across geographical, socioeconomic, religious, and cultural communities. Currently, most democracy aid flows to international NGOs and local human rights NGOs whose agendas align with donors' goals of reforming institutions and bringing about procedural democracy. Yet many NGOs tagged as working solely in socioeconomic development may, in fact, be trying to incubate democratic cultures and nurture democratic citizens. Their focus on collective agency, free expression, and human rights puts many of these organizations squarely in the political reform realm, even if they carefully mask this behind innocuous development projects. Democracy aid workers who have their ears to the ground and who have generated trust among local groups should be able to identify and support such organizations.

Aid agencies could also look beyond formal NGOs to identify other groups working for democratic change. As NGO laws become more and more restrictive, social change actors are turning to other types of groups through which to mobilize citizens for reform. As chapter 2 discussed, *legan*, or popular committees, played a prominent role in building collective civic action in Egypt after the uprisings and many remained active well after the heady days of 2011. Social enterprises are booming throughout the world as activists are seeking more sustainable organizational forms.[24] While laws may prohibit these organizations, which are generally registered as companies, from accepting grants, nonprofit social enterprise incubators often rely on grants to fund own their operations and provide seed funding to social entrepreneurs. Nonprofit support organizations can also channel grant funds to informal initiatives.

To accurately discern the people's priorities and support their democratic aspirations, aid workers would benefit from developing a stronger presence on the ground in target countries. During my first trip to USAID's Egypt headquarters, my taxi driver got lost and it took us ages to find someone who could provide directions. This is conspicuously odd in a country where people on the street can normally point a driver in the right direction and provide landmarks such as trees, markets, and oddly shaped buildings. When we finally did arrive, I passed through X-ray machines and was asked to leave my passport and electronic devices at the entry gate. I was then escorted into an office that resembled a typical workplace in Washington, DC. Even in my nicest field trousers, I felt underdressed.

What I experienced during that visit to USAID conformed with the reputation of US aid workers as being inaccessible to local people—and out of touch with their concerns, their priorities, and their ways of living. Democracy brokers could establish a wider and deeper presence in more far-flung areas. Interactive, mass communications technology provides a quick and straightforward place to start, as it supplies easy access to diverse populations. Aid agencies could structure their communications outreach so that it encourages two-way conversations, and the objective would be to listen and learn, not simply to push their own agenda. A new, humbler approach could begin to build the United States' reputation as a genuine listener.

Aid offices could also expand their physical presence beyond capital and major metropolitan cities and reach more deeply into villages and rural areas. Instead of one large office in a given target country or region, aid agencies could consider having multiple smaller offices that are more easily accessible—while of course being cognizant of potential security concerns. Aid workers could seek out ways to identify local NGOs searching for funds and convene discussions to learn about potential projects. Again, officials will need to be open to new ideas about how democracy can be promoted. When the NGO leader highlighted in chapter 4 told a Western democracy broker that education reform should be part of democracy building, his words should have served as a clue. Instead, the aid worker rejected the organization's education projects as out of scope.

In addition, US aid organizations have growing opportunities to support and learn from local, indigenous philanthropic foundations. Grantmaking foundation sectors are expanding not only in the Arab region but around the world, yet there is often a wide divide between foreign aid and local philanthropy. In Egypt, for example, Western aid agency staff members indicated that they collaborated among themselves through the UNDP's Development Partners Group but rarely with local foundations. Yet these foundations can serve not only as information brokers but also as funding intermediaries. Aid could be channeled to local foundations, which in turn would have discretion over where to grant the funds; presumably with an understanding of which local NGOs and informal groups are doing high-impact work.

The proliferation of community foundations offers particularly promising venues for intermediary grantmaking.[25] The community foundations in the Arab world, for example, practice "community-owned" grantmaking. In this model, the foundation facilitates application processes, but it is the members of the community who pool their resources together and decide which applicants should receive grants. The model offers a unique opportunity for US donors because it guarantees local control of, and accountability for, the grantmaking process and could thus reduce the stigma NGOs face when they accept foreign aid. The practice also, of course, reinforces core democratic values of citizen decision-making.

US diplomats and aid workers are exceptionally well intentioned and genuinely care about the fate of the countries where they are stationed. Yet because USAID houses its staff in luxurious residences, provides them with private drivers, and cordons off aid offices behind barricades and security screens, barriers between aid workers and everyday citizens are quickly, if inadvertently, erected. While aid workers must be mindful of security concerns, they should also be encouraged and given opportunities to break down some of these barriers between themselves and those they seek to understand and assist.[26]

Reform Application and Evaluation Procedures

One of the most common criticisms of democracy aid is that the bureaucracy and monitoring that accompanies aid depoliticizes the work carried out by grant recipients.[27] To secure funding under existing protocols, NGOs must develop project-based proposals structured like business plans. Applicants must clearly summarize the scope of work, lay out a strategic plan, detail a budget, and build a linear logic model that hypothesizes causal links between inputs and outcomes. Throughout the cycle of the grant, organizations must report back to their donors using quantitative metrics to show progress toward stated goals and efficient use of resources. These processes require grant applicants to be professional, managerial institutions with English-speaking staff who are conversant in the language of democracy promotion and trained in evaluation techniques. Office technologies must be sufficient to manage the required forms and data. These requirements prevent many organizations from even applying for grants and are particularly discriminatory against the most locally rooted organizations that are best positioned to ensure that democratic political reform reaches communities beyond capitals and other major cities.

Application and evaluation procedures also diminish and depoliticize the democracy building programs undertaken. They force organizations to take on narrowly defined projects with outcomes that can be quantitatively measured and observed in short periods of time. Moreover, organizations must show that their particular intervention caused a given outcome, or at least produced a concrete output. The trouble is, any given organization's contribution to progress on political reform is incredibly difficult to identify and measure. As a result, democracy aid tends to produce outputs that donors believe contribute to democratic political reform. Reports, workshops, legal defense, and trainings for political party leaders should, in theory, prepare a country for procedural democracy. But as the output becomes the focus, the end goal of democracy tends to get sidelined.

These activities, while ostensibly targeting political reform, actually depoliticize reform processes. They fail to address more fundamental power dynamics and leave grassroots, rural, and marginalized communities out of the conversation. They largely overlook concerns about economic justice. They do not encourage radical re-thinking about the future or incite revolutionary actions. And yet, ironically, they are easy targets for ruling autocrats to suppress. While Mubarak understood that these democracy promotion projects were relatively benign and presented a pretense of liberalization that benefited his continuing rule, subsequent governing regimes used legal codes to terminate them. They were easy targets for a law that forbade political activity, aimed as they were at changing public policies and building democracy.

As my interlocutors regularly asked, how does one measure an organization's impact on people's perceived agency, freedom, justice, and dignity? How does one measure the role a particular organization played in shifting power relations? Surveys such as the World Values Survey and the Arab Barometer provide valuable country-wide data that offer clues about how these aspects of human well-being and social change are faring and evolving. But how can a particular organization prove to its funders that *its* efforts had an impact? How can an organization prove causality between its interventions and social change? In all likelihood, it can't. And yet, evaluations are certainly not going away. Thus, the question becomes, how can evaluations be restructured in ways that make them useful tools for communities, grantee organizations, and donors?

Donors could begin by reassessing grant application systems and by working with local NGO leaders to create applications that are accessible to grassroots organizations and useful for donors and the communities they serve. At the very least, they should be accepted in both English and in the native language of the target country. While logic models are not likely to be abandoned anytime soon, they serve best as visual theories of change subject to revision as on-the-ground realities evolve—not as straitjackets into which grantees must fit all elements of their programming. Evaluations can be retooled to encourage feedback on progress, with a recognition that in many cases citizen-owned processes will be more important than outputs. Many of the activities described in chapter 4—public discussion, arts and culture production, free expression, and rights claiming—are valuable in their own right, regardless of immediate outputs and outcomes.

As part of any evaluation process, donors and grantees can benefit from acting as co-learners, engaging in honest conversations about what seems to work and what does not. If grantees can be honest about the challenges they face, donors can more effectively work with them to try and overcome those obstacles. Strategies may need to change, mid-course, along with fluctuations in the external environment. Donors that can be flexible and accommodating to such changes might serve their grantees better. Such co-learning and adaptability require that donors are accessible to their grantees, which is yet another reason to strive for a wider and more locally rooted presence.

Most donors understand that reform processes happen over the long term. Transformative change, in particular, is unlikely to occur in one-, two-, or three-year grant cycles. Therefore, donors should seek to identify organizations doing good work and support them for the long haul not only with grants for particular programs but also, critically, with core operating support. Grantee organizations cannot conduct projects if they cannot keep their lights on, and it is unrealistic to tell a grantee to find operating support elsewhere. Often, Western aid offers one of the only significant sources of support for local NGOs.

Finally, donors can take the time to seek out honest feedback about their own performance. Rather than hiring evaluation consultants or relying solely on assessments by home government bureaucrats, donors can ask their grantees how people on the ground think they are doing. After all, at the end of the day grantees and the citizens they work with are best positioned to evaluate whether aid is succeeding or failing.[28] Of course, grant recipients tend to be wary of criticizing their donors for fear of biting the hand that feeds them. However, philanthropic foundations in the United States are increasingly using a tool called the Grantee Perception Report® (GPR) to solicit anonymous feedback about how those working in the trenches perceive the foundation's support. Conducted by the nonprofit Center for Effective Philanthropy, the GPR provides comparative data on how a particular foundation is doing, relative to peer institutions, on a variety of measures (e.g., knowledge of the field, impact on the field, communications with grantees). These data are based on anonymous surveys conducted with current grantees. Aid organizations are already well networked and engaged in communicating about best practices, so a GPR for US aid providers is feasible. The question is whether donors are willing to accept criticism and adapt their programs based on feedback.

Drive National Values, Not Institutions

National government institutions do matter, too. Without responsive, accountable, and honest government institutions, democratic governance is impossible and all the civil society in the world will fail to reach its full potential. Freedom, justice, and equality cannot be realized under corrupt governance structures. While aid that targets high-level reform of government institutions and political systems can't be the only approach to democracy building, it does need to be one component of a comprehensive approach. But democratic values and questions of power should be at the core of democracy aid's efforts to reform structures and institutions. The aim should not be to export US structures of democracy to the rest of the world.[29]

Rather, aid can be used to pressure ruling regimes to reconfigure their institutions in ways that local citizens desire. Areas of emphasis might include government responsiveness, accountability, and transparency, with rulers being pressed to reshape their relationships with society in ways that respond and give legitimacy to citizens' demands and dignity. Forcing US institutional structures on other countries without directly addressing underlying power relations is not likely to produce meaningful change and risks perpetuating the notion that the West is out to rule the world.[30]

Aid conditionality can be deployed as part of the pressure applied to stubborn dictators.[31] Giving lip service to democracy and human rights while failing to condition aid on rulers' progress toward these goals will leave the United States perceived as hypocritical and signal to despotic rulers that they will not be punished for carrying on with the status quo. Conditionality can be followed up with hard talk. In August 2017, the United States denied Egypt $95.7 million in aid and delayed an additional $195 million because of its failure to make progress on respecting human rights and democratic norms.[32] Just months later, however, in January 2018, Vice President Mike Pence visited the Egyptian capital and during his meeting with President Sisi, praised the Egyptian leader and declined to mention the country's escalating cases of human rights abuse. In fact, he indicated that ties between the United States and Egypt had "never been stronger."[33] During his visit to Cairo the following month, then–Secretary of State Rex Tillerson failed to criticize Egypt's upcoming elections, which were widely seen as a farce, or even take issue with the regime's human rights abuses.[34] In July 2018, President Trump released the previously withheld $195 million in military aid.

In short, the institutions of democracy are not enough. Principles also matter. If local citizens perceive the United States as weakly pushing for the formal institutions of liberal democracy while failing to call out violations of freedom, justice, and equality, any democracy aid will lack teeth and the United States will come to be seen as irrelevant. If it wants to be an honest, legitimate broker of democracy, the United States will need to relinquish its support for so-called friendly dictators and full-throatedly defend and champion citizens' demands for substantive change.

Delta Democracy

One beauty of the 2011 uprisings is that they were citizen led and citizen maintained. The world was captivated by the courage, scrappiness, and solidarity of the protesters, and Egyptians emerged from Tahrir Square proud and determined to continue in their quest to bring freedom, justice, and equality to Egypt. At this stage, US and other Western donors had a potentially important role to play. But overall, the Western democracy promotion playbook failed the Arab Spring. As organizations that had, theretofore, shied away from addressing political reforms began to build democracy cultivation efforts into their socioeconomic development programs, Western donors could have offered some financial backing. But the democracy aid that poured into Egypt after the uprisings did not flow to these organizations. Instead, the bulk of it went to democracy promotion and human rights NGOs that struggled to maintain their activities—or even their presence in Egypt—in the face of relentless government crackdowns.

Yet even as the democracy promotion industry faces backlashes, in Egypt and elsewhere, citizens around the world continue to take to the streets and to social media to demand their rights and to call for changes to the existing world order. The Arab Spring uprisings reflected a wider, global set of civic revolutions seeking not just to overthrow dictators but to more fundamentally build more sovereign and just societies. They are radically questioning old social orders and calling with common voice across ideological, socioeconomic, political, and national divides for shared values of freedom, justice, and equality. Taking on the policy recommendations provided here can spur and guide US policymakers to reform the country's outdated democracy promotion playbook in ways that make it more relevant and effective in today's world.

In Egypt, the specter of authoritarian revival in the wake of the 2011 uprisings threatened to quell civic energy for reform. As increasingly despotic rulers came to power, Egyptians did not forget their triumph in the revolutionary moment of 2011, when they broke barriers of fear and displayed the power of collective, civic action. Government repression subsequently circumscribed the type of work individuals, groups, and organizations could undertake, but it did not silence their voices or halt their activism. As the organizations featured in this book have shown, civic action carries on in inconspicuous ways: through collaborative decision-making, through shared community development efforts, through art, through demands for basic human rights, and through deliberations around cups of tea. That these acts of engagement and sovereignty continue even in the face of unyielding government suppression suggests that there is no going back to the old social order. Yet change will not happen overnight; it will require protracted struggle.

What will it take for US aid to meaningfully support these ongoing civic revolutions? It will require US foreign policy makers and aid officials to respect the priorities of local citizens and recognize that effective strategies to bring about change are more likely to come from people on the ground than from an increasingly dysfunctional democracy promotion playbook. It will require a better recognition of the interconnectivity of political, economic, and social forces. It will require acknowledging that form follows function, and that the cultivation of democratic values must go hand in hand with, and guide, the construction of democratic institutions. Finally, it will require taking the long view. Democracy—in whatever form it takes—will not transpire with the overthrow of dictators or the hosting of elections. It will evolve incrementally, as citizens continue to declare and claim their collective sovereignty. This is Delta Democracy.

Notes

Introduction

1. Arab Foundations Forum, "Arab Foundations Forum Annual Meeting 2011: Towards Effective Philanthropy in the Arab Region," (Beirut: Arab Foundations Forum, 2011).
2. Participant observation, May 6, 2011.
3. Development NGOs constitute a growing segment of Egypt's NGO sector. Ranging in size from very small, locally focused groups to larger organizations that work throughout Egypt, these organizations distinguish themselves by their efforts to combat entrenched poverty and inequality and develop structures for long-term social and economic development. Since 2002, philanthropic foundations have become increasingly important players in Egypt's NGO sector. Many of these foundations operate their own programs; the approximately twenty Western-style grantmaking foundations in Egypt are the focus of this book. See chapter 1 for more information on the landscape of NGOs in Egypt and on development NGOs and philanthropic foundations in particular.
4. These organizational leaders spoke under the condition of anonymity for themselves and their organizations, but with the understanding that I would be publishing the results of the research project in which they were taking part.
5. For data on USAID's democracy and governance obligations to Egypt by year, see https://explorer.usaid.gov/cd/EGY?fiscal_year=2011&implementing_agency_id=1&measure=Disbursements. For examples of NGOs that left Egypt or were shut down, see for example, Ahram Online, "Al Mawred Al Thaqafy Announces Freeze on All Activities in Egypt for the Present," November 5, 2014; Cairo Institute for Human Rights Studies, "CIHRS Moves Its Regional and International Programs Outside Egypt," News Release, December 9, 2014;Al Jazeera, "Egypt Shuts El Nadeem Centre for Torture Victims," February 9, 2017.
6. Interview, July 9, 2014.
7. Jessica C. Teets, *Civil Society under Authoritarianism: The China Model* (Cambridge: Cambridge University Press, 2014); Jennifer N. Brass, *Allies or Adversaries: NGOs and the State in Africa* (Cambridge: Cambridge University Press, 2016); Kendra E. Dupuy, James Ron, and Aseem Prakash, "Who Survived? Ethiopia's Regulatory Crackdown on Foreign-Funded NGOs," *Review of International Political Economy* 22, no. 2 (2015): 419–56; Saskia Brechenmacher, "Civil Society under Assault: Repression and Responses in Russia, Egypt, and Ethiopia," (Washington, DC: Carnegie Endowment for International Peace, 2017); Daniel Brumberg, "Democratization in the Arab World? The Trap of Liberalized Autocracy," *Journal of Democracy* 13, no. 4 (2002): 56–68.

8. Dean Chahim and Aseem Prakash, "NGOization, Foreign Funding, and the Nicoraguan Civil Society," *VOLUNTAS: International Journal of Voluntary and Nonprofit Organizations* 25, no. 2 (2014): 487–513; Sari Hanafi and Linda Tabar, "The Intifada and the Aid Industry: The Impact of the New Liberal Agenda on the Palestinian NGOs," *Comparative Studies of South Asia, Africa and the Middle East* 23, no. 1&2 (2003): 205–14; Islah Jad, *Palestinian Women's Activism: Nationalism, Secularism, Islamism* (Syracuse, NY: Syracuse University Press, 2018).

9. Amaney A. Jamal, *Barriers to Democracy: The Other Side of Social Capital in Palestine and the Arab World* (Princeton, NJ: Princeton University Press, 2007); Teets, *Civil Society under Authoritarianism*; Vickie Langohr, "Too Much Civil Society, Too Little Politics: Egypt and Liberalizing Arab Regimes," *Comparative Politics* 36, no. 2 (2004): 181–204.

10. Robert D. Putnam, *Making Democracy Work: Civic Traditions in Modern Italy* (Princeton, NJ: Princeton University Press, 1993); Larry Diamond, "Rethinking Civil Society: Toward Democratic Consolidation," *Journal of Democracy* 5 (1994): 4–18.

11. Thomas Carothers, "Revitalizing U.S. Democracy Assistance: The Challenge of USAID," (Washington, DC: Carnegie Endowment for International Peace, 2009); Sarah Sunn Bush, *The Taming of Democracy Assistance: Why Democracy Promotion Does Not Confront Dictators* (Cambridge: Cambridge University Press, 2015).

12. Sheila Carapico, *Political Aid and Arab Activism: Democracy Promotion, Justice, and Representation* (Cambridge: Cambridge University Press, 2014).

13. Sheila Carapico, "Egypt's Civic Revolution Turns 'Democracy Promotion' on Its Head," in *Arab Spring in Egypt: Revolution and Beyond*, ed. Bahgat Korany and Rabab El-Mahdi(Cairo: The American University in Cairo Press, 2012), 199–222; Thomas Carothers and Diane DeGramont, *Development Aid Confronts Politics: The Almost Revolution* (Washington, DC: Carnegie Endowment for International Peace, 2013); Bush, *Taming of Democracy Assistance*.

14. Interview, June 24, 2014.

15. See, for example, Joel Fleishman, *The Foundation: A Great American Secret* (New York: Public Affairs, 2007); Lehn M. Benjamin and Kevin F. F. Quigley, "U.S. Foundations and International Grantmaking," in *American Foundations: Their Roles and Contributions to Society*, ed. Helmut K. Anheier and David C. Hammack (Washington, DC: The Brookings Institution, 2010), 237–62.

16. See, for example, Kristin A. Goss, "Foundations of Feminism: How Philanthropic Patrons Shaped Gender Politics," *Social Science Quarterly* 88, no. 5 (2007): 1174–91; J. Craig Jenkins and Abigail L. Halci, "Grassrooting the System? The Development and Impact of Social Movement Philanthropy," in *Philanthropic Foundations: New Scholarship, New Possibilities*, ed. Ellen Condliffe Lagemann (Bloomington: Indiana University Press, 1999), 229–56; Herbert H. Haines, "Black Radicalization and the Funding of Civil Rights: 1957–1970," *Social Problems* 32, no. 1 (1984): 31–43; J. Craig Jenkins and Craig M. Eckert, "Channeling Black Insurgency: Elite Patronage and Professional Social Movement Organizations in the Development of the Black Movement," *American Sociological Review* 51 (1986): 812–29; Tim Bartley, "How Foundations Shape Social Movements: The Construction of an Organizational Field and the Rise of Forest Certification," *Social Problems* 54, no. 3 (2007): 229–55.

17. Interviews were spread fairly evenly over different types of organizations. I conducted between twenty and twenty-five interviews with representatives from each of the following groups: Egyptian philanthropic foundations, Egyptian development NGOs, international donor agencies, and international NGOs and local human rights organizations. I also spoke with a wide variety of activists, academics, and experts on Egyptian civil society.

18. Gary King, Robert O. Keohane, and Sidney Verba, *Designing Social Inquiry: Scientific Inference in Qualitative Research* (Princeton, NJ: Princeton University Press, 1994).

19. While organization leaders understood that their perspectives, and indeed their quotes, would be included in publications from this research, they were assured that neither they nor their organizations' names would be revealed.

20. This is also prohibited by the protocol on file with my institution's Internal Review Board.

21. See especially Mona Atia, *Building a House in Heaven: Pious Neoliberalism and Islamic Charity in Egypt* (Minneapolis: University of Minnesota Press, 2013); Carrie Rosefsky Wickham, *The Muslim Brotherhood: Evolution of an Islamist Movement* (Princeton, NJ: Princeton University Press, 2013); Nathan J. Brown, *When Victory Is Not an Option: Islamist Movements in Arab Politics* (Ithaca, NY: Cornell University Press, 2012); Tarek Masoud, *Counting Islam: Religion, Class, and Elections in Egypt* (Cambridge: Cambridge University Press, 2014).

22. See, for example, Alexis de Tocqueville, *Democracy in America and Two Essays on America* (London: Penguin Books, (1835) 2003); Robert Putnam, *Bowling Alone: The Collapse and Revival of American Community* (New York: Simon & Schuster, 2000); Larry Diamond, "Rethinking Civil Society: Toward Democratic Consolidation," *Journal of Democracy* 5 (1994): 4–18.

23. Putnam, *Making Democracy Work*; Doug McAdam, *Political Process and the Development of Black Insurgency, 1930–1970* (Chicago, IL: University of Chicago, 1982).

24. Putnam, *Making Democracy Work*; Axel Hadenius and Fredrick Uggla, "Making Civil Society Work, Promoting Democratic Development: What Can States and Donors Do?," *World Development* 24, no. 10 (1996): 1621–39.

25. McAdam, *Political Process and the Development of Black Insurgency, 1930–1970*.

26. Rob Reich, "Repugnant to the Whole Idea of Democracy? On the Role of Foundations in Democratic Societies," *PS: Political Science and Politics* 49, no. 3 (2016): 466–72; Fleishman, *Foundation*; David C. Hammack and Helmut Anheier, "American Foundations: Their Roles and Contributions to Society," in Anheier and Hammack *American Foundations*, 3–28.

27. Daniel Brumberg, "Liberalization versus Democracy: Understanding Arab Political Reform," Middle East Series Working Paper No. 37, (Washington, DC: Carnegie Endowment for International Peace, 2003); Jennifer Gandhi and Ellen Lust-Okar, "Elections under Authoritarianism," *Annual Review of Political Science* 12 (2009): 159–79.

28. Brumberg, "Liberalization versus Democracy," 5.

29. Holger Albrecht, "How Can Opposition Support Authoritarianism? Lessons from Egypt," *Democratization* 12, no. 3 (2005): 378–97; Brumberg, "Liberalization versus Democracy"; Quintan Wiktorowicz, "Civil Society as Social Control: State Power in Jordan," *Comparative Politics* 33, no. 1 (2000): 43–61.

30. Brass, *Allies or Adversaries*.

31. Collaborative government-NGO relationships are not exclusive to non-democratic states. Many governments in established democracies maintain close relationships with NGOs, particularly through government-NGO contracts and partnerships. While scholars have criticized such contracting for altering the civic roles of NGOs, they rarely suggest that leaders of established democracies use NGOs in corrupt ways to maintain power.

32. Jamal, *Barriers to Democracy*; Susan Dicklitch, *The Elusive Promise of NGOs in Africa: Lessons from Uganda* (London: Palgrave Macmillan UK, 1998).

33. Catherine Herrold and Mona Atia, "Competing rather than Collaborating: Egyptian Nongovernmental Organizations in Turbulence," *Nonprofit Policy Forum* 7, no. 3 (2016): 389–407; Catherine Herrold, "NGO Policy in Pre- and Post-Mubarak Egypt: Effects on NGOs' Roles in Democracy Promotion," *Nonprofit Policy Forum* 7, no. 2 (2016): 189–212; Mohamed Agati, "Undermining Standards of Good Governance: Egypt's NGO Law and Its Impact on the Transparency and Accountability of Csos," *International Journal of Not-for-Profit Law* 9, no. 2 (2007): 57–75; Wiktorowicz, "Civil Society as Social Control."

34. Herrold and Atia, "Competing rather than Collaborating."

35. Wiktorowicz, "Civil Society as Social Control."

36. Brumberg, "Liberalization versus Democracy," 6.

37. David Lewis, "Civil Society and the Authoritarian State: Cooperation, Contestation and Discourse," *Journal of Civil Society* 9, no. 3 (2013): 325–40; Joshua Stacher, *Adaptable Autocrats: Regime Power in Egypt and Syria* (Stanford: Stanford University Press, 2012); Christopher Heurlin, "Governing Civil Society: The Political Logic of NGO-State Relations under Dictatorship," *VOLUNTAS: International Journal of Voluntary and Nonprofit Organizations* 21, no. 2 (2010): 220–39.

38. Jamal, *Barriers to Democracy*.

39. Bush, *Taming of Democracy Assistance*; Carapico, "Egypt's Civic Revolution Turns 'Democracy Promotion' on Its Head"; Sarah L. Henderson, *Building Democracy in Contemporary Russia: Western Support for Grassroots Organizations* (Ithaca, NY: Cornell University Press, 2003); Mona Atia and Catherine Herrold, "Governing through Patronage: The Rise of NGOs and the Fall of Civil Society in Palestine and Morocco," *VOLUNTAS: International Journal of Voluntary and Nonprofit Organizations* 29, no. 5 (2018): 1044–54.

40. Carapico, "Egypt's Civic Revolution Turns 'Democracy Promotion' on Its Head."

41. Andrea Cornwall and Celestine Nyamu-Musembi, "Putting the 'Rights-Based Approach' to Development into Perspective," *Third World Quarterly* 25, no. 8 (2004): 1415–37; Giles Mohan and Kristian Stokke, "Participatory Development and Empowerment: The Dangers of Localism," *Third World Quarterly* 21, no. 2 (2000): 247–68; Bina Agarwal, "Participatory Exclusions, Community Forestry, and Gender: An Analysis for South Asia and a Conceptual Framework," *World Development* 29, no. 10 (2001): 1623–48.

42. Alison Mathie and Gord Cunningham, "From Clients to Citizens: Asset-Based Community Development as a Strategy for Community-Driven Development,"

Development in Practice 13, no. 5 (2003): 474–86; John Clark, "The State, Popular Participation, and the Voluntary Sector," *World Development* 23, no. 4 (1995): 593–601.

43. Daniel Sepinuck Immerwahr, *Thinking Small: The United States and the Lure of Community Development* (Cambridge, MA: Harvard University Press, 2015).

44. Robert Chambers, "The Origins and Practice of Participatory Rural Appraisal," *World Development* 22, no. 7 (1994): 953–69.

45. Lisa M. Campbell and Arja Vainio-Mattila, "Participatory Development and Community-Based Conservation: Opportunities Missed for Lessons Learned?," *Human Ecology* 31, no. 3 (2003): 417–37; Agarwal, "Participatory Exclusions, Community Forestry, and Gender"; Erica Kohl-Arenas, *The Self-Help Myth: How Philanthropy Fails to Alleviate Poverty* (Oakland: University of California Press, 2015); John M. Cohen and Norman T. Uphoff, "Participation's Place in Rural Development: Seeking Clarity through Specificity," *World Development* 8, no. 3 (1980): 213–35.

46. Anthony Bebbington, "New States, New NGOs? Crises and Transitions among Rural Development NGOs in the Andean Region," *World Development* 25, no. 11 (1997): 1755–65.

47. Brass, *Allies or Adversaries*; Carole Pateman, *Participation and Democratic Theory* (Cambridge: Cambridge University Press, 1970); Archon Fung and Erik Olin Wright, *Deepening Democracy: Institutional Innovations in Empowered Participatory Governance*, vol. 4 (New York: Verso, 2003); John Gaventa, "Towards Participatory Governance: Assessing the Transformative Possibilities," in *Participation: From Tyranny to Transformation?: Exploring New Approaches to Participation in Development*, ed. Samuel Hickey and Giles Mohan (London: Zed Books, 2004), 25–41.

48. Pateman, *Participation and Democratic Theory*; Ank Michels and Laurens De Graaf, "Examining Citizen Participation: Local Participatory Policy Making and Democracy," *Local Government Studies* 36, no. 4 (2010): 477–91; Michael Edwards and David Hulme, "Scaling up NGO Impact on Development: Learning from Experience," *Development in Practice* 2, no. 2 (1992): 961–73; Clark, "State, Popular Participation, and the Voluntary Sector"; Sidney Verba, Kay Lehman Schlozman, and Henry E. Brady, *Voice and Equality: Civic Voluntarism in American Politics* (Cambridge, MA: Harvard University Press, 1995); Brian Wampler, *Activating Democracy in Brazil: Popular Participation, Social Justice, and Interlocking Institutions* (Notre Dame: University of Notre Dame Press, 2015).

49. Majid Rahnema, "Participatory Action Research: The 'Last Temptation of Saint' Development," *Alternatives* 15, no. 2 (1990): 199–226; James Ferguson, *The Anti-Politics Machine: "Development," Depoliticization, and Bureaucratic Power in Lesotho* (Minneapolis: University of Minnesota Press, 1994); Bill Cooke and Uma Kothari, *Participation: The New Tyranny?* (London: Zed Books, 2001).

50. Khaldoun AbouAssi and Deborah Trent, "Understanding Local Participation Amidst Challenges: Evidence from Lebanon in the Global South," *VOLUNTAS: International Journal of Voluntary and Nonprofit Organizations* 24, no. 4 (2013): 1113–37; Sherry R. Arnstein, "A Ladder of Citizen Participation," *Journal of the American Institute of Planners* 35, no. 4 (1969): 216–24; Cornwall and Nyamu-Musembi, "Putting the 'Rights-Based Approach' to Development into Perspective"; Cooke and Kothari, *Participation*.

51. Bebbington, "New States, New NGOs?"
52. Kendra Dupuy, James Ron, and Aseem Prakash, "Hands Off My Regime! Governments' Restrictions on Foreign Aid to Non-Governmental Organizations in Poor and Middle-Income Countries," *World Development* 84 (2016): 299–311.
53. While the implications of this research are likely relevant for many Western aid agencies, this book targets its policy recommendations to the United States. Democracy aid across Western states features similar characteristics; however, due to nuances in approaches and practices it is difficult to devise a set of policy prescriptions that are universally applicable. Many of the criticisms of democracy aid articulated by my interlocutors were levied at both US and European donors, and their perspectives are included throughout this book. The conclusion's policy recommendations, however, are addressed specifically to US policymakers and funding agencies.

Chapter 1

1. For details about the Islamic *waqf* institution, see for example, Gabriel Baer, "The Waqf as a Prop for the Social System (Sixteenth–Twentieth Centuries)," *Islamic Law and Society* 4, no. 3 (1997): 264–97; Timur Kuran, "The Provision of Public Goods under Islamic Law: Origins, Impact, and Limitations of the Waqf System," *Law and Society Review* 35, no. 4 (2001): 841–98; Oded Peri, "Waqf and Ottoman Welfare Policy," *Journal of the Economic and Social History of the Orient* 35 (1992): 167–86; Daniela Pioppi, "Privatization of Social Services as a Regime Strategy: The Revival of Islamic Endowments (Awqaf) in Egypt," in *Debating Arab Authoritarianism*, ed. Oliver Schlumberger (Stanford, CA: Stanford University Press, 2007), 129–42.
2. Mona Atia, *Building a House in Heaven: Pious Neoliberalism and Islamic Charity in Egypt* (Minneapolis: University of Minnesota Press, 2013).
3. Mine Ener, *Managing Egypt's Poor and the Politics of Benevolence, 1800–1952* (Princeton: Princeton University Press, 2003).
4. Atia, *Building a House in Heaven*.
5. For more on Egypt's political economy under Nasser, see for example, Nadia Ramsis Farah, *Egypt's Political Economy: Power Relations in Development* (Cairo: The American University in Cairo Press, 2009); Atia, *Building a House in Heaven*; John Waterbury, *The Egypt of Nasser and Sadat: The Political Economy of Two Regimes* (Princeton: Princeton University Press, 1993).
6. Following Phillipe Schmitter, this book defines corporatism as, "a system of interest representation in which the constituent units are organized into a limited number of singular, compulsory, non-competitive, hierarchically organized and functionally differentiated categories, recognized or licensed (if not created) by the state and granted a deliberate representational monopoly within their respective categories in exchange for observing certain controls on their selection of leaders and articulation of demands and supports," Phillipe Schmitter and Gerhard Lehmbruch, eds., *Trends toward Corporatist Intermediation* (London: Sage, 1979), 13. For more on the nature of corporatism in Egypt and how the system affected the country's NGO sector,

see for example, Maha Abdelrahman, *Civil Society Exposed: The Politics of NGOs in Egypt* (London: Tauris Academic Studies, 2004); Janine A. Clark, "The Economic and Political Impact of Economic Restructuring on NGO-State Relations in Egypt," in *Economic Liberalization, Democratization and Civil Society in the Developing World*, ed. Remonda Bensabat Kleinberg and Janine A. Clark (Hampshire: Macmillan Press Ltd, 2000), 157–79; Robert Bianchi, *Unruly Capitalism: Associational Life in Twentieth-Century Egypt* (New York: Oxford University Press, 1989).

7. Unable to directly supervise all of the country's NGOs, the government established regional federations of NGOs, each of which served as an umbrella group for all of the NGOs located in a particular governorate. These federations, along with the NGOs they represented, fell under the jurisdiction of the NGO law and were regulated by MOSA (later MOSS). Dennis J. Sullivan, *Private Voluntary Organizations in Egypt: Islamic Development, Private Initiatives, and State Control* (Gainesville: University of Florida Press, 1994).

8. Abdelrahman, *Civil Society Exposed*, 128.

9. For more on Egypt's political economy under Sadat, see for example Atia, *Building a House in Heaven*; Farah, *Egypt's Political Economy*; Waterbury, *Egypt of Nasser and Sadat*.

10. Atia, *Building a House in Heaven*.

11. Ibid.; Abdelrahman, *Civil Society Exposed*.

12. Samer Soliman, *The Autumn of Dictatorship: Fiscal Crisis and Political Change in Egypt under Mubarak* (Stanford, CA: Stanford University Press, 2011); Farah, *Egypt's Political Economy*; Atia, *Building a House in Heaven*.

13. Safinaz El-Tarouty, *Businessmen, Clientelism, and Authoritarianism in Egypt* (New York: Palgrave Macmillan, 2015).

14. Atia, *Building a House in Heaven*.

15. Alan Richards et al., *A Political Economy of the Middle East* (Boulder: Westview Press, 2014).

16. Steven A. Cook, *False Dawn: Protest, Democracy, and Violence in the New Middle East* (New York: Oxford University Press, 2017), 63; Farah, *Egypt's Political Economy*, 42; Soliman, *Autumn of Dictatorship*, 40.

17. Karen Pfeifer et al., "Reform or Reaction? Dilemmas of Economic Development in the Middle East," *Middle East Report* 210 (1999): 14–15; Joel Beinin, "The Working Class and Peasantry in the Middle East: From Economic Nationalism to Neoliberalism," *Social Research* 79, no. 2 (2012): 323–48.

18. Amr Ismail Adly, "Politically Embedded Cronyism: The Case of Post-Liberalization Egypt," *Business and Politics* 11, no. 4 (2009): Article 3; Stephan Roll, "'Finance Matters!' The Influence of Financial Sector Reforms on the Development of the Entrepreneurial Elite in Egypt," *Mediterranean Politics* 15, no. 3 (2010): 349–70.

19. Koenraad Bogaert, "Contextualizing the Arab Revolts: The Politics Behind Three Decades of Neoliberalism in the Arab World," *Middle East Critique* 22, no. 3 (2013): 213–34. Clientelist relationships are those marked by unequal power relations between two actors but that are nonetheless mutually beneficial to both actors. Clientelism, according to Amaney Jamal, "provides clients with paths to exclusive

services and influence in return for their support of their patron." Amaney A. Jamal, *Barriers to Democracy: The Other Side of Social Capital in Palestine and the Arab World* (Princeton: Princeton University Press, 2007), 14. In the case described in this chapter, the Egyptian government acted as the patron while foundation donors were the clients. In exchange for business favors, donors to Egypt's foundations used their philanthropy to help advance the government's economic development agenda.

20. Soliman, *Autumn of Dictatorship*.

21. Farah, *Egypt's Political Economy*.

22. Julia Elyachar, *Markets of Disposition: NGOs, Economic Development and the State in Cairo* (Durham: Duke University Press, 2005); Viviane Fouad, Nadia Ref'at, and Samir Murcos, "From Inertia to Movement: A Study of the Conflict over NGO Law in Egypt," in *NGOs and Governance in the Arab World*, ed. Sarah Ben Nefissa et al. (Cairo: The American University in Cairo Press, 2005), 101–22.

23. Sullivan, *Private Voluntary Organizations in Egypt*.

24. Ehaab Abdou et al., "How Can the U.S. And International Finance Institutions Best Engage Egypt's Civil Society?" (Washington, DC: The Brookings Institution, 2011).

25. Atia, *Building a House in Heaven*.

26. Interview, February 28, 2010.

27. Atia, *Building a House in Heaven*.

28. Scholars have developed a variety of classification schemes, with some overlap but also tremendous variety. See for example: Abdelrahman, *Civil Society Exposed*; Amani Kandil, "Defining the Nonprofit Sector: Egypt," Working Paper No. 1 (Baltimore: The Johns Hopkins Institute for Policy Studies, 1993); Saad Eddin Ibrahim, Amani Kandil, Moheb Zaki, Nagah Hassan, Ola El-Ramly, Sahar Al-Ga'arah, Mohammad Sami, and Ahmed Abu Al-Yazid, eds., *An Assessment of Grass Roots Participation in the Development of Egypt* (Cairo: The American University in Cairo Press, 1997); Atia, *Building a House in Heaven*. Abdelrahman identifies Islamic NGOs, Coptic NGOs, community development associations, advocacy groups, and businessmen associations, and Kandil has a similarly diverse categorization including associations and private foundations, professional groups, business associations, nonprofit foreign foundations, Islamic *waqf*, and Christian charities. Whereas these schemes distinguish organizations primarily by their ideological origins, other scholars group NGOs according to the type of work they conduct. Ibrahim and Atia, for example, distinguish between charitable and development NGOs—the former providing basic welfare services and the latter engaging in broader-based community development activities.

29. Mona Atia and I also lay out this categorization in Catherine Herrold and Mona Atia, "Competing rather than Collaborating: Egyptian Nongovernmental Organizations in Turbulence," *Nonprofit Policy Forum* 7, no. 3 (2016): 389–407.

30. Holger Albrecht, "How Can Opposition Support Authoritarianism? Lessons from Egypt," *Democratization* 12, no. 3 (2005): 378–97.

31. In the United States, private foundations operate separately from corporations and fund their grantmaking through income from their endowments. Corporate foundations generally do not have endowments and rely on their parent corporations to fund their annual grantmaking budgets. Often a corporate foundation's budget is a set percentage of the corporate parent's annual profits.

32. Mona Atia, "The Arab Republic of Egypt," in *From Charity to Social Change: Trends in Arab Philanthropy*, ed. Barbara Lethem Ibrahim and Dina H. Sherif (Cairo: The American University in Cairo Press, 2008), 23–43.

33. Barbara Lethem Ibrahim and Dina H. Sherif, eds., *From Charity to Social Change: Trends in Arab Philanthropy* (Cairo: The American University in Cairo Press, 2008).

34. For additional information about federations, see Sullivan, *Private Voluntary Organizations in Egypt*; Atia, *Building a House in Heaven*; Abdelrahman, *Civil Society Exposed*.

35. Both the United States and European Union considered NGOs to be important partners in democracy building; see for example, Danya Greenfield and Rosa Balfour, "Arab Awakening: Are the US and EU Missing the Challenge?" (Washington, DC: The Atlantic Council of the United States, 2012); Mohamed Elagati, "Foreign Funding in Egypt after the Revolution," (Madrid, Spain: Arab Forum for Alternatives, FRIDE, and HIVOS, 2013); Shadi Hamid, "Civil Society in the Arab World and the Dilemma of Funding" (Washington, DC, The Brookings Institution, 2010). From 2002 to 2010, for example, USAID earmarked between 2.2 per cent and 7.1 percent of its assistance to NGOs: https://explorer. usaid.gov/query?country_name=Egypt&fiscal_year=2016&transaction_type_ name=Obligations&implementing_agency_name=U.S.%20Agency%20for%20 International%20Development.

36. For a more in-depth analysis of Law 84's impact on Egypt's NGO sector, see Catherine Herrold, "NGO Policy in Pre- and Post-Mubarak Egypt: Effects on NGOs' Roles in Democracy Promotion," *Nonprofit Policy Forum* 7, no. 2 (2016): 189–212.

37. Interview, October 22, 2011.

38. Interview, January 28, 2010.

39. Interview, January 31, 2010.

40. Interview, August 7, 2014.

41. Interview, February 6, 2010.

42. Interview, May 15, 2012.

43. Interview, February 21, 2010.

44. Herrold and Atia, "Competing Rather Than Collaborating."

45. Interview, August 7, 2014.

46. Interview, August 6, 2014.

47. Interview, October 22, 2011.

48. Interview, February 7, 2010.

49. M. Cherif Bassiouni, "Corruption Cases against Officials of the Mubarak Regime," (Washington, DC: Egyptian American Rule of Law Association, 2012); Lisa Blaydes, *Elections and Distributive Politics in Mubarak's Egypt* (Cambridge: Cambridge University Press, 2011); Roll, " 'Finance Matters!' "

50. Soliman, *Autumn of Dictatorship*.

51. Interview, February 4, 2010.

52. El-Tarouty, *Businessmen, Clientelism, and Authoritarianism in Egypt*.

53. Ibid.

54. Sai Felicia Krishna-Hensel, *Authoritarian and Populist Influences in the New Media* (London: Routledge, 2018).

55. El-Tarouty, *Businessmen, Clientelism, and Authoritarianism in Egypt.*

56. Joshua Stacher, *Adaptable Autocrats: Regime Power in Egypt and Syria* (Stanford: Stanford University Press, 2012); Christopher Heurlin, "Governing Civil Society: The Political Logic of NGO-State Relations under Dictatorship," *VOLUNTAS: International Journal of Voluntary and Nonprofit Organizations* 21, no. 2 (2010): 220–39.

57. Interview, June 28, 2012.

58. For more on the Mubarak regime's strategy to "divide and throttle" Egypt's NGO sector, see Herrold and Atia, "Competing Rather Than Collaborating."

59. Elyachar, *Markets of Disposition*, 172

60. Interview, February 2, 2010.

61. Interview, March 15, 2010.

62. Interview, February 14, 2012.

63. Interview, April 24, 2012.

64. Interview, February 6, 2010.

65. Interview, January 23, 2010.

66. Interview, August 4, 2014.

67. Interview, August 12, 2014.

68. Interview, February 26, 2012.

69. Interview, July 4, 2011.

70. Interview, June 19, 2014.

71. Interview, June 24, 2014.

72. For a longer discussion of NGO competition in Egypt, see Herrold and Atia, "Competing rather than Collaborating."

73. Interview, January 28, 2010.

74. Interview, February 7, 2012.

75. Interview, March 12, 2012.

76. Interview, January 28, 2010.

77. Interview, July 14, 2011.

78. Herrold and Atia, "Competing rather than Collaborating."

79. Holger Albrecht and Oliver Schlumberger, "'Waiting for Godot': Regime Change without Democratization in the Middle East," *International Political Science Review* 25, no. 4 (2004): 371–92.

80. Daniel Brumberg, "Liberalization versus Democracy: Understanding Arab Political Reform," Middle East Series Working Paper No. 37 (Washington, DC: Carnegie Endowment for International Peace, 2003), 6.

81. Interview, February 20, 2012.

Chapter 2

1. Steven A. Cook, *The Struggle for Egypt: From Nasser to Tahrir Square* (New York: Oxford University Press, 2012), 286–87.

2. Neil Ketchley, *Egypt in a Time of Revolution: Contentious Politics and the Arab Spring* (Cambridge: Cambridge University Press, 2017), 46–77.

3. Gause makes the point that most political scientists were surprised by the Arab uprisings in part because they had been so focused on explaining the persistence of undemocratic rulers in the region: F. Gregory Gause, "Why Middle East Studies Missed the Arab Spring: The Myth of Authoritarian Stability," *Foreign Affairs* 90, no. 4 (2011): 81–84, 85–90. For examples of the scholarship to which Gause refers, see for example, Jason Brownlee, *Authoritarianism in an Age of Democratization* (Cambridge: Cambridge University Press, 2007); Jillian Schwedler, *Faith in Moderation: Islamist Parties in Jordan and Yemen* (Cambridge: Cambridge University Press, 2006); Holger Albrecht, "How Can Opposition Support Authoritarianism? Lessons from Egypt," *Democratization* 12, no. 3 (2005): 378–97; Ellen Lust-Okar, "Divided They Rule: The Management and Manipulation of Political Opposition," *Comparative Politics* 36, no. 2 (2004): 403–22; Eva Bellin, *Stalled Democracy: Capital, Labor, and the Paradox of State-Sponsored Development* (Ithaca, NY: Cornell University Press, 2002); Daniel Brumberg, "Democratization in the Arab World? The Trap of Liberalized Autocracy," *Journal of Democracy* 13, no. 4 (2002): 56–68.

4. Nahed Eltantawy and Julie B. Wiest, "Social Media in the Egyptian Revolution: Reconsidering Resource Mobilization Theory," *International Journal of Communication* 5 (2011): 1207–24; Merlyna Lim, "Clicks, Cabs, and Coffee Houses: Social Media and Oppositional Movements in Egypt, 2004–2011," *Journal of Communication* 62, no. 2 (2012): 231–48.

5. Joel Beinin and Frederic Vairel, eds., *Social Movements, Mobilization, and Contestation in the Middle East and North Africa*, 2nd ed. (Stanford: Stanford University Press, 2013).

6. Jason Brownlee, Tarek Masoud, and Andrew Reynolds, *The Arab Spring: Pathways of Repression and Reform* (New York: Oxford University Press, 2015).

7. See, for example, Ketchley, *Egypt in a Time of Revolution*; Brownlee, Masoud, and Reynolds, *Arab Spring*; Marc Lynch, ed., *The Arab Uprisings Explained: New Contentious Politics in the Middle East* (New York: Columbia University Press, 2014).

8. Many scholars have made this argument. See especially Mark Beissinger, Amaney A. Jamal, and Kevin Mazur, "Explaining Divergent Revolutionary Coalitions: Regime Strategies and the Structuring of Participation in the Tunisian and Egyptian Revolutions," *Comparative Politics* 48, no. 1 (2015): 1–44; Bessma Momani, *Arab Dawn: Arab Youth and the Demographic Dividend They Will Bring* (Toronto: University of Toronto Press, 2015); Alan Richards et al., *A Political Economy of the Middle East* (Boulder: Westview Press, 2014); Magdi Amin et al., *After the Spring: Economic Transitions in the Arab World* (New York: Oxford University Press, 2012); Jane Kinninmont, "'Bread, Dignity and Social Justice': The Political Economy of Egypt's Transition," (London: Royal Institute of International Affairs, 2012); Safinaz El-Tarouty, *Businessmen, Clientelism, and Authoritarianism in Egypt* (New York: Palgrave Macmillan, 2015).

9. Richards et al., *Political Economy of the Middle East*.

10. https://data.worldbank.org/indicator/NY.GDP.PCAP.CD?locations=EG.

11. https://data.worldbank.org/indicator/BX.KLT.DINV.WD.GD.ZS.

12. Richards et al., *Political Economy of the Middle East*, 250; Kinninmont, "'Bread, Dignity and Social Justice.'"

13. Richards et al., *Political Economy of the Middle East*, 252; El-Tarouty, *Businessmen, Clientelism, and Authoritarianism in Egypt*; Stephan Roll, "Egypt's Business Elite after Mubarak: A Powerful Player between Generals and Brotherhood," (Berlin: Stiftung Wissenschaft und Politik, German Institute for International and Security Affairs, 2013).

14. Noha El-Mikawy, Mohamed Mohieddin, and Sarah El-Ashmaouy, "Egypt: The Protracted Transition from Authoritarianism to Democracy and Social Justice," in *Democratic Transitions in the Arab World*, ed. Ibrahim Elbadawi and Samir Makdisi (Cambridge: Cambridge University Press, 2017), 133–83; Amin et al., *After the Spring*.

15. Richards et al., *Political Economy of the Middle East*; El-Tarouty, *Businessmen, Clientelism, and Authoritarianism in Egypt*.

16. Kinninmont, "'Bread, Dignity and Social Justice.'"

17. Richards et al., *Political Economy of the Middle East*; Momani; Amin et al., *After the Spring*; Jeroen Gunning and Ilan Zvi Baron, *Why Occupy a Square? People, Protests and Movements in the Egyptian Revolution* (New York: Oxford University Press, 2014); Kinninmont, "'Bread, Dignity and Social Justice.'"

18. Jennifer Bremer, "Egypt: Civil Society Success or Spontaneous Combustion?," *Inside ISTR* 19, no. 1 (2011): 70–92.

19. Maha Abdelrahman, *Egypt's Long Revolution: Protest Movements and Uprisings* (Oxfordshire: Routledge, 2015); Gunning and Baron, *Why Occupy a Square?*; Tarek Masoud, "The Road to (and from) Liberation Square," *Journal of Democracy* 22, no. 3 (2011): 20–34; Dina Shehata, "The Fall of the Pharaoh: How Hosni Mubarak's Region Came to an End," *Foreign Affairs* 90, no. 3 (2011): 26–32.

20. Abdelrahman, *Egypt's Long Revolution*.

21. Brownlee, *Arab Spring*.

22. Gunning and Baron, *Why Occupy a Square?*.

23. For more on the March 9 group, see Abdelrahman, *Egypt's Long Revolution*; Ann M. Lesch, "Egypt's Spring: Causes of the Revolution," *Middle East Policy* 18, no. 3 (2011): 35–48.

24. For more on Kefaya, see Abdelrahman, *Egypt's Long Revolution*; Gunning and Baron, *Why Occupy a Square?*; Killian Clarke, "Saying "Enough": Authoritarianism and Egypt's Kefaya Movement," *Mobilization: An International Quarterly* 16, no. 4 (2011): 397–416; Manar Shorbagy, "Understanding Kefaya: The New Politics in Egypt," *Arab Studies Quarterly* 29, no. 1 (2007): 39–60; Sherif Mansour, "Enough Is Not Enough: Achievements and Shortcomings of Kefaya, the Egyptian Movement for Change," in *Civilian Jihad: Nonviolent Struggle, Democratization, and Governance in the Middle East*, ed. Maria Stepan (New York: Palgrave Macmillan, 2009), 205–18.

25. El-Tarouty, *Businessmen, Clientelism, and Authoritarianism in Egypt*; Brownlee, *Arab Spring*; Mansour, "Enough Is Not Enough."

26. Gunning and Baron, *Why Occupy a Square?*

27. Cook, *Struggle for Egypt*, 196.

28. Thomas Carothers, "Promoting Democracy and Fighting Terror," *Foreign Affairs* 82, no. 1 (2003): 84–97.

29. William Lafi Youmans, "An Unwilling Client: How Hosni Mubarak's Egypt Defied the Bush Administration's 'Freedom Agenda,'" *Cambridge Review of International Affairs* 29, no. 4 (2016): 1209–32; Jason Brownlee, *Democracy Prevention: The Politics of the U.S.-Egyptian Alliance* (Cambridge: Cambridge University Press, 2012).

30. Cook, *Struggle for Egypt*, 264.

31. Joel Beinin, "Egyptian Workers and January 25th: A Social Movement in Historical Context," *Social Research* 79, no. 2 (2012): 323–48.

32. Joel Beinin, "Workers' Protest in Egypt: Neo-Liberalism and Class Struggle in 21st Century," *Social Movement Studies* 8, no. 4 (2009): 449–54.

33. For more on the Misr Spinning and Weaving Company strikes, see Abdelrahman, *Egypt's Long Revolution*; Beinin, "Egyptian Workers and January 25th: A Social Movement in Historical Context"; Beinin, "Workers' Protest in Egypt: Neo-Liberalism and Class Struggle in 21st Century."

34. Abdelrahman, *Egypt's Long Revolution*, 57. The Egyptian Trade Union Federation (ETUF) nominally represented all organized workers but was in reality an arm of the state.

35. Ibid., 55.

36. Gunning and Baron, *Why Occupy a Square?*, 67; Beinin, "Egyptian Workers and January 25th: A Social Movement in Historical Context."

37. Beinin, "Egyptian Workers and January 25th: A Social Movement in Historical Context," 335.

38. Jack Shenker, "Supporters Give Mohamed Elbaradei Hero's Welcome at Cairo Airport," *Guardian*, February 19, 2010.

39. Abigail Hauslohner, "Ready for Change in Egypt," *Time*, July 12, 2010.

40. Kara Alaimo, "How the Facebook Arabic Page 'We Are All Khaled Said' Helped Promote the Egyptian Revolution," *Social Media + Society*, July–December (2015): 1–10.

41. Riccardo Alcaro, "Introduction. Bouazizi's Inextinguishable Fire," in *Re-Thinking Western Policies in Light of the Arab Uprisings*, ed. Riccardo Alcaro and Miguel Haubrich-Seco (Rome: Edizioni Nuova Cultura, 2012), 11–20.

42. The previous section focused on instances of collective action that were high profile and maintained some level of organization. Other scholars have highlighted the everyday practices that Egyptians have long used to more subtly resist state dominance. See, for example, Asef Bayat, *Life as Politics: How Ordinary People Change the Middle East* (Stanford, CA: Stanford University Press, 2009); Salwa Ismail, *Political Life in Cairo's New Quarters: Encountering the Everyday State* (Minneapolis: University of Minnesota Press, 2006); Diane Singerman, *Avenues of Participation: Family, Politics, and Networks in Urban Quarters of Cairo* (Princeton, NJ: Princeton University Press, 1995).

43. Diana Fu, *Mobilizing Without the Masses: Control and Contention in China* (Cambridge: Cambridge University Press, 2018).

44. Sheila Carapico, "Egypt's Civic Revolution Turns 'Democracy Promotion' on Its Head," in *Arab Spring in Egypt: Revolution and Beyond*, ed. Bahgat Korany and Rabab El-Mahdi (Cairo: The American University in Cairo Press, 2012), 199–222.

45. Charles J. Hanley, "US Training Quietly Nurtured Young Arab Democrats," *Washington Post*, March 13, 2011.

46. Sheila Carapico, "Foreign Aid for Promoting Democracy in the Arab World," *Middle East Journal* 56, no. 3 (2002): 379–95.

47. High Representative of the European Union for Foreign Affairs and Security Policy, "Joint Communication to the European Parliament, the Council, the European Economic and Social Committee and the Committee of the Regions" (Brussels: European Commission, 2011), 4.

48. Interview, September 26, 2011.

49. Interview, March 4, 2012.

50. Interview, February 7, 2012.

51. Interview, April 24, 2012.

52. Interview, May 22, 2012.

53. Interview, June 3, 2012.

54. Asya El-Meehy, "Egypt's Popular Committees: From Moments of Madness to NGO Dilemmas," *Middle East Report* 42, Winter (2012): 29–33.

55. See, for example, Jennifer Bremer, "Leadership and Collective Action in Egypt's Popular Committees: Emergence of Authentic Civic Activism in the Absence of the State," *International Journal of Not-for-Profit Law* 13, no. 4 (2011): 70–92; El-Meehy, "Egypt's Popular Committees"; Jeannie Sowers, "Egypt in Transformation," in *The Journey to Tahrir: Revolution, Protest, and Social Change in Egypt*, ed. Jeannie Sowers and Chris Toensing (London: Verso, 2012), 1–20.

56. Bremer, "Leadership and Collective Action in Egypt's Popular Committees," 71.

57. Interview, July 14, 2011.

58. El-Meehy, "Egypt's Popular Committees."

59. Interview, June 28, 2012.

60. Interview, June 24, 2014.

61. Interview, February 16, 2012.

62. Cook, *Struggle for Egypt*, 285.

63. Ketchley, *Egypt in a Time of Revolution*, 59.

64. Cook, *Struggle for Egypt*, 286; Ketchley, *Egypt in a Time of Revolution*, 67.

65. Ketchley, *Egypt in a Time of Revolution*, 46–47.

66. Chris McGreal, "Egypt's Military Rejects Swift Transfer of Power and Suspends Constitution," *Guardian*, 2011. The state of emergency in Egypt extends police powers, suspends constitutional rights, legalizes censorship and limits free speech, restricts street demonstrations, and allows civilians to be tried in military courts.

67. Steve Inskeep, "Ramy Essam: The Singer of the Egyptian Revolution," *National Public Radio*, March 15, 2011.

68. Ketchley, *Egypt in a Time of Revolution*.

69. Kristen A. Stilt, "The End of 'One Hand': The Egyptian Constitutional Declaration and the Rift between the 'People' and the Supreme Council of the Armed Forces," Faculty Working Paper No. 208 (Chicago: Northwestern University Pritzker School of Law, 2012).

70. Robert Springborg, "The Political Economy of the Arab Spring," *Mediterranean Politics* 16, no. 3 (2011): 427–33; Brownlee, Masoud, and Reynolds, *Arab Spring*.

71. H. A. Hellyer, "Egypt: The Politics of Remembering Death," (Washington, DC: The Brookings Institution, 2013).

72. David D. Kirkpatrick, "Egypt's Military Expands Power, Raising Alarms," *New York Times*, October 14, 2011.

73. Yezid Sayigh, "The Specter of 'Protected Democracy' in Egypt," (Washington, DC: Carnegie Endowment for International Peace, 2011).

74. Interview, September 26, 2011.

75. Interview, July 31, 2011.

76. Interview, March 4, 2012.

77. Interview, July 4, 2011.

78. Lisa Blaydes, *Elections and Distributive Politics in Mubarak's Egypt* (Cambridge: Cambridge University Press, 2011), 149; Nathan J. Brown, *When Victory Is Not an Option: Islamist Movements in Arab Politics* (Ithaca, NY: Cornell University Press, 2012), 24. The Muslim Brotherhood itself was prohibited from forming a party unto itself, since Article 5 of Egypt's constitution banned religious parties. In 2011, the Freedom and Justice Party—widely perceived to be the Brotherhood's party—claimed to be a party for people of all faiths.

79. Nathan J. Brown, "The Transition: From Mubarak's Fall to the 2014 Presidential Election," in *Egypt after the Spring: Revolt and Reaction*, ed. Emile Hokayem (London: Routledge, 2016), 15–32.

80. BBC, "Egypt's Islamist Parties Win Elections to Parliament," January 21, 2012.

81. The term "civil state" (*dawla madanīya*) was used synonymously with "secular state," however the former was the term preferred by my interviewees.

82. Al Jazeera, "Egypt PM Appoints New Key Ministers," March 6, 2011.

83. Al-Fagar, "Official Report to the Prosecutor Uncovers Names and Amounts: 1.34 Billion Egyptian Pounds Given from the United States, Europe and the Gulf to Egyptian Organizations in the Last Four Months," September 26, 2011.

84. *Akhbar al-Youm* is a semi-official newspaper owned by the Shura Council, Egypt's Upper House of Parliament.

85. Al-Masry al-Youm, "Ministry Sources: NGOs Received Le1.7 Bn in Foreign Funds since June 2010," December 24, 2011. In her book, Carapico cited a figure of $150 million, Sheila Carapico, *Political Aid and Arab Activism: Democracy Promotion, Justice, and Representation* (Cambridge: Cambridge University Press, 2014), 150.

86. Al Jazeera, "Egypt Security Forces Storm NGO Offices," December 29, 2011.

87. Daily News Egypt, "Judge Says NGOs Were Lawfully Inspected, Not 'Raided,'" February 8, 2012.

88. Al-Arabiya News, "Egypt Slaps Travel Ban on U.S. NGO Staff, Washington Urges Lifting Ban 'Immediately,'" January 26, 2012.

89. Ernesto Londoño and William Wan, "American Pro-Democracy Organization Workers in Cairo Take Shelter at U.S. Embassy," *Washington Post*, January 29, 2012. One of the US employees was Sam LaHood, a prominent figured connected to the US government via his father, Ray LaHood, who at the time was the US Secretary of Transportation.

90. Associated Press, "Egypt Sends 43 NGO Workers to Trial over Funds," *Salon*, February 5, 2012.

91. David D. Kirkpatrick and Steven Lee Myers, "U.S. Defendants Leave Egypt Amid Growing Backlash," *New York Times*, March 1 2012. Note that one American, Robert Becker of NDI, stayed behind to stand trial with his Egyptian colleagues.

92. Max Strasser, "Egypt Warns of Foreign Meddling as US Pushes on with Democracy Programs," *Al-Masry al-Youm*, July 5, 2011.

93. These organizations included the NDI, the IRI, Freedom House, the International Center for Journalists, and the Konrad Adenauer Foundation. See Kristen Chick, "Why Egypt Is Angry over $65 Million in US Democracy Grants," *Christian Science Monitor*, August 12, 2011.

94. Interview, February 27, 2012.

95. Interview, March 5, 2012.

96. Evan Hill, "Background: Scaf's Last-Minute Power Grab," *Al Jazeera*, June 17, 2012.

97. Ibid.

98. BBC, "Egyptian Voters Back New Constitution in Referendum," December 25, 2012.

99. Ketchley, *Egypt in a Time of Revolution*, 110–13.

100. Kristen Chick, "Convictions Put Egypt's Beleaguered NGOs into Deeper Chill," *Christian Science Monitor*, June 4, 2013.

101. Danya Greenfield and Rosa Balfour, "Arab Awakening: Are the US and EU Missing the Challenge?" (Washington, DC: The Atlantic Council of the United States, 2012); Khaled Amin, "International Assistance to Egypt after the 2011 and 2013 Uprisings: More Politics and Less Development," *Mediterranean Politics* 19, no. 3 (2014): 392–412.

102. Interview, June 22, 2011.

103. Interview, March 28, 2012.

104. Interview, February 14, 2012.

105. Interview, February 27, 2012.

106. Jeremy Sharp, "Egypt: Background and U.S. Relations," (Washington, DC: The Congressional Research Service, 2012), 11.

107. For more details on USAID's response to the Egyptian uprisings, see Greenfield and Balfour, "Arab Awakening"; United States Government Accountability Office, "Democracy Assistance: Lessons Learned from Egypt Should Inform Future U.S. Plans," (Washington, DC: United States Government Accountability Office, 2014).

108. https://ec.europa.eu/neighbourhood-enlargement/neighbourhood/countries/egypt_en

109. Laine Škoba, "European Endowment for Democracy: Hopes and Expectations," (Brussels: Library of the European Parliament, 2013).

110. https://www.wilsoncenter.org/deauville-partnership-arab-countries-transition

111. Greenfield and Balfour, "Arab Awakening."

112. United States Government Accountability Office, "Democracy Assistance."

113. Rania Hamoud, "Time of Up-Rise: Threat or Opportunity?" Paper presented at the Takaful 2012: Second Annual Conference on Arab Philanthropy and Civic Engagement, Cairo, 2012.

114. Interview, April 10, 2012.

115. International Republican Institute, "Egyptian Public Opinion Survey: April 14–April 27, 2011," (Washington, DC: International Republican Institute, 2011).

116. Interview, October 27, 2011.

117. Joshua Stacher, *Adaptable Autocrats: Regime Power in Egypt and Syria* (Stanford, CA: Stanford University Press, 2012).

118. Ken Stier, "Egypt's Pursuit of the Corrupt: Justice or a Witch Hunt?," *Time*, February 22, 2011.

119. Roll, "Egypt's Business Elite after Mubarak."

120. Springborg, "Political Economy of the Arab Spring," 431.

121. Interview, July 4, 2011.

122. Ibtessam Zayed and Salma Hussein, "Mohamed Mansour: A Tarnished Captain of Industry," *Ahram Online*, March 20, 2011; Roll, "Egypt's Business Elite after Mubarak."

123. These included Yasser el-Mallawany of the EFG-Hermes Foundation and Mohammed Mansour of the Mansour Foundation for Development. See Yasmine Saleh and Dina Zayed, "Mubarak's Sons Back in Court on Graft Charges," (2012); Zina Moukheiber, "Billionaire Egyptian Family Faces Potential Blow to Reputation," *Forbes*, April 25, 2011.

124. Ibrahim Saif, "Challenges of Egypt's Economic Transition," The Carnegie Papers (Washington, DC: Carnegie Endowment for International Peace, 2011).

125. One Egyptian woman serving at a checkpoint during a Tahrir Square protest in May 2011 remarked upon seeing my US passport, "Please tell your friends to visit Egypt. We don't want your country's aid or advice but please send your tourists."

126. https://tradingeconomics.com/egypt/gdp-growth, accessed September 10, 2017.

127. http://www.focus-economics.com/countries/egypt, accessed September 10, 2017.

128. Interview, June 24, 2014.

129. Participant observation, May 6, 2011.

130. Interview, April 10, 2012.

Chapter 3

1. Interview, February 14, 2011.

2. Ibid.

3. Sheila Carapico's excellent book on political aid to the Arab region elucidates these contradictions in great depth. Sheila Carapico, *Political Aid and Arab Activism: Democracy Promotion, Justice, and Representation* (Cambridge: Cambridge University Press, 2014).

4. Ibid.

5. Interview, October 26, 2011.

6. Interview, November 14, 2011.

7. Interview, July 28, 2011.

8. Interview, July 28, 2011.

9. Interview, February 14, 2012.

10. Interview, June 3, 2012.

11. Interview, July 28, 2011.

12. European Commission, "European Neighbourhood and Partnership Instrument 2007–2013: Overview of Activities and Results," (Brussels: European Commission, 2014), 22.

13. The Westminster Foundation for Democracy Limited, "Annual Report and Accounts 2011/12" (London: Westminster Foundation for Democracy, 2012); and https://www.kas.de/web/guest/einzeltitel/-/content/from-tahrir-square-to-open-space1.

14. While translation was offered, the vast majority of audience members listened in English. Only a scattered few wore headsets that broadcast the Arabic translation.

15. Andrea Teti, "The EU's First Response to the 'Arab Spring': A Critical Discourse Analysis of *The Partnership for Democracy and Shared Prosperity*," *Mediterranean Politics* 17, no. 3 (2012): 266–84; Steven Heydemann, "America's Response to the Arab Uprisings: US Foreign Assistance in an Era of Ambivalence," *Mediterranean Politics* 19 (2014): 299–317; Stephen J. Golub, "Democracy as Development: A Case for Civil Society Assistance in Asia," in *Funding Virtue: Civil Society Aid and Democracy Promotion*, ed. Marina Ottaway and Thomas Carothers (Washington, DC: Carnegie Endowment for International Peace, 2000), 135–58.

16. Sarah Sunn Bush, *The Taming of Democracy Assistance: Why Democracy Promotion Does Not Confront Dictators* (Cambridge: Cambridge University Press, 2015); Sheila Carapico, "Foreign Aid for Promoting Democracy in the Arab World," *Middle East Journal* 56, no. 3 (2002): 379–95; Sheila Carapico, "Egypt's Civic Revolution Turns 'Democracy Promotion' on Its Head," in *Arab Spring in Egypt: Revolution and Beyond*, ed. Bahgat Korany and Rabab El-Mahdi (Cairo: The American University in Cairo Press, 2012), 199–222; Sheila Carapico, "What Does It Mean 'Promoting Democratization'?," *International Journal of Middle East Studies* 41, no. 1 (2009): 7–9; *Political Aid and Arab Activism: Democracy Promotion, Justice, and Representation*; Khaled Amin, "International Assistance to Egypt after the 2011 and 2013 Uprisings: More Politics and Less Development," *Mediterranean Politics* 19, no. 3 (2014): 392–412; Erin A. Snider and David M. Faris, "The Arab Spring: U.S. Democracy Promotion in Egypt" *Middle East Policy* 18, no. 3 (2013): 49–62; Thomas Carothers, "Democracy Assistance: Political vs. Developmental?," *Journal of Democracy* 20, no. 1 (2009): 5–19.

17. Thomas Carothers and Diane DeGramont, *Development Aid Confronts Politics: The Almost Revolution* (Washington, DC: Carnegie Endowment for International Peace, 2013); Carapico, "What Does It Mean 'Promoting Democratization'?"; James M. Scott and Carie A. Steele, "Assisting Democrats or Resisting Dictators? The Nature and Impact of Democracy Support by the United States National Endowment for Democracy, 1990–99," *Democratization* 12, no. 4 (2005): 439–60.

18. Joel D. Barkan, "Democracy Assistance: What Recipients Think," *Journal of Democracy* 23, no. 1 (2012): 129–37; Kristina Kausch, "Assessing Democracy Assistance: Egypt," (Madrid, Spain: FRIDE, 2010).

19. Imco Brouwer, "Weak Democracy and Civil Society Promotion: The Cases of Egypt and Palestine," in Ottaway and Carothers, *Funding Virtue*, 21–48; Bush, *Taming of Democracy Assistance*; Sarah L. Henderson, *Building Democracy in Contemporary Russia: Western Support for Grassroots Organizations* (Ithaca, NY: Cornell University Press, 2003).

20. Carapico, "Egypt's Civic Revolution Turns 'Democracy Promotion' on Its Head"; Manal A. Jamal, "Democracy Promotion, Civil Society Building, and the Primacy of Politics," *Comparative Political Studies* 45, no. 1 (2012): 3–31; Amy Hawthorne, "Middle Eastern Democracy: Is Civil Society the Answer?," Carnegie Papers: Middle East Series No. 4 (Washington, DC: Carnegie Endowment for International Peace, 2004); Sarah L. Henderson, "Selling Civil Society: Western Aid and the Nongovernmental Organization Sector in Russia," *Comparative Political Studies* 35, no. 2 (2002): 139–67; Bush, *Taming of Democracy Assistance*.

21. David Suárez and Mary Kay Gugerty, "Funding Civil Society? Bilateral Government Support for Development NGOs," *VOLUNTAS: International Journal of Voluntary and Nonprofit Organizations* 27, no. 6 (2016): 2617–40; Willem Elbers and Bas Arts, "Keeping Body and Soul Together: Southern NGOs' Strategic Responses to Donor Constraints," *International Review of Administrative Sciences* 77, no. 4 (2011): 713–32; Alnoor Ebrahim, "Accountability Myopia: Losing Sight of Organizational Learning," *Nonprofit and Voluntary Sector Quarterly* 34, no. 1 (2005): 56–87; David Hulme and Michael Edwards, "Too Close for Comfort? The Impact of Official Aid on Nongovernmental Organizations," *World Development* 24, no. 6 (1996): 961–73.

22. Interview, March 15, 2010.

23. Hilary Gilbert and Mohammed Khedr Al-Jebaali, "Not Philanthropists but Revolutionaries: Promoting Bedouin Participation in the New Egypt: A Case Study from South Sinai" (Cairo: John D. Gerhart Center for Philanthropy and Civic Engagement at the American University in Cairo, 2012), 40.

24. Interview, July 14, 2011.

25. Interview, January 31, 2012.

26. Interview, August 12, 2014.

27. Interview, June 30, 2014

28. Interview, July 14, 2011.

29. Interview, March 28, 2012.

30. Interview, October 24, 2011.

31. Interview, February 7, 2010.

32. Interview, June 22, 2011.

33. One major US private foundation, The Ford Foundation, was committed to the development of Egypt's foundation sector and provided grants to the Arab Foundations Forum to support the expansion of institutionalized philanthropy throughout the region.

34. Interview, October 26, 2011.

35. Interview, November 14, 2011.

36. Interview, July 28, 2011.

Chapter 4

1. https://www.youtube.com/watch?v=GucIyK94RwI.

2. Bassem is a pseudonym.

3. Interview, March 12, 2012.

4. Hilary Gilbert and Mohammed Khedr Al-Jebaali, "Not Philanthropists but Revolutionaries: Promoting Bedouin Participation in the New Egypt: A Case Study from South Sinai," (Cairo: John D. Gerhart Center for Philanthropy and Civic Engagement at the American University in Cairo, 2012).

5. Nathan J. Brown, *When Victory Is Not an Option: Islamist Movements in Arab Politics* (Ithaca, NY: Cornell University Press, 2012), 217.

6. Lisa Wedeen, *Peripheral Visions: Publics, Power, and Performance in Yemen* (Chicago, IL: University of Chicago Press, 2008), 105. Wedeen defines the stripped-down notions of democracy as contested elections, referencing Adam Przeworski et al., *Democracy and Development: Political Institutions and Well-Being in the World, 1950–1990* (Cambridge: Cambridge University Press, 2000).

7. Gamal Abdel Gawad Soltan, Ahmed Nagui Qamha, and Subhi 'Asilah, "The Arab Barometer Project: Arab Republic of Egypt Public Opinion Report on the Most Important Political and Social Issues in Egypt," (Cairo: Al-Ahram Center for Political and Strategic Studies, 2011), 4.

8. Wedeen, *Peripheral Visions*, 104.

9. Ibid., 105.

10. Brown, *When Victory Is Not an Option*, 218.

11. Thomas Mann, *The Coming Victory of Democracy* (New York: Alfred A Knopf, 1938), 18–19.

12. Brown, *When Victory Is Not an Option*, 221.

13. Wedeen, *Peripheral Visions*, 109.

14. Interview, July 18, 2011.

15. Interview, April 24, 2012.

16. Interview, February 2, 2010.

17. Sheila Carapico, *Civil Society in Yemen: The Political Economy of Activism in Modern Arabia* (Cambridge: Cambridge University Press, 1998), 118.

18. Brown, *When Victory Is Not an Option*.

19. Interview, March 12, 2012.

20. Gilbert and Al-Jebaali point out that Bedouin women's voices are rarely heard outside the home. Gilbert and Al-Jebaali, "Not Philanthropists but Revolutionaries," 14.

21. Ibid.; Heba Aziz, "Employment in a Bedouin Community: The Case of the Town of Dahab in South Sinai," *Nomadic Peoples* 4, no. 2 (2000): 28–47; Ruth Kark and Seth J. Frantzman, "Empire, State and the Bedouin of the Middle East, Past and Present: A Comparative Study of Land and Settlement Policies," *Middle Eastern Studies* 48, no. 4 (2012): 487–510.

22. Interview, June 19, 2014.

23. Ali Aslam, *Ordinary Democracy: Sovereignty & Citizenship Beyond the Neoliberal Impasse* (New York: Oxford University Press, 2017), 162.

24. Ibid.

25. Asef Bayat, *Life as Politcs: How Ordinary People Change the Middle East* (Stanford: Stanford University Press, 2009).

26. Diana Fu, *Mobilizing Without the Masses: Control and Contention in China* (Cambridge: Cambridge University Press, 2018).

27. Political scientist Diana Fu found a similar strategy among NGOs in China. There, organization leaders coached participants in their programs to make demands on the state as individuals or as small groups acting outside of the formal NGO. Fu, *Mobilizing Without the Masses.*

28. Egypt was experiencing positive GDP growth in the years leading up to the 2011 uprisings, https://tradingeconomics.com/egypt/gdp-growth. However scholars have argued that Egyptians' perceptions of growing inequality, wrought by neoliberalism, was a key driver of the uprisings. See, for example, Alan Richards et al., *A Political Economy of the Middle East* (Boulder, CO: Westview Press, 2014); Hazem Fahmy, "An Initial Perspective on "the Winter of Discontent": The Root Causes of the Egyptian Revolution," *Social Research* 79, no. 2 (2012): 349–376; Mark Beissinger, Amaney A. Jamal, and Kevin Mazur, "Explaining Divergent Revolutionary Coalitions: Regime Strategies and the Structuring of Participation in the Tunisian and Egyptian Revolutions," *Comparative Politics* 48, no. 1 (2015): 1–44; Dina Shehata, "The Fall of the Pharaoh: How Hosni Mubarak's Reign Came to an End," *Foreign Affairs* 90, no. 3 (2011): 26–32.

29. Interview, October 21, 2017.

30. Interview, September 26, 2011.

31. Interview, July 18, 2011.

32. Interview, June 29, 2011.

33. Interview, May 22, 2012.

34. Interview, July 18, 2011.

35. Soltan, Qamha, and 'Asilah, "Arab Barometer Project." The next most commonly cited challenges were security and stability and financial corruption, coming in at 7 percent. While survey results came from only 1,220 respondents, they reflected sentiments expressed in everyday conversations at the time.

36. Tarek Masoud, *Counting Islam: Religion, Class, and Elections in Egypt* (Cambridge: Cambridge University Press, 2014).

37. Ibid., 126.

38. Interview, March 8, 2012.

39. Interview, March 28, 2012.

40. Operating foundations are established with an endowment but, like NGOs, mainly provide services instead of making grants.

41. Interview, March 28, 2012.

42. Ibid.

43. Andrea Teti, "The EU's First Response to the 'Arab Spring': A Critical Discourse Analysis of *the Partnership for Democracy and Shared Prosperity*," *Mediterranean Politics* 17, no. 3 (2012): 266–84; Steven Heydemann, "America's Response to the Arab Uprisings: US Foreign Assistance in an Era of Ambivalence," *Mediterranean Politics* 19 (2014): 299–317; Samuel Moyn, *Not Enough: Human Rights in an Unequal World* (Cambridge, MA: The Belknap Press of Harvard University Press, 2018).

44. Interview, March 12, 2012.

45. Interview, October 22, 2011.

46. Ibid.

47. Ibid.

48. Aziz, "Employment in a Bedouin Community."

49. Interview, October 22, 2011.

50. The donor, a smaller aid organization, was amenable to this.

51. Marwan Muasher, *The Second Arab Awakening and the Battle for Pluralism* (New Haven, CT: Yale University Press, 2014).

52. Interview, June 24, 2011.

53. Official statistics suggest that around one quarter of Egyptians are illiterate, however many of my interlocutors believed that official counts drastically underreported the true number of Egyptians who could not read or write.

54. Interview, July 1, 2014.

55. Interview, July 14, 2011.

56. Ibid.

57. Ibid.

58. Interview, March 8, 2012.

59. The transliteration of "h" in Arabic is often depicted as "7."

60. Silvia Mollicchi, "Al-Fan Midan Brings the Arts to the Streets," *Egypt Independent*, May 10, 2011.

61. Interview, June 24, 2014.

62. Interview, October 27, 2011.

63. Interview, June 28, 2012.

64. Participant observation, May 6, 2011.

65. Interview, June 30, 2011.

66. Jennifer Bremer, "Leadership and Collective Action in Egypt's Popular Committees: Emergence of Authentic Civic Activism in the Absence of the State," *International Journal of Not-for-Profit Law* 13, no. 4 (2011): 72.

67. Interview, July 10, 2014.

68. Interview, August 6, 2014.

69. Ibid.

70. Ibid.

71. Interview, October 22, 2011.

72. Interview, February 2, 2010.

73. Ibid.

74. Aslam, *Ordinary Democracy*, 82.

75. Interview, June 19, 2014.

76. Ibid.

77. Ibid.

78. Interview, September 26, 2011.

79. Interview, June 24, 2014.

80. Interview, August 12, 2014.

81. Ibid.

82. Interview, March 5, 2012.

83. Ibid.

84. For more on the concept of active citizenship, see Bayat, *Life as Politcs*.

85. A point also made by Gilbert and Al-Jebaali, "Not Philanthropists but Revolutionaries."

86. Aslam, *Ordinary Democracy*, 162.

87. James Ferguson, *The Anti-Politics Machine: "Development," Depoliticization, and Bureaucratic Power in Lesotho* (Minneapolis: University of Minnesota Press, 1994).

88. One NGO director lamented that Western donors "make things difficult. They want us to evaluate results. How to do this? Happier people? We can't [evaluate results] here in the Sinai as everything is connected." Interview, March 12, 2012.

89. Sarah Sunn Bush, *The Taming of Democracy Assistance: Why Democracy Promotion Does Not Confront Dictators* (Cambridge: Cambridge University Press, 2015).

Chapter 5

1. As chapter 2 noted, Tamarrod was largely co-opted by the Egyptian military, Interior Ministry, and state security services.

2. Ian Black and Patrick Kingsley, "Egypt: Interim Presidency Appoints PM and Vice-President," *Guardian*, July 10, 2013.

3. Kareem Fahim and Mayy El Sheikh, "Egyptian General Calls for Mass Protests," *New York Times*, July 24, 2013.

4. Human Rights Watch, "All According to Plan: The Rab'a Massacre and Mass Killings of Protesters in Egypt," (New York: Human Rights Watch, August 12, 2014).

5. David D. Kirkpatrick, "Egyptian Court Shuts Down the Muslim Brotherhood and Seizes Its Assets," *New York Times*, September 23, 2013.

6. Interview, July 9, 2014.

7. Ibid.

8. Interview, June 24, 2014.

9. Reem Gehad, "Egypt Amends Penal Code to Stipulate Harsher Punishments on Foreign Funding," *Ahram Online*, September 23, 2014.

10. Ahmed Naji, "Egypt's NGO Laws Continue to Threaten Civil Society," (Washington, DC: Tahrir Institute for Middle East Policy, 2014).

11. Merrit Kennedy, "Egypt's Civil Society Fears It Will Be Silenced," *ABC News*, October 4, 2014.

12. Interview, July 9, 2014.

13. Soyia Ellison, "Carter Center Closes Egypt Office; Calls for Stronger Protections for Democratic Rights and Freedoms," Carter Center News Release, October 14, 2014; Ahram Online, "Al-Mawred Al-Thaqafy Announces Freeze on All Activities in Egypt for the Present," November 5, 2014; Egypt Independent, "Rights Group Suspends Work, Cites 'Unfavorable Environment,'" November 10, 2014.

14. Cairo Institute for Human Rights Studies, "CIHRS Moves Its Regional and International Programs Outside Egypt," News Release, December 9, 2014.

15. Erin Cunningham, "Under Egypt's Sisi, Crackdown on Human Rights Groups Expands," *Washington Post*, May 21, 2015. EDA's CEO, Hossam el-Din Ali, was barred from traveling for a second time in February 2016 when he attempted to board a flight to the United States to attend an international conference on fighting corruption.

16. Egyptian Commission for Rights and Freedom, "A Sudden Search at the Egyptian Commission for Rights and Freedoms Headquarter in Cairo: A New Chapter in the State's Plan to Terminate Human Rights Work in Egypt," News Release, October 21, 2016.

17. Human Rights Watch, "Egypt: Renewed Crackdown on Independent Groups," (New York: Human Rights Watch, June 15, 2015).

18. Laura King and Ingy Hassieb, "Egyptian Court Bans Muslim Brotherhood, Orders Its Assets Confiscated," *Los Angeles Times*, September 23, 2013.

19. Mada Masr, "With Latest Crackdown, State Dissolves 380 NGOs in Just 2 Months," March 18, 2015.

20. Al-Masry al-Youm, "Social Solidarity Ministry Opens Foreign NGO Surveillance Unit," March 17, 2016.

21. Al-Shorouk, "Case 173 Foreign Financing," March 16, 2016.

22. Mada Masr, "2011 NGO Case Reopened against Hossam Bahgat, Gamal Eid and Others," March 17, 2016.

23. Mada Masr, "Judge Imposes Gag Order on NGO Foreign Funding Case," March 21, 2016.

24. Mada Masr, "New Regulation Mandates NGOs Consult Ministry Security Department Regarding Activities." August 25, 2016.

25. Cairo Institute for Human Rights Studies, "Egypt: A Letter and Legal Memorandum to the President; Demanding the Repeal of the NGO Law," News Release, December 4, 2016.

26. Personal communication, June 1, 2017.

27. "Egypt: A Letter and Legal Memorandum to the President."

28. While the Sisi regime's security measures were extreme, it is important to note that they were not entirely politically driven. The government had been battling an insurgent group called the Sinai Province (Wilayat Sinai) in the North Sinai, but attacks linked to the group were also reported in Cairo and other Nile Valley provinces. See BBC, "Sinai Province: Egypt's Most Dangerous Group," May 12, 2016; Jake Greene, "Wilayat Sinai's Tale of Control," (Washington, DC: The Tahrir Insitute for Middle East Policy, March 14, 2016).

29. Participant observation, October 19, 2017.

30. Participant observation, October 18, 2017.

31. Participant observation, October 19, 2017.

32. Ibid.

33. Participant observation, October 18, 2017.

34. Interview, October 16, 2017.

35. Ibid.

36. Ibid.

37. Participant observation, October 18, 2017.

38. Ibid.
39. Ibid.
40. Interview, October 16, 2017.
41. Ibid.
42. Participant observation, October 19, 2017.
43. Correspondence, January 17, 2017.
44. Interview, August 6, 2014.
45. Interview, July 10, 2014.
46. These included women in business suits speaking in public and shaking Sisi's hand.
47. Eman Maklad's Facebook page, https://www.facebook.com/eman.maklad.31/videos/1530378903710197/, accessed February 18, 2018.
48. Asef Bayat, *Revolution without Revolutionaries: Making Sense of the Arab Spring* (Stanford, CA: Stanford University Press, 2017), 224.

Conclusion

1. See especially Marc Lynch, ed. *The Arab Uprisings Explained: New Contentious Politics in the Middle East* (New York: Columbia University Press, 2014). A conference held June 4–6, 2011, at AUC entitled, "From Tahrir: Revolution or Democratic Transition?" offers one example of the many seminars that were held, http://www.transicion.org/20actividades/SeminarioEgipto/Democratic_Transition_Conference.pdf.
2. Steven A. Cook, *False Dawn: Protest, Democracy, and Violence in the New Middle East* (New York: Oxford University Press, 2017); Jason Brownlee, Tarek Masoud, and Andrew Reynolds, *The Arab Spring: Pathways of Repression and Reform* (New York: Oxford University Press, 2015); Robert Springborg, *Egypt* (Cambridge: Polity, 2018).
3. Brownlee, Masoud, and Reynolds, *Arab Spring*, 227–28.
4. Sheila Carapico, *Civil Society in Yemen: The Political Economy of Activism in Modern Arabia* (Cambridge: Cambridge University Press, 1998), 118.
5. Vincent Durac, "Social Movements, Protest Movements and Cross-Ideological Coalitions—the Arab Uprisings Re-Appraised," *Democratization* 22, no. 2 (2015): 239–58.
6. Mona Atia, *Building a House in Heaven: Pious Neoliberalism and Islamic Charity in Egypt* (Minneapolis: University of Minnesota Press, 2013), xviii.
7. Shadi Hamid, "Civil Society in the Arab World and the Dilemma of Funding," (Washington, DC: The Brookings Institution, October 21, 2010); Sarah Sunn Bush, *The Taming of Democracy Assistance: Why Democracy Promotion Does Not Confront Dictators* (Cambridge: Cambridge University Press, 2015); Sarah L. Henderson, *Building Democracy in Contemporary Russia: Western Support for Grassroots Organizations* (Ithaca, NY: Cornell University Press, 2003); Julie Hearn, "Aiding Democracy? Donors and Civil Society in South Africa," *Third World Quarterly* 21, no. 5 (2003): 815–30; Rosemary Hollis, "No Friend of Democratization: Europe's Role in the Genesis of the 'Arab Spring,'" *International Affairs* 88, no. 1 (2012): 81–94; Erin A.

Snider and David M. Faris, "The Arab Spring: U.S. Democracy Promotion in Egypt," *Middle East Policy* 18, no. 3 (2013): 49–62; Sheila Carapico, "Egypt's Civic Revolution Turns 'Democracy Promotion' on Its Head," in *Arab Spring in Egypt: Revolution and Beyond*, ed. Bahgat Korany and Rabab El-Mahdi (Cairo: The American University in Cairo Press, 2012), 199–222.

8. Michael Bratton, "The Politics of Government-NGO Relations in Africa," *World Development* 17, no. 4 (1989): 569–87; Larry Diamond, "Rethinking Civil Society: Toward Democratic Consolidation," *Journal of Democracy* 5 (1994): 4–18; Robert D. Putnam, *Making Democracy Work: Civic Traditions in Modern Italy* (Princeton, NJ: Princeton University Press, 1993).

9. Anthony Bebbington, "New States, New NGOs? Crises and Transitions among Rural Development NGOs in the Andean Region," *World Development* 25, no. 11 (1997): 1755–65; Gerard Clarke, "Non-Governmental Organizations (NGOs) and Politics in the Developing World," *Political Studies* XLVI (1998): 36–52; Jude Howell and Jenny Pearce, *Civil Society and Development: A Critical Exploration* (Boulder, CO: Lynne Rienner Publishers, Inc., 2001).

10. Henderson, *Building Democracy in Contemporary Russia*; David Suárez and Mary Kay Gugerty, "Funding Civil Society? Bilateral Government Support for Development NGOs," *VOLUNTAS: International Journal of Voluntary and Nonprofit Organizations* 27, no 6 (2016): 2617–40; Masooda Bano, "Dangerous Correlations: Aid's Impact on NGOs' Performance and Ability to Mobilize Members in Pakistan," *World Development* 36, no. 11 (2008): 2297–313.

11. Khaldoun AbouAssi, "Hands in the Pockets of Mercurial Donors: NGO Response to Shifting Funding Priorities," *Nonprofit and Voluntary Sector Quarterly* 42, no. 3 (2013): 584–602; Gina Porter, "NGOs and Poverty Reduction in a Globalizing World: Perspectives from Ghana," *Progress in Development Studies* 3, no. 2 (2003): 131–45; Dean Chahim and Aseem Prakash, "NGOization, Foreign Funding, and the Nicaraguan Civil Society," *VOLUNTAS: International Journal of Voluntary and Nonprofit Organizations* 25, no. 2 (2014): 487–513.

12. Asef Bayat, *Revolution without Revolutionaries: Making Sense of the Arab Spring* (Stanford, CA: Stanford University Press, 2017); Carapico, "Egypt's Civic Revolution Turns 'Democracy Promotion' on Its Head"; Mona Atia and Catherine Herrold, "Governing through Patronage: The Rise of NGOs and the Fall of Civil Society in Palestine and Morocco," *VOLUNTAS: International Journal of Voluntary and Nonprofit Organizations* 29, no. 5 (2018): 1044–54.

13. Quintan Wiktorowicz, "Civil Society as Social Control: State Power in Jordan," *Comparative Politics* 33, no. 1 (2000): 43–61; Kendra Dupuy, James Ron, and Aseem Prakash, "Hands Off My Regime! Governments' Restrictions on Foreign Aid to Non-Governmental Organizations in Poor and Middle-Income Countries," *World Development* 84 (2016): 299–311.

14. See especially Carapico, "Egypt's Civic Revolution Turns 'Democracy Promotion' on Its Head"; Bush, *Taming of Democracy Assistance*.

15. Mary Kaldor and Ivan Vejvoda, "Democratization in Central and East European Countries," *International Affairs* 73, no. 1 (1997): 59–82.

16. The United States is not the only donor to come under fire for the ineffectiveness of its democracy aid. Similar criticisms have been levied against European donors. However, given the nuanced approaches and practices of different donor agencies, these policy recommendations focus only on the United States rather than attempting to be more broadly instructive.

17. Carapico describes democracy promotion organizations as resembling think tanks: Sheila Carapico, *Political Aid and Arab Activism: Democracy Promotion, Justice, and Representation* (Cambridge: Cambridge University Press, 2014).

18. For example, Black Lives Matter, #MeToo, Occupy Wall Street, the Color Revolutions, the Anti-extradition Bill Movement in Hong Kong, etc.

19. Scholars agree with this assessment. See in particular Steven Heydemann, "America's Response to the Arab Uprisings: US Foreign Assistance in an Era of Ambivalence," *Mediterranean Politics* 19, no. 3 (2014): 299–317; Andrea Teti, "The EU'S First Response to the 'Arab Spring': A Critical Discourse Analysis of *The Partnership for Democracy and Shared Prosperity*," *Mediterranean Politics* 17, no. 3 (2012): 266–84.

20. See, for example, Bush, *Taming of Democracy Assistance*; Thomas Carothers and Diane DeGramont, *Development Aid Confronts Politics: The Almost Revolution* (Washington, DC: Carnegie Endowment for International Peace, 2013); Tamara Cofman Wittes, *Freedom's Unsteady March: America's Role in Building Arab Democracy* (Washington, DC: The Brookings Institution, 2008).

21. Dupuy, Ron, and Prakash, "Hands Off My Regime!"; Susan Appe and Christopher L. Pallas, "Aid Reduction and Local Civil Society: Causes, Comparisons, and Consequences," *VOLUNTAS: International Journal of Voluntary and Nonprofit Organizations* 29, no. 2 (2018): 245–55.

22. See, for example, Gardiner Harris, "Trump Administration Cuts More than $200 Million in Aid for Palestinians," *New York Times*, August 24, 2018; Jack Corrigan and Government Executive, "The Hollowing out of the State Department Continues," *Atlantic*, February 11, 2018; Carol Morello and Karoum Demirjian, "Trump Administration Is Considering Pulling Back $3 Billion in Foreign Aid," *Washington Post*, August 17, 2018.

23. Some private foundations have already begun removing silos. For example the Ford Foundation recently eliminated traditional program areas (arts and culture, democracy, education, etc.) and structured all of its grantmaking around efforts to challenge inequality. See https://www.fordfoundation.org/work/challenging-inequality/.

24. Jacques Defourny and Marthe Nyssens, "Mapping Social Enterprise Models: Some Evidence from the 'Icsem' Project," *Social Enterprise Journal* 13, no. 4 (2017): 318–28.

25. For more on the global proliferation of community foundations and their theorized roles as change agents, see Jenny Harrow, Tobias Jung, and Susan D. Phillips, "Community Foundations: Agility in the Duality of Foundation and Community," in *The Routledge Companion to Philanthropy*, ed. Tobias Jung, Susan D. Phillips, and Jenny Harrow (London: Routledge, 2016), 308–21; Catherine Herrold, "A Conceptual Model of Foundations' Leadership Capacity in Times of Change: Lessons from Egypt," *Nonprofit and Voluntary Sector Quarterly* 47, no. 2 (2018): 286–303.

26. For more on how international staff carry out and negotiate US foreign policies in target countries, and how these practices affect the impact and effectiveness of the aid provided, see Susanna P. Campbell, *Global Governance and Local Peace: Accountability and Performance in International Peacebuilding* (Cambridge: Cambridge University Press, 2018); Séverine Autesserre, *Peaceland: Conflict Resolution and the Everyday Politics of International Intervention* (Cambridge: Cambridge University Press, 2014). While these books focus on peacebuilding, their arguments are relevant for the policies and practices of democracy aid as well.

27. Atia and Herrold, "Governing through Patronage"; Islah Jad, *Palestinian Women's Activism: Nationalism, Secularism, Islamism* (Syracuse, NY: Syracuse University Press, 2018); Sari Hanafi and Linda Tabar, "The Intifada and the Aid Industry: The Impact of the New Liberal Agenda on the Palestinian NGOs," *Comparative Studies of South Asia, Africa and the Middle East* 23, no. 1&2 (2003): 205–14; Bush, *Taming of Democracy Assistance*; Carapico, *Political Aid and Arab Activism*.

28. Sheila Carapico also makes this point. See *Political Aid and Arab Activism*.

29. As Steven Cook notes, a number of people abroad believe that US democratic institutions have not lived up to their promise of delivering a "free, equal, and tolerant" society. Steven Cook, "The Middle East Doesn't Admire America Anymore: What a Late-Night Meal in Italy Taught Me About U.S. Power in the Arab World," *Foreign Policy,* February 5, 2019.

30. The perils of persisting in a strategy of domination are set forth in Seteven Weber and Bruce W. Jentleson, *The End of Arrogance: America in the Global Competition of Ideas* (Cambridge, MA: Harvard University Press, 2010).

31. Andrew Miller and Seth Binder, "The Case for Arms Embargoes against Uncooperative Partners," *War On The Rocks*, May 10, 2019.

32. Arshad Mohammed and Warren Strobel, "Exclusive: U.S. To Withhold up to $290 Million in Egypt Aid" *Reuters*, August 22, 2017; Nicole Gaouette, "US, Citing Human Rights, Cuts Some Egypt Aid," *CNN,* August 23, 2017.

33. Jenna Johnson, "In Cairo, Pence Praises the Friendship and Partnership between the U.S. And Egypt," *Washington Post*, January 20, 2018.

34. After various candidates were eliminated due to repressive tactics by the Sisi regime, only one "opposition" candidate remained: Mousa Mostafa Mousa, Ghad party leader who has long supported Sisi. For more see Ruth Michaelson, "Egypt Election: Sole Challenger to Sisi Registers at Last Minute," *Guardian*, January 29, 2018; Declan Walsh, "Visiting Egypt, Tillerson Is Silent on Its Wave of Repression," *New York Times*, February 12, 2018.

Bibliography

Abdelrahman, Maha. *Civil Society Exposed: The Politics of NGOs in Egypt*. London: Tauris Academic Studies, 2004.

Abdelrahman, Maha. *Egypt's Long Revolution: Protest Movements and Uprisings*. Oxfordshire: Routledge, 2015.

Abdou, Ehaab, Mona Atia, Noha Hussein, Home Kharas, and Amira Maaty. "How Can the U.S. and International Finance Institutions Best Engage Egypt's Civil Society?" Washington, DC: The Brookings Institution, 2011.

AbouAssi, Khaldoun. "Hands in the Pockets of Mercurial Donors: NGO Response to Shifting Funding Priorities." *Nonprofit and Voluntary Sector Quarterly* 42, no. 3 (2013): 584–602.

AbouAssi, Khaldoun, and Deborah Trent. "Understanding Local Participation Amidst Challenges: Evidence from Lebanon in the Global South." *VOLUNTAS: International Journal of Voluntary and Nonprofit Organizations* 24, no. 4 (2013): 1113–37.

Adly, Amr Ismail. "Politically Embedded Cronyism: The Case of Post-Liberalization Egypt." *Business and Politics* 11, no. 4 (2009): Article 3.

Agarwal, Bina. "Participatory Exclusions, Community Forestry, and Gender: An Analysis for South Asia and a Conceptual Framework." *World Development* 29, no. 10 (2001): 1623–48.

Agati, Mohamed. "Undermining Standards of Good Governance: Egypt's NGO Law and Its Impact on the Transparency and Accountability of Csos." *International Journal of Not-for-Profit Law* 9, no. 2 (2007): 56–75.

Ahram Online. "Al Mawred Al Thaqafy Announces Freeze on All Activities in Egypt for the Present." November 5, 2014.

Al-Arabiya News. "Egypt Slaps Travel Ban on U.S. NGO Staff, Washington Urges Lifting Ban 'Immediately.'" January 26, 2012.

Al-Fagar. "Official Report to the Prosecutor Uncovers Names and Amounts: 1.34 Billion Egyptian Pounds Given from the United States, Europe and the Gulf to Egyptian Organizations in the Last Four Months." September 26, 2011.

Al Jazeera. "Egypt PM Appoints New Key Ministers." March 6, 2011.

Al Jazeera. "Egypt Security Forces Storm NGO Offices." December 29, 2011.

Al Jazeera. "Egypt Shuts El Nadeem Centre for Torture Victims." February 9, 2017.

Al-Masry al-Youm. "Ministry Sources: NGOs Received Le1.7 Bn in Foreign Funds since June 2010." December 24, 2011.

Al-Masry al-Youm. "Social Solidarity Ministry Opens Foreign NGO Surveillance Unit." March 17, 2016.

Al-Shorouk. "Case 173 Foreign Financing." March 16, 2016.

Alaimo, Kara. "How the Facebook Arabic Page 'We Are All Khaled Said' Helped Promote the Egyptian Revolution." *Social Media + Society*, July–December (2015): 1–10.

Albrecht, Holger. "How Can Opposition Support Authoritarianism? Lessons from Egypt." *Democratization* 12, no. 3 (2005): 378–97.

Albrecht, Holger, and Oliver Schlumberger. "'Waiting for Godot': Regime Change without Democratization in the Middle East." *International Political Science Review* 25, no. 4 (2004): 371–92.

Alcaro, Riccardo. "Introduction. Bouazizi's Inextinguishable Fire." In *Re-Thinking Western Policies in Light of the Arab Uprisings*, edited by Riccardo Alcaro and Miguel Haubrich-Seco, 11–20. Rome: Edizioni Nuova Cultura, 2012.

Amin, Khaled. "International Assistance to Egypt after the 2011 and 2013 Uprisings: More Politics and Less Development." *Mediterranean Politics* 19, no. 3 (2014): 392–412.

Amin, Magdi, Ragui Assaad, Nazar Al-Baharna, Kemal Dervis, Raj M. Desai, Navtej S. Dhillon, Ahmed Galal, Hafez Ghanem, and Carol Graham. *After the Spring: Economic Transitions in the Arab World*. New York: Oxford University Press, 2012.

Appe, Susan, and Christopher L. Pallas. "Aid Reduction and Local Civil Society: Causes, Comparisons, and Consequences." *VOLUNTAS: International Journal of Voluntary and Nonprofit Organizations* 29, no. 2 (2018): 245–55.

Arab Foundations Forum. "Arab Foundations Forum Annual Meeting 2011: Towards Effective Philanthropy in the Arab Region." Beirut: Arab Foundations Forum, 2011.

Arnstein, Sherry R. "A Ladder of Citizen Participation." *Journal of the American Institute of Planners* 35, no. 4 (1969): 216–24.

Aslam, Ali. *Ordinary Democracy: Sovereignty & Citizenship Beyond the Neoliberal Impasse*. New York: Oxford University Press, 2017.

Associated Press. "Egypt Sends 43 NGO Workers to Trial over Funds." *Salon*, February 5, 2012.

Atia, Mona. *Building a House in Heaven: Pious Neoliberalism and Islamic Charity in Egypt*. Minneapolis: University of Minnesota Press, 2013.

Atia, Mona. "The Arab Republic of Egypt." In *From Charity to Social Change: Trends in Arab Philanthropy*, edited by Barbara Lethem Ibrahim and Dina H. Sherif, 23–43. Cairo: The American University in Cairo Press, 2008.

Atia, Mona, and Catherine Herrold. "Governing through Patronage: The Rise of NGOs and the Fall of Civil Society in Palestine and Morocco." *VOLUNTAS: International Journal of Voluntary and Nonprofit Organizations* 29, no. 5 (2018): 1044–54.

Autesserre, Séverine. *Peaceland: Conflict Resolution and the Everyday Politics of International Intervention*. Cambridge: Cambridge University Press, 2014.

Aziz, Heba. "Employment in a Bedouin Community: The Case of the Town of Dahab in South Sinai." *Nomadic Peoples* 4, no. 2 (2000): 28–47.

Aziz, Sahar F. "Military Electoral Authoritarianism in Egypt." *Election Law Journal* 16, no. 2 (2017): 280–95.

Baer, Gabriel. "The Waqf as a Prop for the Social System (Sixteenth–Twentieth Centuries)." *Islamic Law and Society* 4, no. 3 (1997): 264–97.

Balboa, Cristina M. *The Paradox of Scale: How NGOs Build, Maintain, and Lose Authority in Environmental Governance*. Cambridge, MA: MIT Press, 2018.

Bano, Masooda. "Dangerous Correlations: Aid's Impact on NGOs' Performance and Ability to Mobilize Members in Pakistan." *World Development* 36, no. 11 (2008): 2297–313.

Barkan, Joel D. "Democracy Assistance: What Recipients Think." *Journal of Democracy* 23, no. 1 (2012): 129–37.

Bartley, Tim. "How Foundations Shape Social Movements: The Construction of an Organizational Field and the Rise of Forest Certification." *Social Problems* 54, no. 3 (2007): 229–55.

Bassiouni, M. Cherif. "Corruption Cases against Officials of the Mubarak Regime." Washington, DC: Egyptian American Rule of Law Association, 2012.

Bayat, Asef. *Life as Politics: How Ordinary People Change the Middle East.* Stanford, CA: Stanford University Press, 2009.

Bayat, Asef. *Revolution without Revolutionaries: Making Sense of the Arab Spring.* Stanford, CA: Stanford University Press, 2017.

BBC. "Egypt's Islamist Parties Win Elections to Parliament." January 21, 2012.

BBC. "Egyptian Voters Back New Constitution in Referendum." December 25, 2012.

BBC. "Sinai Province: Egypt's Most Dangerous Group." May 12, 2016.

Bebbington, Anthony. "New States, New NGOs? Crises and Transitions among Rural Development NGOs in the Andean Region." *World Development* 25, no. 11 (1997): 1755–65.

Beinin, Joel. "Egyptian Workers and January 25th: A Social Movement in Historical Context." *Social Research* 79, no. 2 (2012): 323–48.

Beinin, Joel. "The Working Class and Peasantry in the Middle East: From Economic Nationalism to Neoliberalism." *Middle East Report* 210 (1999): 18–22.

Beinin, Joel. *Workers and Thieves: Labor Movements and Popular Uprisings in Tunisia and Egypt.* Stanford, CA: Stanford University Press, 2015.

Beinin, Joel. "Workers' Protest in Egypt: Neo-Liberalism and Class Struggle in 21st Century." *Social Movement Studies* 8, no. 4 (2009): 449–54.

Beinin, Joel, and Frederic Vairel, eds. *Social Movements, Mobilization, and Contestation in the Middle East and North Africa.* 2nd ed. Stanford, CA: Stanford University Press, 2013.

Beissinger, Mark, Amaney A. Jamal, and Kevin Mazur. "Explaining Divergent Revolutionary Coalitions: Regime Strategies and the Structuring of Participation in the Tunisian and Egyptian Revolutions." *Comparative Politics* 48, no. 1 (2015): 1–44.

Bellin, Eva. *Stalled Democracy: Capital, Labor, and the Paradox of State-Sponsored Development.* Ithaca, NY: Cornell University Press, 2002.

Ben-Nefissa, Sarah, Nabil Abd Al-Fattah, Sari Hanafi, and Carlos Milani, eds. *NGOs and Governance in the Arab World.* Cairo: The American University in Cairo Press, 2005.

Benjamin, Lehn M., and Kevin F. F. Quigley. "U.S. Foundations and International Grantmaking." In *American Foundations: Their Roles and Contributions to Society,* edited by Helmut K. Anheier and David C. Hammack, 237–62. Washington, DC: The Brookings Institution, 2010.

Bermeo, Sarah Blodgett. *Targeted Development: Industrialized Country Strategy in a Globalizing World.* New York: Oxford University Press, 2018.

Bianchi, Robert. *Unruly Capitalism: Associational Life in Twentieth-Century Egypt.* New York: Oxford University Press, 1989.

Black, Ian, and Patrick Kingsley. "Egypt: Interim Presidency Appoints PM and Vice-President." *Guardian,* July 10, 2013.

Blaydes, Lisa. *Elections and Distributive Politics in Mubarak's Egypt.* Cambridge: Cambridge University Press, 2011.

Bleich, Erik, and Robert Pekkanen. "How to Report Interview Data." In *Interview Research in Political Science,* edited by Layna Mosley, 84–105. Ithaca, NY: Cornell University Press, 2013.

Bogaert, Koenraad. "Contextualizing the Arab Revolts: The Politics Behind Three Decades of Neoliberalism in the Arab World." *Middle East Critique* 22, no. 3 (2013): 213–34.

Bonner, Michael, Mine Ener, and Amy Singer, eds. *Poverty and Charity in Middle East Contexts*. Albany: State University of New York Press, 2003.

Brass, Jennifer N. *Allies or Adversaries: NGOs and the State in Africa*. Cambridge: Cambridge University Press, 2016.

Bratton, Michael. "The Politics of Government-NGO Relations in Africa." *World Development* 17, no. 4 (1989): 569–87.

Brechenmacher, Saskia. "Civil Society under Assault: Repression and Responses in Russia, Egypt, and Ethiopia." Washington, DC: Carnegie Endowment for International Peace, 2017.

Bremer, Jennifer. "Egypt: Civil Society Success or Spontaneous Combustion?" *Inside ISTR* 19, no. 1 (2011): 1, 4.

Bremer, Jennifer. "Leadership and Collective Action in Egypt's Popular Committees: Emergence of Authentic Civic Activism in the Absence of the State." *International Journal of Not-for-Profit Law* 13, no. 4 (2011): 70–92.

Brouwer, Imco. "Weak Democracy and Civil Society Promotion: The Cases of Egypt and Palestine." In *Funding Virtue: Civil Society Aid and Democracy Promotion*, edited by Marina Ottaway and Thomas Carothers, 21–48. Washington, DC: Carnegie Endowment for International Peace, 2000.

Brown, Nathan J. "The Transition: From Mubarak's Fall to the 2014 Presidential Election." In *Egypt after the Spring: Revolt and Reaction*, edited by Emile Hokayem, 15–32. London: Routledge, 2016.

Brown, Nathan J. *When Victory Is Not an Option: Islamist Movements in Arab Politics*. Ithaca, NY: Cornell University Press, 2012.

Brownlee, Jason. *Authoritarianism in an Age of Democratization*. Cambridge: Cambridge University Press, 2007.

Brownlee, Jason. *Democracy Prevention: The Politics of the U.S.-Egyptian Alliance*. Cambridge: Cambridge University Press, 2012.

Brownlee, Jason, Tarek Masoud, and Andrew Reynold. *The Arab Spring: Pathways of Repression and Reform*. New York: Oxford University Press, 2015.

Brumberg, Daniel. "Democratization in the Arab World? The Trap of Liberalized Autocracy." *Journal of Democracy* 13, no. 4 (2002): 56–68.

Brumberg, Daniel. "Liberalization Versus Democracy: Understanding Arab Political Reform." Middle East Series Working Paper No. 37. Washington, DC: Carnegie Endowment for International Peace, 2003.

Bush, Sarah Sunn. *The Taming of Democracy Assistance: Why Democracy Promotion Does Not Confront Dictators*. Cambridge: Cambridge University Press, 2015.

Cairo Institute for Human Rights Studies. "CIHRS Moves Its Regional and International Programs Outside Egypt." News Release, December 9, 2014.

Cairo Institute for Human Rights Studies. "Egypt: A Letter and Legal Memorandum to the President; Demanding the Repeal of the NGO Law." News Release, December 4, 2016.

Campbell, Lisa M., and Arja Vainio-Mattila. "Participatory Development and Community-Based Conservation: Opportunities Missed for Lessons Learned?" *Human Ecology* 31, no. 3 (2003): 417–37.

Campbell, Susanna P. *Global Governance and Local Peace: Accountability and Performance in International Peacebuilding*. Cambridge: Cambridge University Press, 2018.

Carapico, Sheila. *Civil Society in Yemen: The Political Economy of Activism in Modern Arabia*. Cambridge: Cambridge University Press, 1998.

Carapico, Sheila. "Egypt's Civic Revolution Turns 'Democracy Promotion' on Its Head." In *Arab Spring in Egypt: Revolution and Beyond*, edited by Bahgat Korany and Rabab El-Mahdi, 199–222. Cairo: The American University in Cairo Press, 2012.

Carapico, Sheila. "Foreign Aid for Promoting Democracy in the Arab World." *Middle East Journal* 56, no. 3 (2002): 379–95.

Carapico, Sheila. *Political Aid and Arab Activism: Democracy Promotion, Justice, and Representation*. Cambridge: Cambridge University Press, 2014.

Carapico, Sheila. "What Does It Mean 'Promoting Democratization'?" *International Journal of Middle East Studies* 41, no. 1 (2009): 7–9.

Carothers, Thomas. "Democracy Assistance: Political Vs. Developmental?" *Journal of Democracy* 20, no. 1 (2009): 5–19.

Carothers, Thomas. "Promoting Democracy and Fighting Terror." *Foreign Affairs* 82, no. 1 (2003): 84–97.

Carothers, Thomas. "Revitalizing U.S. Democracy Assistance: The Challenge of USAID." Washington, DC: Carnegie Endowment for International Peace, 2009.

Carothers, Thomas, and Diane DeGramont. *Development Aid Confronts Politics: The Almost Revolution*. Washington, DC: Carnegie Endowment for International Peace, 2013.

Chahim, Dean, and Aseem Prakash. "NGOization, Foreign Funding, and the Nicaraguan Civil Society." *VOLUNTAS: International Journal of Voluntary and Nonprofit Organizations* 25 (2014): 487–513.

Chambers, Robert. "The Origins and Practice of Participatory Rural Appraisal." *World Development* 22, no. 7 (1994): 953–69.

Chick, Kristen. "Convictions Put Egypt's Beleaguered NGOs into Deeper Chill." *Christian Science Monitor*, June 4, 2013.

Chick, Kristen. "Why Egypt Is Angry over $65 Million in US Democracy Grants." *Christian Science Monitor*, August 12, 2011.

Clark, Janine. *Islam, Charity, and Activism: Middle-Class Networks and Social Welfare in Egypt, Jordan, and Yemen*. Bloomington: Indiana University Press, 2004.

Clark, Janine. "The Economic and Political Impact of Economic Restructuring on NGO-State Relations in Egypt." In *Economic Liberalization, Democratization and Civil Society in the Developing World*, edited by Remonda Bensabat Kleinberg and Janine A. Clark, 157–79. Hampshire: Macmillan Press Ltd, 2000.

Clark, John. "The State, Popular Participation, and the Voluntary Sector." *World Development* 23, no. 4 (1995): 593–601.

Clarke, Gerard. "Non-Governmental Organizations (NGOs) and Politics in the Developing World." *Political Studies* XLVI (1998): 36–52.

Clarke, Killian. "Saying 'Enough': Authoritarianism and Egypt's Kefaya Movement." *Mobilization: An International Quarterly* 16, no. 4 (2011): 397–416.

Cohen, John M., and Norman T. Uphoff. "Participation's Place in Rural Development: Seeking Clarity through Specificity." *World Development* 8, no. 3 (1980): 213–35.

Cook, Steven A. *False Dawn: Protest, Democracy, and Violence in the New Middle East*. New York: Oxford University Press, 2017.

Cook, Steven A. "The Middle East Doesn't Admire America Anymore: What a Late-Night Meal in Italy Taught Me About U.S. Power in the Arab World." *Foreign Policy*, February 5, 2019.

Cook, Steven A. *The Struggle for Egypt: From Nasser to Tahrir Square*. New York: Oxford University Press, 2012.

Cooke, Bill, and Uma Kothari. *Participation: The New Tyranny?* London: Zed Books, 2001.

Cornwall, Andrea, and Celestine Nyamu-Musembi. "Putting the 'Rights-Based Approach' to Development into Perspective." *Third World Quarterly* 25, no. 8 (2004): 1415–37.

Corrigan, Jack, and Government Executive. "The Hollowing out of the State Department Continues." *Atlantic*, February 11, 2018.

Cunningham, Erin. "Under Egypt's Sisi, Crackdown on Human Rights Groups Expands." *Washington Post*, May 21, 2015.

Daily News Egypt. "Judge Says NGOs Were Lawfully Inspected, Not 'Raided.'" February 8, 2012.

Defourny, Jacques, and Marthe Nyssens. "Mapping Social Enterprise Models: Some Evidence from the 'Icsem' Project." *Social Enterprise Journal* 13, no. 4 (2017): 318–28.

Diamond, Larry. "Rethinking Civil Society: Toward Democratic Consolidation." *Journal of Democracy* 5 (1994): 4–18.

Dicklitch, Susan. *The Elusive Promise of NGOs in Africa: Lessons from Uganda.* London: Palgrave Macmillan UK, 1998.

Dupuy, Kendra, James Ron, and Aseem Prakash. "Hands Off My Regime! Governments' Restrictions on Foreign Aid to Non-Governmental Organizations in Poor and Middle-Income Countries." *World Development* 84 (2016): 299–311.

Dupuy, Kendra E., James Ron, and Aseem Prakash. "Who Survived? Ethiopia's Regulatory Crackdown on Foreign-Funded NGOs." *Review of International Political Economy* 22, no. 2 (2015): 419–56.

Durac, Vincent. "Social Movements, Protest Movements and Cross-Ideological Coalitions—the Arab Uprisings Re-appraised." *Democratization* 22, no. 2 (2015): 239–58.

Ebrahim, Alnoor. "Accountability Myopia: Losing Sight of Organizational Learning." *Nonprofit and Voluntary Sector Quarterly* 34, no. 1 (2005): 56–87.

Edwards, Michael, and David Hulme. "Scaling up NGO Impact on Development: Learning from Experience." *Development in Practice* 2, no. 2 (1992): 77–91.

Egypt Independent. "Rights Group Suspends Work, Cites 'Unfavorable Environment.'" November 10, 2014.

Egyptian Commission for Rights and Freedom. "A Sudden Search at the Egyptian Commission for Rights and Freedoms Headquarter in Cairo: A New Chapter in the State's Plan to Terminate Human Rights Work in Egypt." News Release, October 21, 2016.

El-Meehy, Asya. "Egypt's Popular Committees: From Moments of Madness to NGO Dilemmas." *Middle East Report* 42, Winter (2012): 29–33.

El-Mikawy, Noha, Mohamed Mohieddin, and Sarah El-Ashmaouy. "Egypt: The Protracted Transition from Authoritarianism to Democracy and Social Justice." In *Democratic Transitions in the Arab World*, edited by Ibrahim Elbadawi and Samir Makdisi, 133–83. Cambridge: Cambridge University Press, 2017.

El-Tarouty, Safinaz. *Businessmen, Clientelism, and Authoritarianism in Egypt.* New York: Palgrave Macmillan, 2015.

Elagati, Mohamed. "Foreign Funding in Egypt after the Revolution." Madrid, Spain: Arab Forum for Alternatives, FRIDE, and HIVOS, 2013.

Elbers, Willem, and Bas Arts. "Keeping Body and Soul Together: Southern NGOs' Strategic Responses to Donor Constraints." *International Review of Administrative Sciences* 77, no. 4 (2011): 713–32.

Ellison, Soyia. "Carter Center Closes Egypt Office; Calls for Stronger Protections for Democratic Rights and Freedoms." Carter Center News Release, October 14, 2014.

Eltantawy, Nahed, and Julie B. Wiest. "Social Media in the Egyptian Revolution: Reconsidering Resource Mobilization Theory." *International Journal of Communication* 5 (2011): 1207–24.

Elyachar, Julia. *Markets of Disposition: NGOs, Economic Development and the State in Cairo.* Durham, NC: Duke University Press, 2005.

Ener, Mine. *Managing Egypt's Poor and the Politics of Benevolence, 1800–1952.* Princeton, NJ: Princeton University Press, 2003.

European Commission. "European Neighbourhood and Partnership Instrument 2007–2013: Overview of Activities and Results." Brussels: European Commission, September 8, 2014.

Fahim, Kareem, and Mayy El Sheikh. "Egyptian General Calls for Mass Protests." *New York Times*, July 24, 2013.

Fahmy, Hazem. "An Initial Perspective on "the Winter of Discontent": The Root Causes of the Egyptian Revolution." *Social Research* 79, no. 2 (2012): 349–376.

Farah, Nadia Ramsis. *Egypt's Political Economy: Power Relations in Development.* Cairo: The American University in Cairo Press, 2009.

Ferguson, James. *The Anti-Politics Machine: "Development," Depoliticization, and Bureaucratic Power in Lesotho.* Minneapolis: University of Minnesota Press, 1994.

Fleishman, Joel. *The Foundation: A Great American Secret.* New York: Public Affairs, 2007.

Fouad, Viviane, Nadia Ref'at, and Samir Murcos. "From Inertia to Movement: A Study of the Conflict over NGO Law in Egypt." In *NGOs and Governance in the Arab World*, edited by Sarah Ben Nefissa, Nabil Abd Al-Fattah, Sari Hanafi and Carlos Milani, 101–22. Cairo: The American University in Cairo Press, 2005.

Fu, Diana. *Mobilizing Without the Masses: Control and Contention in China.* Cambridge: Cambridge University Press, 2018.

Fung, Archon, and Erik Olin Wright. *Deepening Democracy: Institutional Innovations in Empowered Participatory Governance.* Vol. 4. New York: Verso, 2003.

Gandhi, Jennifer, and Ellen Lust-Okar. "Elections under Authoritarianism." *Annual Review of Political Science* 12 (2009): 403–22.

Gaouette, Nicole. "US, Citing Human Rights, Cuts Some Egypt Aid." *CNN*, August 23, 2017.

Gause, F. Gregory. "Why Middle East Studies Missed the Arab Spring: The Myth of Authoritarian Stability." *Foreign Affairs* 90, no. 4 (2011): 81–84, 85–90.

Gaventa, John. "Towards Participatory Governance: Assessing the Transformative Possibilities." In *Participation: From Tyranny to Transformation?: Exploring New Approaches to Participation in Development*, edited by Samuel Hickey and Giles Mohan, 25–41. London: Zed Books, 2004.

Gehad, Reem. "Egypt Amends Penal Code to Stipulate Harsher Punishments on Foreign Funding." *Ahram Online*, September 23, 2014.

Gilbert, Hilary, and Mohammed Khedr Al-Jebaali. "Not Philanthropists but Revolutionaries: Promoting Bedouin Participation in the New Egypt: A Case Study from South Sinai." Cairo: John D. Gerhart Center for Philanthropy and Civic Engagement at the American University in Cairo, 2012.

Golub, Stephen J. "Democracy as Development: A Case for Civil Society Assistance in Asia." In *Funding Virtue: Civil Society Aid and Democracy Promotion*, edited by Marina Ottaway and Thomas Carothers, 135–58. Washington, DC: Carnegie Endowment for International Peace, 2000.

Goss, Kristin A. "Foundations of Feminism: How Philanthropic Patrons Shaped Gender Politics." *Social Science Quarterly* 88, no. 5 (2007): 1174–91.

Greene, Jake. "Wilayat Sinai's Tale of Control." Washington, DC, The Tahrir Institute for Middle East Policy, March 14, 2016.

Greenfield, Danya, and Rosa Balfour. "Arab Awakening: Are the US and EU Missing the Challenge? " Washington, DC: The Atlantic Council of the United States, 2012.

Gunning, Jeroen, and Ilan Zvi Baron. *Why Occupy a Square? People, Protests and Movements in the Egyptian Revolution*. New York: Oxford University Press, 2014.

Hadenius, Axel, and Fredrick Uggla. "Making Civil Society Work, Promoting Democratic Development: What Can States and Donors Do?" *World Development* 24, no. 10 (1996): 1621–39.

Haines, Herbert H. "Black Radicalization and the Funding of Civil Rights: 1957–1970." *Social Problems* 32, no. 1 (1984): 31–43.

Hamid, Shadi. "Civil Society in the Arab World and the Dilemma of Funding." Washington, DC, The Brookings Institution, October 21, 2010.

Hammack, David C., and Helmut Anheier. "American Foundations: Their Roles and Contributions to Society." In *American Foundations: Roles and Contributions*, edited by Helmut K. Anheier and David C. Hammack, 3–28. Washington, DC: The Brookings Institution, 2010.

Hamoud, Rania. "Time of Up-Rise: Threat or Opportunity?" Paper presented at the Takaful 2012: Second Annual Conference on Arab Philanthropy and Civic Engagement, Cairo, 2012.

Hanafi, Sari, and Linda Tabar. "The Intifada and the Aid Industry: The Impact of the New Liberal Agenda on the Palestinian NGOs." *Comparative Studies of South Asia, Africa and the Middle East* 23, no. 1&2 (2003): 205–14.

Hanley, Charles J. "US Training Quietly Nurtured Young Arab Democrats." *Washington Post*, March 13, 2011.

Harris, Gardiner. "Trump Administration Cuts More Than $200 Million in Aid for Palestinians." *New York Times*, August 24, 2018.

Harrow, Jenny, Tobias Jung, and Susan D. Phillips. "Community Foundations: Agility in the Duality of Foundation and Community." In *The Routledge Companion to Philanthropy*, edited by Tobias Jung, Susan D. Phillips, and Jenny Harrow, 308–21. London: Routledge, 2016.

Hauslohner, Abigail. "Ready for Change in Egypt." *Time*, July 12, 2010.

Hawthorne, Amy. "Middle Eastern Democracy: Is Civil Society the Answer?" Carnegie Papers: Middle East Series 44. Washington, DC: Carnegie Endowment for International Peace, 2004.

Hearn, Julie. "Aiding Democracy? Donors and Civil Society in South Africa." *Third World Quarterly* 21, no. 5 (2003): 815–30.

Hellyer, H. A. "Egypt: The Politics of Remembering Death." Washington, DC: The Brookings Institution, 2013.

Henderson, Sarah L. *Building Democracy in Contemporary Russia: Western Support for Grassroots Organizations*. Ithaca, NY: Cornell University Press, 2003.

Henderson, Sarah L. "Selling Civil Society: Western Aid and the Nongovernmental Organization Sector in Russia." *Comparative Political Studies* 35, no. 2 (2002): 139–67.

Herrold, Catherine. "A Conceptual Model of Foundations' Leadership Capacity in Times of Change: Lessons from Egypt." *Nonprofit and Voluntary Sector Quarterly* 47, no. 2 (2018): 286–303.

Herrold, Catherine. "NGO Policy in Pre- and Post-Mubarak Egypt: Effects on NGOs' Roles in Democracy Promotion." *Nonprofit Policy Forum* 7, no. 2 (2016): 189–212.

Herrold, Catherine, and Mona Atia. "Competing rather than Collaborating: Egyptian Nongovernmental Organizations in Turbulence." *Nonprofit Policy Forum* 7, no. 3 (2016): 389–407.

Heurlin, Christopher. "Governing Civil Society: The Political Logic of NGO-State Relations under Dictatorship." *VOLUNTAS: International Journal of Voluntary and Nonprofit Organizations* 21, no. 2 (2010): 220–39.

Heydemann, Steven. "America's Response to the Arab Uprisings: US Foreign Assistance in an Era of Ambivalence." *Mediterranean Politics* 19, no. 3 (2014): 299–317.

High Representative of the European Union for Foreign Affairs and Security Policy. "Joint Communication to the European Parliament, the Council, the European Economic and Social Committee and the Committee of the Regions." Brussels: European Commission, 2011.

Hill, Evan. "Background: SCAF's Last-Minute Power Grab." *Al Jazeera*, June 17, 2012.

Hoexter, Miriam. "Charity, the Poor, and Distribution of Alms in Ottoman Algiers." In *Poverty and Charity in Middle Eastern Contexts*, edited by Mine Ener, Michael Bonner, and Amy Singer, 145–64. Albany: State University of New York Press, 2003.

Hollis, Rosemary. "No Friend of Democratization: Europe's Role in the Genesis of the 'Arab Spring.'" *International Affairs* 88, no. 1 (2012): 81–94.

Howell, Jude. "Shall We Dance? Welfarist Incorporation and the Politics of State-Labour NGO Relations." *China Quarterly* 223 (2015): 702–23.

Howell, Jude, and Jenny Pearce. *Civil Society and Development: A Critical Exploration.* Boulder, CO: Lynne Rienner Publishers, Inc., 2001.

Hulme, David, and Michael Edwards. "Too Close for Comfort? The Impact of Official Aid on Nongovernmental Organizations." *World Development* 24, no. 6 (1996): 961–73.

Human Rights Watch. "All According to Plan: The Rab'a Massacre and Mass Killings of Protesters in Egypt." New York: Human Rights Watch, August 12, 2014.

Human Rights Watch. "Egypt: Renewed Crackdown on Independent Groups." New York: Human Rights Watch, June 15, 2015.

Ibrahim, Barbara Lethem, and Dina H. Sherif, eds. *From Charity to Social Change: Trends in Arab Philanthropy.* Cairo: The American University in Cairo Press, 2008.

Ibrahim, Saad Eddin. *Egypt, Islam, and Democracy: Critical Essays.* Cairo: The American University in Cairo Press, 2002.

Ibrahim, Saad Eddin, Amani Kandil, Moheb Zaki, Nagah Hassan, Ola El-Ramly, Sahar Al-Ga'arah, Mohammad Sami, and Ahmed Abu Al-Yazid, eds. *An Assessment of Grassroots Participation in the Development of Egypt.* Cairo: The American University in Cairo Press, 1997.

Immerwahr, Daniel Sepinuck. *Thinking Small: The United States and the Lure of Community Development.* Cambridge, MA: Harvard University Press, 2015.

Inskeep, Steve. "Ramy Essam: The Singer of the Egyptian Revolution." *National Public Radio*, March 15, 2011.

International Republican Institute. "Egyptian Public Opinion Survey: April 14–April 27, 2011." Washington, DC: International Republican Institute, 2011.

Ismail, Salwa. *Political Life in Cairo's New Quarters: Encountering the Everyday State.* Minneapolis: University of Minnesota Press, 2006.

Jad, Islah. *Palestinian Women's Activism: Nationalism, Secularism, Islamism.* Syracuse, NY: Syracuse University Press, 2018.

Jamal, Amaney A. *Barriers to Democracy: The Other Side of Social Capital in Palestine and the Arab World*. Princeton, NJ: Princeton University Press, 2007.

Jamal, Amaney A. *Of Empires and Citizens: Pro-American Democracy or No Democracy at All?* Princeton, NJ: Princeton University Press, 2012.

Jamal, Manal A. "Democracy Promotion, Civil Society Building, and the Primacy of Politics." *Comparative Political Studies* 45, no. 1 (2012): 3–31.

Jenkins, J. Craig, and Abigail L. Halci. "Grassrooting the System? The Development and Impact of Social Movement Philanthropy." In *Philanthropic Foundations: New Scholarship, New Possibilities*, edited by Ellen Condliffe Lagemann, 229–56. Bloomington: Indiana University Press, 1999.

Jenkins, J. Craig, and Craig M. Eckert. "Channeling Black Insurgency: Elite Patronage and Professional Social Movement Organizations in the Development of the Black Movement." *American Sociological Review* 51 (1986): 812–29.

Johnson, Jenna. "In Cairo, Pence Praises the Friendship and Partnership between the U.S. And Egypt." *Washington Post*, January 20, 2018.

Kaldor, Mary, and Ivan Vejvoda. "Democratization in Central and East European Countries." *International Affairs* 73, no. 1 (1997): 59–82.

Kandil, Amani. "Defining the Nonprofit Sector: Egypt." Working Paper No. 10. Baltimore: The Johns Hopkins Institute for Policy Studies, 1993.

Kark, Ruth, and Seth J. Frantzman. "Empire, State and the Bedouin of the Middle East, Past and Present: A Comparative Study of Land and Settlement Policies." *Middle Eastern Studies* 48, no. 4 (2012): 487–510.

Kausch, Kristina. "Assessing Democracy Assistance: Egypt." Madrid, Spain: FRIDE, 2010.

Kennedy, Merrit. "Egypt's Civil Society Fears It Will Be Silenced." *ABC News,* October 4, 2014.

Ketchley, Neil. *Egypt in a Time of Revolution: Contentious Politics and the Arab Spring* Cambridge: Cambridge University Press, 2017.

King, Gary, Robert O. Keohane, and Sidney Verba. *Designing Social Inquiry: Scientific Inference in Qualitative Research*. Princeton, NJ: Princeton University Press, 1994.

King, Laura, and Ingy Hassieb. "Egyptian Court Bans Muslim Brotherhood, Orders Its Assets Confiscated." *Los Angeles Times*, September 23, 2013.

Kinninmont, Jane. " 'Bread, Dignity, and Social Justice': The Political Economy of Egypt's Transition." London: Royal Institute of International Affairs, 2012.

Kirkpatrick, David D. "Egyptian Court Shuts Down the Muslim Brotherhood and Seizes Its Assets." *New York Times*, September 23, 2013.

Kirkpatrick, David D. "Egypt's Military Expands Power, Raising Alarms." *New York Times*, October 14, 2011.

Kirkpatrick, David D., and Steven Lee Myers. "U.S. Defendants Leave Egypt Amid Growing Backlash." *New York Times*, March 1, 2012.

Kohl-Arenas, Erica. *The Self-Help Myth: How Philanthropy Fails to Alleviate Poverty*. Oakland: University of California Press, 2015.

Krishna-Hensel, Sai Felicia. *Authoritarian and Populist Influences in the New Media*. London: Routledge, 2018.

Kuran, Timur. "The Provision of Public Goods under Islamic Law: Origins, Impact, and Limitations of the Waqf System." *Law and Society Review* 35, no. 4 (2001): 841–98.

Lafi Youmans, William. "An Unwilling Client: How Hosni Mubarak's Egypt Defied the Bush Administration's 'Freedom Agenda.'" *Cambridge Review of International Affairs* 29, no. 4 (2016): 1209–32.

Langohr, Vickie. "Too Much Civil Society, Too Little Politics: Egypt and Liberalizing Arab Regimes." *Comparative Politics* 36, no. 2 (2004): 181–204.

Lesch, Ann M. "Egypt's Spring: Causes of the Revolution." *Middle East Policy* 18, no. 3 (2011): 35–48.

Lewis, David. "Civil Society and the Authoritarian State: Cooperation, Contestation and Discourse." *Journal of Civil Society* 9, no. 3 (2013): 325–40.

Lim, Merlyna. "Clicks, Cabs, and Coffee Houses: Social Media and Oppositional Movements in Egypt, 2004–2011." *Journal of Communication* 62, no. 2 (2012): 231–48.

Londoño, Ernesto, and William Wan. "American Pro-Democracy Organization Workers in Cairo Take Shelter at U.S. Embassy." *Washington Post*, January 29, 2012.

Lust-Okar, Ellen. "Divided They Rule: The Management and Manipulation of Political Opposition." *Comparative Politics* 36, no. 2 (2004): 159–79.

Lynch, Marc. "Calvinball in Cairo." *Foreign Policy*, June 18, 2012.

Lynch, Marc, ed. *The Arab Uprisings Explained: New Contentious Politics in the Middle East*. New York: Columbia University Press, 2014.

Mada Masr. "2011 NGO Case Reopened against Hossam Bahgat, Gamal Eid and Others." March 17, 2016.

Mada Masr. "Judge Imposes Gag Order on NGO Foreign Funding Case." March 21, 2016.

Mada Masr. "New Regulation Mandates NGOs Consult Ministry Security Department Regarding Activities." August 25, 2016.

Mada Masr. "With Latest Crackdown, State Dissolves 380 NGOs in Just 2 Months." March 18, 2015.

Mann, Thomas. *The Coming Victory of Democracy*. New York: Alfred A Knopf, 1938.

Mansour, Sherif. "Enough Is Not Enough: Achievements and Shortcomings of Kefaya, the Egyptian Movement for Change." In *Civilian Jihad: Nonviolent Struggle, Democratization, and Governance in the Middle East*, edited by Maria Stepan, 205–18. New York: Palgrave Macmillan, 2009.

Masoud, Tarek. *Counting Islam: Religion, Class, and Elections in Egypt*. Cambridge: Cambridge University Press, 2014.

Masoud, Tarek. "The Road to (and from) Liberation Square." *Journal of Democracy* 22, no. 3 (2011): 20–34.

Mathie, Alison, and Gord Cunningham. "From Clients to Citizens: Asset-Based Community Development as a Strategy for Community-Driven Development." *Development in Practice* 13, no. 5 (2003): 474–86.

McAdam, Doug. *Political Process and the Development of Black Insurgency, 1930–1970*. Chicago, IL: University of Chicago Press, 1982.

McAdam, Doug, Sidney Tarrow, and Charles Tilly. *Dynamics of Contention*. Cambridge: Cambridge University Press, 2001.

McGreal, Chris. "Egypt's Military Rejects Swift Transfer of Power and Suspends Constitution." *Guardian*, February 13, 2011.

Michaelson, Ruth. "Egypt Election: Sole Challenger to Sisi Registers at Last Minute." *Guardian*, January 29, 2018.

Michels, Ank, and Laurens De Graaf. "Examining Citizen Participation: Local Participatory Policy Making and Democracy." *Local Government Studies* 36, no. 4 (2010): 477–91.

Miller, Andrew, and Seth Binder. "The Case for Arms Embargoes against Uncooperative Partners." *War on the Rocks*, May 10, 2019.

Mills, C. Wright. *The Power Elite*. New ed. New York: Oxford University Press, 2000.

Mohammed, Arshad, and Warren Strobel. "Exclusive: U.S. To Withhold up to $290 Million in Egypt Aid." *Reuters*, August 22, 2017.

Mohan, Giles, and Kristian Stokke. "Participatory Development and Empowerment: The Dangers of Localism." *Third World Quarterly* 21, no. 2 (2000): 247–68.

Mollicchi, Silvia. "Al-Fan Midan Brings the Arts to the Streets." *Egypt Independent*, May 10, 2011.

Momani, Bessma. *Arab Dawn: Arab Youth and the Demographic Dividend They Will Bring*. Toronto: University of Toronto Press, 2015.

Morello, Carol, and Karoum Demirjian. "Trump Administration Is Considering Pulling Back $3 Billion in Foreign Aid." *Washington Post*, August 16, 2018.

Mosley, Layna, ed. *Interview Research in Political Science*. Ithaca, NY: Cornell University Press, 2013.

Moukheiber, Zina. "Billionaire Egyptian Family Faces Potential Blow to Reputation." *Forbes*, April 25, 2011.

Moyn, Samuel. *Not Enough: Human Rights in an Unequal World*. Cambridge, MA: The Belknap Press of Harvard University Press, 2018.

Muasher, Marwan. *The Second Arab Awakening and the Battle for Pluralism*. New Haven, CT: Yale University Press, 2014.

Naji, Ahmed. "Egypt's NGO Laws Continue to Threaten Civil Society." Washington, DC, The Tahrir Institute for Middle East Policy, October 17, 2014.

Pateman, Carole. *Participation and Democratic Theory*. Cambridge: Cambridge University Press, 1970.

Peri, Oded. "Waqf and Ottoman Welfare Policy." *Journal of the Economic and Social History of the Orient* 35 (1992): 167–86.

Pfeifer, Karen, Marsha Pripstein-Posusney, Djavad Salehi-Isfahani, and Steve Niva. "Reform or Reaction? Dilemmas of Economic Development in the Middle East." *Middle East Report* 210 (1999): 14–15.

Pioppi, Daniela. "Privatization of Social Services as a Regime Strategy: The Revival of Islamic Endowments (Awqaf) in Egypt." In *Debating Arab Authoritarianism*, edited by Oliver Schlumberger, 129–42. Stanford, CA: Stanford University Press, 2007.

Porter, Gina. "NGOs and Poverty Reduction in a Globalizing World: Perspectives from Ghana." *Progress in Development Studies* 3, no. 2 (2003): 131–45.

Przeworski, Adam, Michael E. Alvarez, Jose Antonio Cheibub, and Fernando Limongi. *Democracy and Development: Political Institutions and Well-Being in the World, 1950–1990*. Cambridge: Cambridge University Press, 2000.

Putnam, Robert D. *Bowling Alone: The Collapse and Revival of American Community*. New York: Simon & Schuster, 2000.

Putnam, Robert D. *Making Democracy Work: Civic Traditions in Modern Italy*. Princeton, NJ: Princeton University Press, 1993.

Rahnema, Majid. "Participatory Action Research: The 'Last Temptation of Saint' Development." *Alternatives* 15, no. 2 (1990): 199–226.

Reich, Rob. "Repugnant to the Whole Idea of Democracy? On the Role of Foundations in Democratic Societies." *PS: Political Science and Politics* 49, no. 3 (2016): 466–72.

Reimann, Kim D. "A View from the Top: International Politics, Norms and the Worldwide Growth of NGOs." *International Studies Quarterly* 50, no. 1 (2006): 45–67.

Richards, Alan, John Waterbury, Melani Cammett, and Ishac Diwan. *A Political Economy of the Middle East*. Boulder, CO: Westview Press, 2014.

Roll, Stephan. "Egypt's Business Elite after Mubarak: A Powerful Player between Generals and Brotherhood." Berlin: Stiftung Wissenschaft und Politik, German Institute for International and Security Affairs, 2013.

Roll, Stephan. "'Finance Matters!' The Influence of Financial Sector Reforms on the Development of the Entrepreneurial Elite in Egypt." *Mediterranean Politics* 15, no. 3 (2010): 349–70.

Saif, Ibrahim. "Challenges of Egypt's Economic Transition." The Carnegie Papers. Washington, DC: Carnegie Endowment for International Peace, 2011.

Salamon, Lester. "The Rise of the Nonprofit Sector." *Foreign Affairs* 73, no. 3 (1994): 111–24.

Saleh, Yasmine, and Dina Zayed. "Mubarak's Sons Back in Court on Graft Charges." *Reuters,* July 9, 2012.

Sayigh, Yezid. "The Specter of 'Protected Democracy' in Egypt." Washington, DC: Carnegie Endowment for International Peace, December 15, 2011.

Schatz, Edward. *Political Ethnography: What Immersion Contributes to the Study of Power.* Chicago, IL: University of Chicago Press, 2013.

Schedler, Andreas, ed. *Electoral Authoritarianism: The Dynamics of Unfree Competition.* Boulder, CO: Lynne Rienner, 2006.

Schmitter, Phillipe, and Gerhard Lehmbruch, eds. *Trends toward Corporatist Intermediation.* London: Sage, 1979.

Schwedler, Jillian. *Faith in Moderation: Islamist Parties in Jordan and Yemen.* Cambridge: Cambridge University Press, 2006.

Scott, James M., and Carie A. Steele. "Assisting Democrats or Resisting Dictators? The Nature and Impact of Democracy Support by the United States National Endowment for Democracy, 1990–99." *Democratization* 12, no. 4 (2005): 439–60.

Sen, Amartya. *Development as Freedom.* New York: Anchor Books, 1999.

Sharp, Jeremy. "Egypt: Background and U.S. Relations." Washington, DC: The Congressional Research Service, 2012.

Shehata, Dina. "The Fall of the Pharaoh: How Hosni Mubarak's Region Came to an End." *Foreign Affairs* 90, no. 3 (2011): 26–32.

Shenker, Jack. "Supporters Give Mohamed Elbaradei Hero's Welcome at Cairo Airport." *Guardian,* February 19, 2010.

Shorbagy, Manar. "Understanding Kefaya: The New Politics in Egypt." *Arab Studies Quarterly* 29, no. 1 (2007): 39–60.

Singer, Amy. *Charity in Islamic Societies.* Cambridge: Cambridge University Press, 2008.

Singerman, Diane. *Avenues of Participation: Family, Politics, and Networks in Urban Quarters of Cairo.* Princeton, NJ: Princeton University Press, 1995.

Škoba, Laine. "European Endowment for Democracy: Hopes and Expectations." Brussels: Library of the European Parliament, 2013.

Snider, Erin A., and David M. Faris. "The Arab Spring: U.S. Democracy Promotion in Egypt." *Middle East Policy* 18, no. 3 (2013): 49–62.

Soliman, Samer. *The Autumn of Dictatorship: Fiscal Crisis and Political Change in Egypt under Mubarak.* Stanford, CA: Stanford University Press, 2011.

Sowers, Jeannie. "Egypt in Transition." In *Journey to Tahrir: Revolution, Protest, and Social Change in Egypt,* edited by Jeannie Sowers and Chris Toensing, 1–20. London: Verso, 2012.

Soltan, Gamal Abdel Gawad, Ahmed Nagui Qamha, and Subhi 'Asilah. "The Arab Barometer Project: Arab Republic of Egypt Public Opinion Report on the Most

Important Political and Social Issues in Egypt." Cairo, Egypt: Al-Ahram Center for Political and Strategic Studies, June 2011.

Springborg, Robert. *Egypt*. Cambridge: Polity, 2018.

Springborg, Robert. "The Political Economy of the Arab Spring." *Mediterranean Politics* 16, no. 3 (2011): 427–33.

Stacher, Joshua. *Adaptable Autocrats: Regime Power in Egypt and Syria*. Stanford, CA: Stanford University Press, 2012.

Stier, Ken. "Egypt's Pursuit of the Corrupt: Justice or a Witch Hunt?" *TIME*, February 22, 2011.

Stilt, Kristen A. "The End of 'One Hand': The Egyptian Constitutional Declaration and the Rift between the 'People' and the Supreme Council of the Armed Forces." Faculty Working Paper No. 208. Chicago: Northwestern University Pritzker School of Law, 2012. https://scholarlycommons.law.northwestern.edu/cgi/viewcontent.cgi?article=1 207&context=facultyworkingpapers

Strasser, Max. "Egypt Warns of Foreign Meddling as US Pushes on with Democracy Programs." *Al-Masry al-Youm*, July 5, 2011.

Suárez, David, and Mary Kay Gugerty. "Funding Civil Society? Bilateral Government Support for Development NGOs." *VOLUNTAS: International Journal of Voluntary and Nonprofit Organizations* 27, no. 6 (2016): 2617–40.

Sullivan, Dennis J. *Private Voluntary Organizations in Egypt: Islamic Development, Private Initiatives, and State Control*. Gainesville: University of Florida Press, 1994.

Swedlund, Haley J. *The Development Dance: How Donors and Recipients Negotiate the Delivery of Foreign Aid*. Ithaca, NY: Cornell University Press, 2017.

Teets, Jessica C. *Civil Society under Authoritarianism: The China Model*. Cambridge: Cambridge University Press, 2014.

Teti, Andrea. "The EU's First Response to the 'Arab Spring': A Critical Discourse Analysis of *The Partnership for Democracy and Shared Prosperity*." *Mediterranean Politics* 17, no. 3 (2012): 266–84.

Tocqueville, Alexis de. *Democracy in America and Two Essays on America*. London: Penguin Books, 2003. First published 1835.

United States Government Accountability Office. "Democracy Assistance: Lessons Learned from Egypt Should Inform Future U.S. Plans." Washington, DC: United States Government Accountability Office, July 24, 2014.

Verba, Sidney, Kay Lehman Schlozman, and Henry E. Brady. *Voice and Equality: Civic Voluntarism in American Politics*. Cambridge, MA: Harvard University Press, 1995.

Walsh, Declan. "Visiting Egypt, Tillerson Is Silent on Its Wave of Repression." *New York Times*, February 12, 2018.

Wampler, Brian. *Activating Democracy in Brazil: Popular Participation, Social Justice, and Interlocking Institutions*. Notre Dame, IN: University of Notre Dame Press, 2015.

Waterbury, John. *The Egypt of Nasser and Sadat: The Political Economy of Two Regimes*. Princeton, NJ: Princeton University Press, 1993.

Weber, Steven, and Bruce W. Jentleson. *The End of Arrogance: America in the Global Competition of Ideas*. Cambridge, MA: Harvard University Press, 2010.

Wedeen, Lisa. *Peripheral Visions: Publics, Power, and Performance in Yemen*. Chicago, IL: University of Chicago Press, 2008.

Westminster Foundation for Democracy Limited. "Annual Report and Accounts 2011/ 12." London: Westminster Foundation for Democracy, 2012.

Wiarda, Howard J. "Arab Fall or Arab Winter?" *American Foreign Policy Interests* 34, no. 3 (2012): 134–37.

Wickham, Carrie Rosefsky. "Beyond Democratization: Political Change in the Arab World." *PS: Political Science and Politics* 27, no. 3 (1994): 507–9.

Wickham, Carrie Rosefsky. *Mobilizing Islam: Religion, Activism, and Political Change in Egypt.* New York: Columbia University Press, 2002.

Wickham, Carrie Rosefsky. *The Muslim Brotherhood: Evolution of an Islamist Movement.* Princeton, NJ: Princeton University Press, 2013.

Wiktorowicz, Quintan. "Civil Society as Social Control: State Power in Jordan." *Comparative Politics* 33, no. 1 (2000): 43–61.

Wittes, Tamara Cofman. *Freedom's Unsteady March: America's Role in Building Arab Democracy.* Washington, DC: The Brookings Institution, 2008.

Yom, Sean L. "Civil Society and Democratization in the Arab World." *Middle East Review of International Affairs* 9, no. 4 (2005): 14–33.

Zayed, Ibtessam, and Salma Hussein. "Mohamed Mansour: A Tarnished Captain of Industry." *Ahram Online*, March 20, 2011.

Index

For the benefit of digital users, indexed terms that span two pages (e.g., 52–53) may, on occasion, appear on only one of those pages.

Figures are indicated by *f* following the page number

accountability
  foreign aid and, 84–86
  government, 9–10, 93–94, 120,
    132–33, 155
  grantmaking and, 151
agency (human quality), 94, 95–96, 100,
    120–22, 148, 153
  collective, 4–5, 103–4, 113–16, 118, 120,
    121, 138–39, 140–41, 148, 149
Ahram, al, 127
aid
  bilateral and multilateral, 19, 38, 83
  competing for, 46, 49
  conditionality of, 155
  democracy vs. economic, 4, 148
  military, 54, 155
  withholding, 155
  See also democracy aid
Ali, Mohammed, 28–30
American University in Cairo, 11, 13,
    81–83, 82*f*
Arab
  culture, 1
  region or world, 24, 52, 104,
    138–39, 151
Arab Barometer, 153
Arab Foundations Forum, 1, 11, 12, 13,
    37–38, 90, 112–13
Arab Penal Reform Organization, 127
Arab Spring, 1, 138, 144–45, 156
Arabic, 12, 13–14, 81, 105–6
Arabic Network for Human Rights
    Information, 128–29
army, 50, 51, 58, 61–62, 63–64, 74–75,
    79, 138
  See also military

art, 108–10, 111–12, 133, 137, 147, 156–57
  and culture, 4–5, 14, 19, 20, 34, 35, 103,
    126, 133, 147, 148, 153
  See also graffiti
Aslam, Ali, 95–96
associations. See *gam'iyyat*
AUC. *See* American University in Cairo
austerity, 32
Australia, 38, 83
authoritarianism, 4–5, 6, 7–8, 18–19, 49,
    52, 53, 71, 77–78, 93, 96, 114–15, 120,
    135–36, 137, 138–39, 156–57
  as regime or government, 1–3, 15, 77,
    83, 95–96, 124
autocrat. *See* dictator

Bahgat, Hossam, 128–29
Baradei, Mohammed el-, 55–56
Bayat, Asef, 95–96, 137
Bedouin, 47, 69, 90–91, 94–95,
    100–3, 104–5
Beirut, 1–2
ben Ali, Zine el-Abidine, 1–2, 50, 138
bias, 11–12, 91–92
board (of foundation), 10–11, 13, 36, 73–74,
    76, 77, 85
  co-optation of, 8, 17–18, 34, 38, 39, 40–41,
    42–43, 75, 129
Bouazizi, Mohammed, 56, *See also* Tunisia
boycott, 85
Brazil, 12
bread, 53, 96–97, 100–1, 117,
    135–36, 142–43
Bread Riots, 32
Britain. *See* United Kingdom
Brown, Nathan, 91–92, 94–95

budget, 70, 127–28, 136–37, 151–52
    civil society and, 2, 20, 24, 69, 72, 76,
        138, 139
    Egyptian foundations and,
        36–37, 75–76
    national, 31–32, 70
    participatory democracy and, 22
    Western donor, 2, 5, 20, 23, 24, 72–73,
        78, 84, 138, 139–40, 145, 146
bureaucracy, 23, 29–31, 39, 44, 52,
    79–80, 151–52
Bush, George W., 54

Cairo
    income inequality in, 135–37
    NGO centralization in, 13–14, 35–36,
        72, 110, 134
    rural Egypt vs, 101, 110, 115,
        119–20, 132–33
    shanty towns of, 69, 99
Cairo Institute for Human Rights Studies
    (CIHRS), 127–29
Canada, 38, 83, 146
capitalism
    crony, 16, 31–32, 42, 96–97
Carapico, Sheila, 20, 94
CARE International, 38
Caritas Internationalis, 38
Carnegie Endowment, 8, 36
charity
    development vs., 34, 44–47, 120
    Egyptian culture and, 27–29,
        34–35, 44–45
    NGOs and, 34–35, 48–49, 87–88
    politics and, 98–99
    private, 29–30, 94
church, 34–35, 46–47, 63
CIHRS. See Cairo Institute for Human
    Rights Studies
cities, 33–34, 135, 145, 148, 150–52
civic life, 146
    political life and, 57–58, 147
    see also under civil society: participation in
civil society
    activists, 8–9, 11, 59, 70, 138
    authoritarianism and, 6, 15, 71, 77,
        136–37, 138–40
    control over, 1, 3, 24–26, 48, 51, 63–64,
        77, 118, 123, 125, 135–36

democracy and, 2, 6–7, 15–16, 20, 24,
    51, 56–57, 69, 72, 77, 79, 83–84, 113,
    141–42, 154–55
    leaders, 2, 129
    NGOs and, 7, 17, 32–33, 38, 44, 56–57,
        76–78, 79, 141–42
    organizations, 2, 7, 12, 15, 20, 25, 51, 71
    participation in, 15–16, 17–18,
        49, 51, 69
    theories of, 6–7, 15–16
class (social), 10, 31, 32, 36, 56, 77, 96–97,
    99, 112–15, 135–36, 140
collective action, 113, 118. see also under
    agency: collective
colonialism, 30. see also under foundation:
    community
community
    business, 37, 74–75
    development, 14, 21, 34, 37, 59–60,
        148, 156–57
    infrastructure, 4, 102–3, 113–14, 120, 148
    international, 22, 38, 49, 73
    meetings, 4, 101–2
    organizing, 59–60
constitution, 39–40, 59, 80,
    83–84, 121–22
    Egyptian, 62–63, 70–71, 123–24, 130
co-optation, 15, 18–19, 24, 33, 39
corporate foundation. See foundation
corruption, 140, 154–55. see also under
    capitalism: crony
coup, 124, 125–26

debate
    democracy and, 4–5, 91, 104,
        144–45, 148
    policy, 39–40, 43
    public, 9–10, 22, 50, 139, 140–41, 143
debt, 31–32, 52
deliberation. See debate
democracy (types of)
    participatory, 22–24
    procedural, 20, 92, 149, 152
    substantive, 7, 93
    See also qāt
Democracy Academy, 81
democracy aid
    characteristics of Western, 20, 80–81,
        83, 121, 145

criticism of, 7, 25, 79–80, 86–87, 89,
    141, 144
definition of, 83–84
reform of, 7, 14–15, 20–21, 144–55
democracy promotion
    budget for, 5, 24, 72–73, 138
    language of, 20, 82–83, 86
    suppression of, 5, 56–57, 65–69
    Western playbook, 80, 83–84, 89, 121–22,
        145, 146, 156–57
    See also budget; non-governmental
        organization
development
    community, 14, 21, 34, 37, 59–60,
        148, 156–57
    experts, 21–23, 37
    international, 21, 23–24
    participatory democracy and, 3–4, 10–11,
        19, 21–23
    socioeconomic, 2–4, 6, 10, 17, 18–19,
        20, 73, 77, 78, 83, 89, 103, 120–21,
        136–37, 140–41, 142, 143, 148,
        149, 156
    sustainable, 21, 32–33, 35–38, 118–19
Development Partners Group
    (DPG), 38, 73
dictator, 1–2, 6, 7, 20, 25, 39, 84–85, 121–22,
    138–39, 144, 155, 156, 157
dignity, 53, 69, 91–93, 96, 102–3, 115, 116,
    120, 138–39, 143–44, 148, 149, 153, 155
discussion. See debate
disenfranchisement, 5, 91
donors
    criticism of, 154
    local, 14, 40, 134–35, 141
    Western, 2, 5, 13–14, 32–33, 35–36,
        45–46, 57, 72, 73–74, 78, 81–82,
        86–87, 88, 100–1, 103, 121,
        139–40, 156
DPG. See Development Partners Group

Economic Reform and Structural
    Adjustment Program
    (ERSAP), 31–32
economy
    of charity, 28–29
    downturn in, 3, 25, 32, 51, 75–76, 77
    inequality and, 10, 96–98
    privatization and, 31–32, 52

ECRF. See Egyptian Commission for
    Rights and Freedoms
education
    democracy aid and, 19, 20, 81, 101–2,
        103–5, 147
    NGOs and, 35, 68–69, 101, 119, 140,
        148, 150–51
    welfare state and, 29–30, 43, 99–100
EFG Hermes Foundation, 36, 42–43, 74
EFG Hermes Holding Company, 36
Egyptian Commission for Rights and
    Freedoms (ECRF), 127–28
Egyptian Democratic Academy, 127–29
Egyptian Initiative for Personal
    Rights, 128–29
Egyptian Trade Union Federation
    (ETUF), 55
Eid, Gamal, 128–29
Eid al-Adha, 27, 28f, 48–49
elections
    2012, 51, 65, 70, 79
    2014, 124
    authoritarianism and, 20–21, 93, 138
    contested, 92, 93–94
    free and fair, 16, 18–19, 20, 59, 65, 83–84
    Islamists and, 62, 64–65, 98
    monitoring of, 53–54, 80–82, 84
    NGO programming and, 4, 20, 80,
        103, 120
    rigged, 91
    voting in, 20–21, 70, 101, 102–3, 104,
        105–6, 120
equality, 96, 115–16, 132–33, 143–45,
    149, 154–56
ERSAP. See Economic Reform and
    Structural Adjustment Program
European Neighborhood Partnership
    Initiative, 72–73
European Union (EU), 4, 57, 85–86, 105–6,
    119, 125, 130

façade, 3–4, 43, 135–37
Facebook, 50, 53, 55–56, 108–10, See also
    social media
Fan Midan, al- 110–11
fear, 52, 61, 66–67, 93, 125–26,
    139, 156–57
    culture of, 2–3, 13, 48, 50–51, 88,
        133–34, 142

federation. See *ittihad*

Ford Foundation, 36, 38

foundation (types of)
community, 13, 37, 44–45, 48, 59–60, 151
corporate, 36–37
modern origins of Egyptian, 1, 8
private, 19, 30, 33, 35–38, 39–40, 44, 147
See also board; donors; grants; non-governmental organization

fragmentation
of NGO sector, 9, 44, 46, 115–16
of society, 93, 113–14

free market doctrine, 149

free speech. *See under* freedom: of expression

freedom
academic, 53–54
of expression, 4–5, 7, 10, 72–73, 103, 110–11, 121, 124, 144–45, 147, 148, 149, 153
as protest slogan ("bread, freedom and human dignity"), 53, 96–97, 142–43
socioeconomic justice and, 5, 91–92, 100–1, 102–3, 120–21, 140, 142–43, 149
See also art; graffiti

Freedom and Justice Party, 51, 64–65, 70.
See also Muslim Brotherhood

funding. *See* aid; grants

Gaddafi, Muammar, 52, 138

gam'iyyat, 9, 22, 31, 33–34, 127

gas (cooking and heating), 59–60, 108–10, 117, 135–36

General Federation of NGOs and Foundations, 30–31, 38

Gerhart Center for Philanthropy and Civic Engagement at the AUC, 11, 13, 37–38

Ghazl al-Mahallah, 55

Ghonim, Wael, 56

Global Fund for Community Foundations, 13

Global South, 6, 21–22, 142

GONGO. *See* government-organized NGO

government-organized NGO, 18, 43

graffiti, 50, 108*f*, 108–10, 109*f*, 110*f*, 111*f*, 112*f*

grants
administration of, 19, 76, 83, 144
application for, 84, 86, 148–49, 151–55
evaluation of, 84, 151–55
silos and, 147–49
See also aid; foundation; non-governmental organization

happiness, 121–22

Hassan, Bahey, 127–28

healthcare, 10, 30, 98–99, 100, 102, 116, 147
NGO programming in, 4, 18–19, 20, 21–22, 34–35, 119, 120, 148

Hermes. *See* EFG Hermes

Hicham Mubarak Law Center, 128–29

human rights
basic, 10, 100, 138–40, 156–57
claiming of, 4–5, 7, 10, 23–24, 57–58, 92, 96, 100, 103, 121, 136–37, 143, 148, 153
Egyptian organizations focused on, 2, 8–9, 24, 78, 87

imperialism, 85

infrastructure, 27–29, 102–3, 113–14, 120, 148

institutions
bureaucratic, 6
democratic, 80, 91–92, 138–39, 146, 155, 157
national-political, 4–5, 10–11, 20, 83–84, 86–87
religious, 27–29
semi-governmental, 42

International Monetary Fund (IMF), 31–32, 52

International Republican Institute (IRI), 38, 66–67

internet, 55–56, 81, 100–1

intifada, 53

IRI. *See* International Republican Institute

Islamic endowments. See *waqf*

Islamic organizations, 14
Islamism, 51, 64–65, 78, 79, 98–99, 124,
    See also Freedom and Justice Party;
    Muslim Brotherhood
ittihad, 33–34, 38

jail. *See* prison
journalist, 56–57
justice
    economic, 33, 92, 98, 100, 102, 105, 121,
        136–37, 140, 152–53
    social, 53, 77, 88, 91, 139–40,
        142–43, 144–45
    See also freedom

Kefaya, 54, 55–56
Kenya, 6, 17, 22

Law (specific laws)
    32, 30–31, 34
    49, 30, 129–30, 131–32, 134, 136–37
    84, 33–34, 35–36, 38, 39–40, 42, 58,
        63–64, 65–66, 124, 127
    348, 30–31
law (general), 31, 39, 45–46, 48, 51, 65,
        85–86, 128–29, 142, 145–46
    electoral, 81–83, 82*f*, 91–92
    rule of, 18–19, 35–36, 80
Lebanon, 1
legan, 59–60, 113, 149–50
libraries, 4–5, 37, 117–18
Libya, 138–39
literacy, 19, 103–4, 105, 117, 126,
        144–45, 147
local, 31, 37–38, 95, 103, 141, 148, 151–52,
        153. *See also* community

Mann, Thomas, 93
Mansour Foundation for Development,
    36, 42–43, 74
Mansour Group, 36, 42–43
March 9 Movement for Academic
    Freedom, 53–54
martyr, 80–81, 106–8
Masry al-Youm, al-, 42–43, 54, 65–67
media, 42–43, 52, 69, 70, 80–81, 91–92, 99,
        128–29, 148. *See also* social media;
    television

MEPI. *See* U.S.-Middle East Partnership
    Initiative
Mercy Corps, 38
micro-practices, 95–96
military, 63, 70–71, 74–75, 80–81,
        123–24, 125–26
    junta, 124
    rule, 123–24
Ministry of Endowments, 29–30, 33
Ministry of Social Affairs (MOSA), 30–31
Ministry of Social Solidarity (MOSS),
        39, 40–41, 68, 85–86, 125, 127,
        128–31, 133–34
Misr Spinning and Weaving Company. See
    Ghazl al-Mahallah
monarchy, 1, 16, 37–38
Morsi, Mohammed, 51, 70–71,
        123–24, 125
MOSA. *See* Ministry of Social Affairs
mosque, 29, 44–45, 46–47, 81–82
MOSS. *See* Ministry of Social Solidarity
Mubarak, Gamal, 37, 42–43, 54
Mubarak, Hosni, 1–2, 31–32, 39, 50, 138
Mubarak, Suzanne, 37, 42, 43
Muslim Brotherhood, 58–59, 64–65, 98–99,
        105–6, 123–24, 128
    See also Freedom and Justice Party;
    Islamism
mu'assasat, 8, 33–34, 36

Nadeem Center for Rehabilitation
    of Victims of Violence and
    Torture, 128–29
Naga, Fayza Abou el-, 65
Nasser, Gamal Abdel, 30–31, 33, 52, 94–95
National Council for Childhood and
    Motherhood, 42–43, *See also*
    Mubarak, Suzanne
National Democratic Institute (NDI),
    38, 66–67
National Democratic Party (NDP),
    32, 62–63
National Endowment for
    Democracy, 38, 83
national security, 30–31, 90, 126, 129, 130,
    135. *See also* security state
Nazra for Feminist Studies, 128–29
NDI. *See* National Democratic Institute

NDP. *See* National Democratic Party

neoliberalism, 18–19, 24–25, 31–32, 35, 42–43, 44, 49, 96–97, 100, 113, 114–15, 120

NGO. *See* non-governmental organizations

Nile TV, 135

non-governmental organizations:
  backlash against Western funding, 84–89
  development vs democracy in, 2, 3–7, 19, 23, 78, 118–19
  grassroots, 9–11, 20, 25, 28–29, 44, 46, 59, 69, 86, 102–3, 121, 126, 133, 153
  international, 8–9, 13–14, 24, 39, 66, 68, 73, 80, 81–82, 84, 123, 125, 127, 143, 146
  prosecution of (legal), 5, 66–68, 71, 125
  raids on, 5, 66–67, 123, 125, 127–28, 136–37
  See also charity; human rights; Law (specific laws); SCAF: and NGOs; surveillance

norms, 93, 94, 155

oil, 31–32

Oxfam, 38

Palestine, 17

participatory democracy. *See* democracy (types of)

Participatory Rural Appraisal (PRA), 21–22

Pence, Mike, 155

people. *See shebab*

People's Assembly, 42–43, 65

philanthropic foundations. *See* foundation; *mu'assasat*

philanthropy, 2–3, 37, 38, 73–74, 76–77, 112–13
  charity vs development, 44–46, 120
  local, 88
  private, 33, 37

Police Day, 50

policy
  agendas, 43
  foreign, 7, 19, 141, 145–46, 149, 157
  makers, 11–12, 21, 115, 145–46, 149, 156, 157

public, 22, 35–36, 47, 91, 142
recommendations, 149–50
reforms, 15–16, 47
tools, 19

political economy, 28–29, 33, 45–46, 76

popular committee. See *legan*

Population Council, 38

poverty, 21–22, 35, 52, 114–15. *See also* class

PRA. *See* Participatory Rural Appraisal

prison, 1, 5, 23, 39–40, 48, 71, 88, 124, 125, 126–27

privatization, 16, 24, 31–32, 44, 74, 96–97, 120, 134–35, 140

procedural democracy. *See* democracy (types of)

protest
  Arab Spring and, 12, 52
  art of, 106–10
  culture of, 53
  movements, 55
  sites of, 61
  waves, 54, 55–56
  See also military

public
  life, 92, 94
  policy, 22, 35–36, 47, 91, 142
  sector, 31–32, 44
  services, 27–29
  sphere, 9–10, 15–16, 91, 94, 120, 121
  See also debate

qāt, 93–95

Rab'a al-Adawiya Square, 124

Red Sea, 89, 90–91, 92, 94–95

reform
  democratic political, 52, 58, 60, 61, 70, 78, 88, 90, 98–99, 118–19, 120–21, 138–41, 150–51
  economic, 76–77
  judicial, 2, 91
  see also under democracy aid: reforms

religion, 77, 94, 111–13. *See also* Islam

repression, 5, 10, 20, 23–24, 25–26, 42, 44, 46, 52, 54, 64, 92, 118–19, 120–21, 124, 125–26, 129, 133, 135–36, 139, 140–41, 143, 144–45, 156–57

government, 10, 20, 46, 54, 120–21, 125–26, 135–36, 144–45, 156–57
Rockefeller Foundation, 36
royalty. *See* monarchy

Sabahi, Hamdeen, 124
Sadat, Anwar, 28–29, 31, 32, 52, 94–95
Said, Khaled, 56
Salafist al-Nour Party, 65
Saleh, Ali Abdullah, 52, 138
sampling (statistical), 11–12
Sawiris (family), 36, 42–43, 74
Sawiris Foundation for Social Development. *See* Sawiris (family)
SCAF. *See* Supreme Council of the Armed Forces
security state, 13, 30–31, 41–42, 55–56, 58, 59–60, 65, 66, 68–69, 71, 90, 124, 125, *See also* national security; surveillance
shanty town. *See* slum
shebab, 15, 22, 45–46, 50, 53, 57, 58, 61–62, 64, 71, 74, 77, 79, 99, 118, 126, 132–33, 149, 150
Shorouk, al-, 128–29
Sisi, Abdel Fattah al-, 24, 25–26, 123–24, 126, 127–30, 134–37, 155
slum, 69, 95, 99, 135
social contract, 9–10, 57–58, 120, 139–40, 149
social enterprise, 134–35, 149–50
social media, 56, 64, 108–10, 142–43, 156
social movements, 8, 20, 144–45, 146, 156
social services, 6, 15, 16, 52, 75–76
social welfare, 9, 24–25, 29–30, 32, 34–35
Sohag, 132–33
solidarity, 55, 93, 103, 115–16, 118, 139. See also *takaful*
South Sinai, 47, 69, 90–91, 100–1
sovereignty, 4–5, 67–68, 95–96, 136–37, 139, 156–57
Soviet Union, 83
Stiftung, Konrad Adenauer, 81, 83
strategic plan, 84, 151–52
structural adjustments, 31–32, 52
subsidy, 30, 32, 52, 97–98
suppression. *See* repression

Supreme Council of the Armed Forces (SCAF)
civil society and, 3, 63–64, 70, 118
as government, 50–51, 62–63, 70–71, 72, 74–75, 97–98
Islamists and, 64, 78
NGOs and, 5, 24, 73–74, 90, 125, 139
al-Sisi and, 124
surveillance
government, 36, 40–41, 44, 48, 69, 96, 125–26, 128, 129
phone and email, 41, 68, 69
sustainable development. *See* development
Switzerland, 38

Tahrir Square, 2, 50, 57, 61–62, 63, 64, 76–77, 85, 91, 96–97, 106–10, 115–16, 139, 140–41, 156
takaful, 27
Tamarrod, 71, 123–24
Tantawi, Mohammed Hussein, 70–71, 124
taxes, 31–32, 42, 94
tea, 4–5, 20–21, 90–91, 94–95, 101, 103–4, 121–22, 126, 156–57
technology, 81, 90–91, 100–1, 104, 146, 150. *See also* social media
television, 42–43, 58–59, 63, 90
terrorism, 54, 123–24, 128
Tillerson, Rex, 155
tourism, 3, 75, 90–91, 97–98, 134–35
transparency, 63, 129, 133–34, 155
Trump, Donald, 146, 155
Tunisia, 1–2, 50, 52, 53, 56, 138–39

UNDP. *See* United Nations Development Programme
United Kingdom, 30, 38
United Nations Development Programme (UNDP), 11, 13–14, 38
United States, 13–14, 19, 21, 36, 38, 52, 54, 67–69, 83, 90, 141, 143, 145–46, 150, 154, 155
United States Agency for International Development (USAID), 4, 31, 57, 73, 81–82, 83, 84–87, 146, 150, 151
uprising. *See* protest

USAID. *See* United States Agency for
      International Development
U.S.-Middle East Partnership Initiative
      (MEPI), 54

vernier. *See* façade
volunteerism, 10, 14, 37, 60, 61*f*, 98–99,
      101, 134–35

waqf, 29–30, 33, 37
Wedeen, Lisa, 92, 93–95
welfare state, 6, 30–31, 32–33, 42, 52,
      98, 120

women, 14, 18, 42, 47, 80, 81, 84, 94–95,
      105–6, 108–10, 116–18, 119–20,
      133, 134–35
World Bank, 31–32, 44, 52
World Congress of Muslim
      Philanthropists, 12
World Values Survey, 153

Yemen, 52, 93–94, 138–39
youth, 14, 54, 55, 56, 62, 64–65, 69, 80, 81,
      99, 103, 114–15, 131–33, 134–35

zakat, 27, 44–45. *See also* charity